Riddle Me This, Batman!

RIDDLE ME THIS, BATMAN!

Essays on the Universe of the Dark Knight

Edited by Kevin K. Durand *and* Mary K. Leigh

McFarland & Company, Inc., Publishers
Jefferson, North Carolina, and London

ALSO OF INTEREST

The Universe of Oz: Essays on Baum's Series and Its Progeny edited by Kevin K. Durand and Mary K. Leigh (2010)

Buffy Meets the Academy: Essays on the Episodes and Scripts as Texts edited by Kevin K. Durand (2009)

LIBRARY OF CONGRESS CATALOGUING-IN-PUBLICATION DATA

Riddle me this, Batman! : essays on the universe of the Dark Knight / edited by Kevin K. Durand and Mary K. Leigh.
    p.   cm.
Includes bibliographical references and index.

ISBN 978-0-7864-4629-2
softcover : 50# alkaline paper

1. Batman (Fictitious character) I. Durand, Kevin K. J. (Kevin Karl Jones), 1967– II. Leigh, Mary K.
PN6728.B363R53 2011
741.5'973 — dc22
                                                2011014385

BRITISH LIBRARY CATALOGUING DATA ARE AVAILABLE

© 2011 Kevin K. Durand and Mary K. Leigh. All rights reserved

No part of this book may be reproduced or transmitted in any form or by any means, electronic or mechanical, including photocopying or recording, or by any information storage and retrieval system, without permission in writing from the publisher.

Front cover design by David Landis (Shake It Loose Graphics)

Manufactured in the United States of America

McFarland & Company, Inc., Publishers
  Box 611, Jefferson, North Carolina 28640
    www.mcfarlandpub.com

Contents

Preface
  Mary K. Leigh 1
Introduction: What Has Adorno to Do with Gotham?
  Kevin K. Durand 3

Part One: The Ethics and Anarchy of Batman

1. Virtue in Gotham: Aristotle's Batman
   Mary K. Leigh 17
2. The Dark Knight Errant: Power and Authority in
   Frank Miller's *Batman: The Dark Knight Returns*
   Christopher Bundrick 24
3. Why Adam West Matters: Camp and Classical Virtue
   Kevin K. Durand 41
4. Dark Knight, White Knight, and the King of Anarchy
   Stephanie Carmichael 54
5. Introducing a Little Anarchy: *The Dark Knight* and
   Power Structures on the Verge of a Nervous Breakdown
   Sudipto Sanyal 70

Part Two: Batman and Literary Theory

6. *Batman's* Canon: Hybridity and the Interpretation
   of the Superhero
   Kevin K. Durand 81
7. Seminar on the Purloined Batarang: Batman and Lacan
   Mitch Frye 93

8. Queer Matters in *The Dark Knight Returns*: Why We Insist
    on a Sexual Identity for Batman
    JENÉE WILDE 104

 9. The Hero We Read: *The Dark Knight*, Popular Allegoresis,
    and Blockbuster Ideology
    ANDREA COMISKEY 124

10. Rolling the Boulder in Gotham
    RANDY DUNCAN 147

11. Figuration of the Superheroic Revolutionary:
    The Dark Knight of Negation
    D. T. KOFOED 156

Part Three: Batman and Beyond

12. "One May Smile, and Smile, and Be a Villain":
    Grim Humor and the Warrior Ethos
    MELANIE WILSON 169

13. "And Doesn't All the World Love a Clown?": Finding
    the Joker and the Representation of His Evil
    MICHAEL SMITH 187

14. Call It (Friendo): Flipism and Folklore in *No Country for
    Old Men* and *The Dark Knight*
    MATTHEW FOTIS 201

About the Contributors 219
Index 221

Preface

Mary K. Leigh

In collecting a volume of essays related to *Batman*, there is always the question of how to select the essays and what balance to provide to such a study. In the Introduction, Kevin K. Durand outlines our particular approach to popular culture studies and demonstrates the framework by which the rest of the essays in this collection were selected. This text argues that the Critical Engagement method is the best way to conduct any study of popular culture, advocating for what the interpretation says about the text itself, not how we may use a text to provide examples for a theory. This is not to say that examples for a theory are not useful or important, but that a disciplined study of popular culture needs to take the next step and provide an analysis of what the application of a type of analysis allows the audience to understand about the text under consideration, in this case, the world of *Batman* in its many conceptions and re-conceptions.

In this collection, several essays begin by providing examples at the outset before turning to engage the text in the more rigorous way that Durand terms the Critical Engagement method. In Part One, "The Ethics and Anarchy in *Batman*," my essay, "Virtue in Gotham" for example, engages the text and the reader with an analysis of *The Dark Knight* that, while Aristotelian, is not merely a starting point. Christopher Bundrick's essay, "The Dark Knight Errant," explores the psychoanalytic development of Bruce Wayne, providing a lens through which to view his ethical standpoint. Focusing on a particular incarnation of Batman, Durand argues in "Why Adam West Matters" that the Batman of Adam West is particularly noteworthy for its depiction of a theory of friendship that differs markedly from the standard philosophy of friendship from Aristotle forward, drawing together and furthering the ideals presented earlier. In "Dark Knight, White Knight, and the King of Anarchy" Stephanie Carmichael leads readers through an engaging character analysis designed to allow them to create connections and devise many theoretical approaches on their own. Ethics also leads to analysis of anarchy; thus, in "Introducing a Little Anarchy," Sudipto Sanyal explores the psychological dysfunction of the Joker and Harvey Dent, respectively, as tools for grappling with the nature of power.

Part Two, "Batman and Literary Theory," opens with an urgent question in literary criticism — what constitutes the canon when there are so many different texts vying for readership and viewership? Durand argues in "*Batman's* Canon" that *Batman* presents us with a most interesting moment in literary criticism, a canon in flux that necessarily must include most interpretations of the story, even those that may contradict each other. The following essays approach the canon from many theoretical frameworks, from Mitch Frye's Lacanian analysis of Batman in the midst of mental crisis in "Seminar on the Purloined Batarang" to "Queer Matters in *The Dark Knight Returns*," Jenée Wilde's careful interpretation of our insistence on a sexual identity for Batman. Andrea Comiskey provides an analysis of popular culture through the medium of popular culture, addressing the many allegorical interpretations of *Batman*, not just in typical scholarship, but also in the work of journalists, film critics, and online bloggers in "The Hero We Read." Randy Duncan, "Rolling the Boulder in Gotham," and D. T. Kofoed, "Figuration of the Superheroic Revolutionary," complete the literary criticism by analyzing the deeply complex world of *Batman* in comic books, analyzing the role of Gotham as a city to the development of *Batman* and the reality of a superhero revolutionary created through careful use of comic book artistry, respectively.

Part Three, "Batman and Beyond," demonstrates not only what we may learn about *Batman* itself, but also what we may understand about *Batman* when studying it in relation to another text. Melanie Wilson, "'One May Smile, and Smile, and Be a Villain,'" and Michael Smith, "'And Doesn't All the World Love a Clown?,'" each take on the nature of the smiling villain, alluding to Shakespeare as they explore the concepts of good and evil. Finally, in "Call It (Friendo)," Matthew Fotis places *Batman* in the concept of another piece of popular culture, *No Country for Old Men*, drawing readers into a discussion of coin-flipping, a tradition so ingrained in cultures that we often do not see its potential significance for understanding psychological motivation.

While all of these essays clearly relate to one another, they also stand as independent examinations of *Batman* and the universe it has inspired as texts in themselves. As scholars who wish to approach popular culture through the Critical Engagement method, it is the hope of the contributors to this volume that the decision to engage the universe of the Batman as a text is in keeping with this choice.

Introduction
What Has Adorno to Do with Gotham?
Kevin K. Durand

Superheroes dot the landscape of the 20th and 21st Century imagination. Batman, Superman, the X-Men, Watchmen, and so many others vie for our time and attention, endure multiple reimaginings at the hands of writers, directors, and actors, and continue as a staple of reading and viewing pleasure. However, Batman occupies a particular privilege of place in the superhero pantheon. It is that privilege of place that this volume seeks to explore — to understand what Batman has for our conversations of good, evil, society, individuality, heroic virtue, and thoughts of home. There are those who would quickly dismiss Batman and the rest of the superheroes. They might suggest that they are nothing but comics, caped clowns, easily discarded pop culture artifacts — summer blockbuster, scholarly popcorn that doesn't last through the movie itself, much less into deep reflection on questions of serious import. Such views clearly are on the wane, but one still encounters them in the quest of truth, meaning, and understanding through the examination of popular culture. Indeed, anytime one comes to popular culture, one is faced with the question of popular culture scholarship — to what extent is popular culture scholarship merely an academic playground in which self-important folks read far more into a work than it contains? Or, perhaps, the question is even more fundamental — is popular culture scholarship worthwhile scholarship at all?

There are those who dismiss all things Batman as comic-book culture, as trifling fancy, as superfluous distraction from more important matters. To those "critics," I will not discuss Batman's legacy, the psychoanalytic investigations of good and evil, the mirror of the world of Gotham and our own, or the grip that Batman has on the imagination of countless people. Instead, rather than pointing at Batman at all, I should like to introduce these "critics" to the greatest philosopher of all time, Plato, and one of the foremost literary critics of the 20th Century, Theodor Adorno.

In Plato's *Ion*, we have the seeds of the discipline that has come to be known as Literary Criticism. Taken together with his discussions of rhetoric in *Phaedrus* and the reflections of the sorts of scholars/critics that analyze the popular culture contemporary to him, we have a genealogy of theory that has taken popular culture seriously — both as exemplary of particular views and as independently developing ideas about what it means to live the good life, what it means to be a good person, and what it means to live within human society. While Plato clearly could not have anticipated Michel Foucault, Jacques Lacan, Julia Kristeva, or bell hooks, all literary critics owe the founding of our art to Plato. Whatever his reaction to the theatre and literature of his day (e.g., Aristophanes's *The Clouds*, Homer's *Iliad*) as works of art and entertainment, one thing is clear — he took them seriously. One could suppose that part of that concern for the seriousness of the theatric and literary forms lay in the role Aristophanes's *The Clouds* played (or at least was thought to have played) in the prejudicial opinions of the Athenian jury that convicted Plato's mentor, Socrates, and ultimately condemned Socrates to a hemlock death. In *Apology*, Plato has Socrates say,

> If the rumormongers were actual accusers, their indictment would be: Socrates is guilty of wrongdoing because he inquires into the things of heaven and beneath the earth; makes the weaker argument appear the stronger; and teaches the young to do the same thing. You of the jury know these things to be true for you have seen Aristophanes's play just as we have [*Footnotes to Plato* 46].

On Plato's view, the role of the theater was such that its images, themes, dialogue, plot, and story could so move the soul that people were liable to take what they saw on stage as the reality that either inspired or was parodied by the play. Thus, the "Socrates" of *The Clouds* becomes the Socrates on trial who, ultimately, is sentenced to death by a mob/jury that couldn't distinguish between the two.

The tense relationship between the poets (all writers, for the ancients, not simply those who would be called poets today) and Plato continued throughout his career. In fact, in his great work *Republic* (from his middle period), Plato has Socrates constructing the "ideal city" in a thought experiment, and in that experiment, he has Socrates and his interlocutors cast out the writers because their work was so potentially ensnaring of the mind. At the same time, a brief reflection on Plato's own work would leave a scholar to wonder whether or not he would have had those interlocutors consign him to banishment as well. In other words, Plato was a fair spinner of words and yarns himself. Whatever the case of Plato's view about writers, his view of those who critique the theater is of one voice.

These critics, or as Plato describes them, the "lovers of sights and sounds," are a considerable danger on Plato's view. He argues that they practice the art of rhetoric in such a way that they seem to know a great many things about the art forms they criticize. Their claims about what is good and bad, what is to be desired and what is undesirable are were highly sought and greatly prized, perhaps because the object of their commentary was the very popular theater of the day. After all, "water cooler" conversations about the latest summer blockbuster are not at all uncommon. Unfortunately, these cultural critics enjoyed a sort of prestige that went far beyond the theater. They held forth on all sorts of matters that were of national importance — whether Athens should go to war with Sparta, for example. The prestige they gained as critics of the theater bought them influence in other areas. While this is clearly problematic, Plato argues that they don't even understand the theater itself. Insulated within the world of drama, their reviews become self-referential — this play of Sophocles isn't as good as that play of Euripides because it doesn't take the proper form of the plays of Aeschylus — and, in becoming self-referential, they also became like monologues in an echo chamber, utterly detached from the world, even the world supposedly reflected in the plays.

Leaving Plato and Aristotle and the ancients, let's turn to a more contemporary source. There is a strange convergence of Platonic critical theory and the work of Theodor Adorno that has an almost prescient grasp of the role of Batman, the role of the cultural critic that easily discards it, and the role of the scholar who seeks the "something deeper" that the essays in this volume suggest is there.

Theodor Adorno, one of the most prominent and influential social and literary critics of the 20th century, writes of the "cultural critic" in much the same way that Plato writes of the "lovers of sights and sounds." Following a generally Marxist critical line, Adorno argues that the sort of cultural criticism that is generally employed is oddly self-contradictory. The cultural critic has, at first, begun as something of a reporter, simply giving an overview of some particular cultural event, be it a movie, a book, or a soiree of some sort. However, very shortly, that reporter gains status with those whom he is "critiquing" and becomes a very part of the social scene itself. Thus, as he ascends to the label "critic," he becomes a purveyor of the very culture he purports to critique; he enters the echo chamber of self-reference and self-importance. This might be benign, except that as "cultural critic," he also levels criticism at that "culture" that is beneath the elite. He must denigrate "low" culture as a necessary feature of upholding the "high" (bourgeois) culture of which he has become a part. Adorno writes:

> What makes the cultural criticism inappropriate is not so much lack of respect for that which is criticised as the dazzled and arrogant recognition which criticism surreptitiously confers on culture. The cultural critic can hardly avoid the imputation that he has the culture which culture lacks [19].

One cannot help but notice the affinity for Plato's view here. The cultural critic, like the lover of sights and sounds, isn't interested in whether or not "culture" reflects truth or knowledge or even the good life. And, as "critics" achieve some prominence, there is a sort of pecking order (and vicious internecine battle) that goes on among them as each tries to both secure his place in the pantheon of the elite critics and, in so doing, secure his place among the elite. Thus, the critic begins to criticize not only "lower" culture, but the critic's own kind. Adorno continues, "Knowledge and understanding were not primary, but at most by-products, and the more they were lacking, the more they were replaced by Oneupmanship and conformity" (20). The search is not for truth about the human condition. Indeed, it becomes at some remove from the "culture" it purports to critique. Substance is no longer the issue, but style and style points.

In a battlefield such as this, the tools of battle are language and information and access. Having gained access to the elite bourgeois culture, and by power of rhetoric, secured that place, he is likely (Plato and Adorno would agree "inevitably") to come to understand his views as something more than merely commentary, but to suppose that they have come to represent reality and truth themselves. Adorno describes this transition thusly, "The prerogatives of information and position permit them to express their opinion as if it were objectivity. But it is solely the objectivity of the ruling mind. They help to weave the veil" (19).

In a further connection to his Platonic ancestor, Adorno critiques not only the bourgeois position of the cultural critic, because, after all, it might be the case that merely charging the critic with being a member of the elite does not, of its own, refute their views. To be sure, their perspective is rightly questioned, but what of their views themselves. Plato argues that the "lovers of sights and sounds" cannot possibly have access to the truth because, insulated within their echo chamber, they cannot perceive reality, only the shadows of it. Adorno's criticism is similar. He argues that their views are marginalized precisely because of the ways in which they climbed into the echo chamber. He writes, "Their agility, which gained them privileged positions in the general competition — privileged, since the fate of those judged depends largely on their vote — invests their judgments with the semblance of competence" (19).

It is important to note that Adorno here relates the very *competence* of the critic to the ways in which the position of cultural critic was attained. On his view, it must be the case that one so badly damages one's perspective in the journey to elevated status that the perspective from the elevated perch is incapable of rendering even competent judgments about culture or, by extension, the several elements of it.

The criticism Adorno levels at the cultural critic can be distinguished, however, from the cultural critic's own criticism. Adorno, like Plato, makes the distinction between the lovers of sights and sounds and the philosopher, or, for Adorno, between the cultural critic and the dialectical critic. The philosopher and the dialectical critic both seek greater understanding of the world, of humankind, and of life. Neither is constrained by a class to which he belongs, because he is as likely as not to bring his critical apparatus to bear on his own class as on that of the bourgeois. However, it is a very fine line that must be walked. The dialectical critic can very easily be seduced into the mode of cultural critic. Adorno describes this dialectic in this way: "The dialectical critic of culture must both participate in culture and not participate. Only then does he do justice to his object and to himself" (33). In this, the dialectical critic (and the philosopher) balances his work on the edge of a knife, neither falling into cultural idol- or status-worship, nor failing to critically analyze the world at all. But, Adorno's closing admonition sums up very nicely the plight of the one who seeks to examine culture, including popular culture, in an analytical way: "Critical intelligence cannot be equal to this challenge as long as it confines itself to self-satisfied contemplation" (34).

Where Plato and Adorno meet is the place where good popular culture criticism must reflect on its own practice. The foregoing argument also serves as a critique of at least a goodly portion of what passes for popular culture studies. It does not, it should be noted, reject popular culture criticism, itself. Like Plato before him and Adorno much later after him, Aristotle is famed for taking seriously the popular culture of the day. Should the three be dropped into the 21st Century, they would likely take seriously many of the works of popular culture scholarship of today. Similarly, they would undoubtedly reject much of what passes as popular culture scholarship as the echo chamber ramblings of lovers of sights and sounds and cultural critics.

The foregoing argument is different in object from arguments I have made elsewhere. In *Buffy Meets the Academy* and *The Universe of Oz*, my concern was the argument that popular culture studies is not only an appropriate field, but that it is both a time-honored and informative one. That is, it is something to be engaged by the scholar, not for its entertainment value, but as a text to be engaged in much the same way one would engage a work by

William Faulkner or John Locke or St. Augustine. They are texts that seek to understand the world, to explore the limits of human knowledge, and to give a view, and perhaps insight, into the good life and how people should live.

As a matter of importance and meaning, there is no question that popular culture vehicles are among the most effective for exploring topics of critical importance. Plato used Homer to discuss the nature of the good life, of becoming a good human being. So, too, the Batman universe provides a template for much of the same conversation. In Homer, we find notions of heroic virtue; in Batman, we see those virtues of the hero — courage, strength, wisdom — reimagined in a 20th and 21st Century context. In Aristotle, we see an argument about the nature of friendship illustrated with examples drawn from the popular opinion of Athens. In Batman, we see a different view of the nature of friendship than we find in Aristotle. For Aristotle, Batman and Robin, Bruce Wayne and Dick Grayson, could never be truly friends, as they are both of unequal social status and differing age and maturity levels. This sort of view is similar to much of the Batman universe, but not all. And, in the 1960s television incarnation, a different philosophy of friendship is forged; one, I argue, that is perhaps more worthwhile even than Aristotle's.

Having argued for taking popular culture seriously, it is of some importance to explore further the matter of why, even among those sympathetic to the foregoing argument, popular culture studies are often relegated to special topics classes taught infrequently and to distinctly second-class status with academia. I have argued elsewhere that the primary reason for this is the shape of popular culture studies itself. I alluded to this in the discussion of Plato, Adorno, and Aristotle, and here, return the argument from the theoretical discussion of the kinds of critics that one encounters to the object of the criticism itself. Obviously, there are some important distinctions that will need to be made as we turn from discussing *Buffy* or *Oz* to *Batman*. I will not rehearse those distinctions at any great length here, but point only to the essay *Batman's Canon*, where they take central stage. Suffice to say here that the Batman universe of texts — movies, graphic novels, cartoons (including the wonderful cross-over from the 1960s live action television show to a cartoon appearance with Scooby-Doo and the Globetrotters), books, magazines, fan fiction, and blogs aplenty, is unmatched in its variety by either *Buffy* or *Oz*.

There is not a universally accepted approach to popular culture studies. There is, also, no universally accepted approach to studies of Socrates, Medieval literature, cultural history, or basket-weaving. When one engages the foregoing, (with the possible exception of basket-weaving) however, it is clear that there is a seriousness to the scholarship that is often absent from the treatment of popular culture. While even Faulkner, for example, dabbled in screenplay writing, it is not his Hollywood career that is fodder for the American Literature course. Scholars engage the text under examination in a deliberative fashion with a critical framework, or perhaps a pluralistic approach to critical frameworks, and thus, more than one. They attend closely to the text, dig carefully to unearth subtext, and provide analyses of the text that both illuminate the text and the reader. This is often not the case in popular culture studies. Too often, popular culture studies are drowned in fluff.

I think we can safely divide the field of popular culture studies into five general sorts, defined by the way in which the scholar (or "scholar") approaches the object of her investigations. I have called these five approaches: Critical Engagement, Theory Exemplar/Corrective, Point of Departure, Cultural Solipsism, and "Isn't that neat?" The "Isn't that neat?" category can, potentially, have a somewhat different character when the discussion is a text that moves from literary to visual instead of one that is almost wholly visual. While a group of friends sitting around watching television might well draw "neat" parallels between the various episodes, the "water cooler" discussion surrounding a text that becomes visual actually harkens back to an ancient phenomenon roundly criticized by Plato — the practice of the "lovers of sights and sounds." When the text is *Batman*, the conversation runs the very real risk of entering the echo chamber, as each "critic" uses a different basis for arguing that the movie is a faithful adaptation of his favored view of Batman. Thus, Michael Keaton's Batman is either a better or worse adaptation depending on whether or not one has in mind, as the foundational Batman myth, the graphic novels or the Adam West television show. Such a conversation can quickly become circular.

It is important to keep in mind the rejection of the "cultural critic" here. A brief digression into the world of the classical Siskels, Eberts, and Roepers is helpful for our discussion. Imagine ancient theatergoers returning from a stirring performance of *Oedipus, the King*. Gathering in the *agora*, they begin to discuss how well the actors have done in their varying roles, comparing them to previous actors in earlier productions, discussing the sets, the singing of the choruses, and the general tone of the production. With a certain self-satisfaction, they conclude not only that this was a better-than-average performance, but that it lacked some certain panache of the best performances. In other words, what takes place is a conversation that is nearly entirely self-referential with little or no introduction of the apparatus of critical theory. Indeed, these "lovers of sights and sounds" have been fascinated with what Aristotle called "the spectacle," and their reflections are little deeper than superficial. Further, when they do come to something like agreement, it is the agreement that their preferred form of entertainment — the theatre — is far to be preferred to the entertainment of the lower masses. After all, the theatre is *culture*, and the low humor of the masses is just that — low and beneath cultural notice.

It is this sort of criticism that both Adorno and Plato so ably dispatch. It is clear that we still encounter this manner of criticism regularly, and, for all its staying power, it sheds little light for all its heat and bother. When discussing a popular culture text as deeply layered and textured as *Batman*, such a conversation might well be little more than a discussion of how well the movie captures the graphic novel, whether the late 1990's cartoon saved *Batman* from a campy fate, whether the scene effects render Gotham a Burtonian nightmare or a more Darwinian one. Clearly, such criticism is hardly worth the label. All too often, unfortunately, in popular culture studies, it is precisely this sort of work that is offered as popular culture scholarship. Plato's criticism of his ancient adversary is applicable here as well. While the work can seem clever and even quite fun to read, it fails to plumb the depths of a work's meaning precisely because it remains at a superficial level. Before long, this kind of work becomes a self-congratulatory exercise in the self-referential pointing out of neat connections or clever turns of phrase or interesting references. Fortunately, and by design, the essays of this volume explicitly eschew this approach to popular culture studies.

If we have consigned the "lovers of sights and sounds" and the "cultural critics" to the sidelines of scholarship, there is a related form of "examination" of a popular culture text that, while more substantial than "Isn't that neat?," is only slightly more. At those times, when it does seem a little more, it can appear as little more than Cultural Solipsism. One of the easiest essays to construct is the one that traces elements of some show or other to other shows that it references. Then, one takes those references and traces them to still others. In some rare cases, the trace comes full circle to the original program under consideration. This is particularly seductive in the case of *Batman*. One can argue that Hollywood launched the Adam West Batman movie as a way of piggy-backing on the popularity of the television show. With nothing more to really do with the storyline, the *Batman* franchise languished until the 1980s and the oddly appropriate Michael Keaton in the Caped Crusader role. However, four movies and three Batmen into the franchise, the shark had been jumped, not once, but repeatedly, and the series had devolved into a cartoonish parody of itself. Meanwhile the cartoon, with its anime influences and strangely affecting visuals salvaged much of what was worthwhile from the movie franchise to meld it with the graphic novels, which had long been neglected by the popular masses in favor of the moving visuals and cinematic explosions. The Christopher Nolan and Christian Bale franchise remakes the universe again; again opening with a genesis story for Batman, but leaving the villains curiously origin-free. This is especially true with *The Dark Knight*, but is also true with the first of the new franchise, so originally titled *Batman Begins*. A paper that traces the connections between the various elements of the universe as a whole would likely be an interesting read, but would introduce nothing in particular to the scholarly evaluation of that universe, or of any particular aspect of it. Indeed, it would likely present the scholar with obstacles to offering a coherent view of the world of the Batman. While a good bit of fun, perhaps, such work would hardly be considered either original or particularly worthwhile. It is this sort of Cultural Solipsism that often makes popular culture studies seem less than serious and somewhat less than scholarly.

The third popular sort of pop culture criticism is considerably more beneficial than the first two. I call it the Point of Departure approach. With this model, the "water cooler" conversation of the former sort takes on a greater level of sophistication. Here, the popular culture text becomes an artifact, an example that is helpful in advancing one's own views. Thus, when watching *Batman Forever*, one notes the watered-down version of a Sophie's Choice presented Kilmer's Batman, perhaps as a way of explicating the more sinister and infinitely more tragic one faced by Sophie. The popular culture text is reduced to an instrumental role in which whatever meaning it may have within it is lost in the service of explicating a view independent of it. In a more light-hearted example, my Louisiana kinfolk are deeply rooted in the oral tradition of southern story-telling. It is a time-honored story-telling technique to go on at some length about some particular story only to say, at the conclusion of the tale, "I told you that so that I could tell you this..." and launch into another, one that may be only tangentially related to the first.

At the same time, the Point of Departure approach is helpful, as far as it goes. It is particularly useful as a pedagogical tool. For example, a strong critical work could begin with the Point of Departure as a way of framing the text itself, but then argue for something much deeper, and, in so doing, leave the Point of Departure approach entirely. For example, an Aristotelian notion of the sorts of people who exist could be a very nice way of discussing Batman and Alfred and the Joker. However, unless it delves deeper than merely serving as a launchpad for discussion, it stops short of true scholarship.

The issue for the popular culture critic is this. In this model, the critical attention is not given to the Batman universe. Instead, the attention is on Aristotle or Lacan or Kant, and the popular culture text is rendered merely a convenient artifact, a wholly interchangeable instrument. As I have argued elsewhere, this approach to popular culture criticism has the often unintentional consequence of self-negation. If the subject under study is merely an interchangeable and, thus, essentially unimportant feature of a broader conversation, then it is much easier to conclude that the Batman is essentially unimportant. This troublesome result seems to indict much of the field of popular culture studies by critiquing the way in which much of it proceeds. Such an approach is more substantive than the others, but it still fails to take the text itself seriously enough to justify a separate scholarly investigation of it.

The fourth approach is the Theory Exemplar model. While it has much in common with the Point of Departure model, it has one characteristic that elevates it beyond its cousin. In the Point of Departure approach, the Batman is an instrument for discussing some theoretical point or other raised by some great thinker within the canon. It is a starting point that is soon abandoned for the more serious conversation that it has spawned of the more important text or concept. For example, some years ago I attended a presentation on the nature of piety and impiety in Plato's *Euthyphro*. The young scholar did a marvelous job explicating a close reading of the text that shed light both on the nature of the historical Socrates and the nature of the Socratic elenchus (method of argument) as it related to the quest for understanding the virtues. After the paper was complete, the call for questions was given and an older scholar raised his hand and said, "That was a very nice paper that raises some interesting textual questions. I know what I'm about to ask isn't related to the text itself, but it is a far more interesting philosophical question." The following question proved the man both right and wrong. The question did, indeed, have nothing to do with *Euthyphro*, but it was not a more interesting philosophical question.

On the other hand, the Theory Exemplar recognizes the popular culture text has something of its own to contribute to the conversation. To use the Batman as an example of a theory, one must first actively engage the text itself. A Cartesian scholar, for example, might quickly note the distinctions between the world as it is perceived and the world as it is; it would, at the same time, be quickly recognized by that same scholar if the text did not actually adequately explicate the view. One might, for example, discuss how *The Matrix* helpfully captures the Cartesian Evil Demon aspect of the Method of Doubt, but to do so, one must first engage both Descartes and *The Matrix* at a level that is deeper than simply using the world of computer masters and human batteries as a point of departure for discussing the Cartesian *Cogito*.

The difficulty with this view is similar to the Point of Departure view in that one still uses the Batman or any other popular culture artifact as a vehicle for illustrating a text other than itself. However, in the serious work that must be done to provide a clear comparison, some measure of critical worth is imputed to the popular culture illumination. At the same time, the text is still largely instrumental and its value is largely that of a tool. It is still unclear whether or not the text *itself* contains anything of value.

It has been my experience in a survey of the literature, both published and presented at various conferences, national and international, that the majority of popular culture studies fall into one of these four models. I take it to be that for these reasons, popular culture studies is often relegated to secondary status within the academy and seen as merely an interesting adjunct or sidebar to other disciplines. This volume, like its *Buffy* and *Oz* predecessors, is itself a critique of that approach to popular culture studies. Further, and more importantly, it is a bit of advocacy for another approach to popular culture texts. I call this approach the Critical Engagement approach.

A scholar critically engages a text when she brings her considerable training to the text and asks of the text what it is arguing. The approach is not a matter of discerning ways in which the text may be of instrumental use in some other venue, but rather of asking what intrinsic value may be found. In approaching the Batman this way, one is not asking, "How can Batman be used to discuss good and evil or canon or epistemology?" Instead, one is asking, "What is it that Batman, as a text, is arguing about good and evil? What arguments are to be found within it?" One might conclude that the arguments are flawed, that the theories are specious, or that the text is unworthy of serious scholarly engagement. However, such conclusions would be based on the engagement with the text itself, and thus would represent the same sort of scholarship one expects of the philosopher who analyzes Aristotle's *Nicomachean Ethics* or the literary critic who explores Joyce's *Ulysses*.

The Critical Engagement approach is the one most rarely seen in contemporary popular culture scholarship. Why this is the case is something of a mystery to me. That it is mysterious, however, in no way detracts from the view that one should expect the same level of scholarly rigor from critics of popular culture that one expects from historians of Tudor/Stuart England or from archaeologists of ancient Troy. Popular culture studies will continue to suffer from second-class citizen status within contemporary academic scholarship until the majority of the scholarly work is done in this latter way. Failure to engage the text itself reduces the text and its importance to mere instrument. Such self-negating approaches have the deleterious effect of implying the negation of the entire field. The vast wealth of material to be gleaned from the study of popular culture is reason enough to commend its study and to indicate its own intrinsic value. This was the view of Plato and of Aristotle, the founders of perceptive critical and analytical theory. The choice for the modern critic is the same as the choice for our ancient ancestors — a serious engagement with the text or a capitulation to the view that popular culture studies are, at best, an adjunct to true scholarship, or, at worst, a trifling diversion unworthy of scholarly time and attention.

Works Cited

Adorno, Theodor. "Cultural Criticism and Society." *Prisms*. Cambridge, MA: MIT Press, 1997. Print.

Durand, Kevin. *Footnotes to Plato*. Lanham, MD: University Press of America, 2009. Print.

Part One

The Ethics and Anarchy of Batman

1

Virtue in Gotham
Aristotle's *Batman*

MARY K. LEIGH

The study of popular culture in the context of philosophy can appear on the surface to be an odd juxtaposition. Proposing to examine Aristotelian ideals as found in Christopher Nolan's envisioning of *Batman* may seem even more unusual. However, the idea may not be as far-fetched as it appears at first glance. To say that Aristotle had his own interest in the popular culture of his time period would be quite an understatement. His *Poetics* is an extraordinarily complex work of literary criticism concerning not only classics of the time, but also the poetry and dramatic productions of his era. The *Poetics*, along with Plato's *Ion*, can be seen as the theoretical foundation of literary criticism. There, Aristotle examines, in depth, notions of plot, character, diction, and the like. The work is an analysis of the elements that comprise a dramatic work. This present study, however, is concerned rather with content than structure. In this, Aristotle is, likewise, quite helpful. In this examination, I propose to use Aristotle's *Nicomachean Ethics* to analyze the Christopher Nolan film *The Dark Knight*. Aristotle's method of collection and division applied to the nature of the human good, virtue, and the good life provides a framework within which the character of the characters (Batman, Alfred, The Joker, and Harvey Dent) fit within the four categories of human behavior—the virtuous, the continent, the incontinent, and the vicious. One consequent of this examination provides an example of a highly controversial Aristotelian notion—the truly vicious person who acts viciously because such actions contribute to his own fulfillment.

Before we can begin to determine the virtue of our characters, we first need some theoretical background. Aristotle's method of collection and division works rather straightforwardly—one gathers all of the possibilities and divides them out, classifying them along the way. As perhaps Aristotle's primary method of classification, it is applied to grammar, biology, drama, politics, and metaphysics, to name but a few. However, on first glance, this method seems incompatible with the concept of finding virtue. How does one go about this process without making classifications that are simply arbitrary?

Aristotle avoids arbitrariness in two ways. First, in seeking the highest human good, he collects all those applications of the word "good" made by the common citizens of Athens. Having assembled the collection, he divides the conceptions of the good into three types, establishing that *eudaimonia*, the state of the soul expressing *arete*, or "excellence," is the highest human good. Aristotle is commonly interpreted as supposing that this excellence is a moral excellence, or virtue. However, he suggests that one form of the truly vicious person can exhibit this stable state of the soul, possess intellectual excellence, and yet, also, excel in vice, rather than virtue.

Aristotle's second part of his construction of ethical theory takes place at the level where intuition and the human function, reason, serve as a guide, the Golden Mean. In order to acquire virtue, the virtue must be habituated until it becomes second nature. Thus, the acquisition of virtue requires the practice of virtuous actions. In order to practice, one must both discern the character of the virtuous action and enact it correctly. For Aristotle, the virtuous action will lie between two extremes — excess and deficiency. An example will perhaps bring this idea into sharper focus. If one wants to practice courage, a virtue often thought of highly by the ancient Greeks, then he or she must be courageous correctly. Courage, as defined by Aristotle, amounts to knowing when to fight and knowing when to flee and being able to successfully act on that knowledge. An excess of courage will lead to recklessness; fighting is not always the best option. However, a deficiency of courage will lead to cowardice; retreating is not always the best course of action either. Using reason to find the middle ground between these two extremes is to determine the Golden Mean. Simply put, virtue is doing the right thing at the right time in the right way and for the right reasons, and the application of the Golden Mean to the particular situation will enable the agent to perform those virtuous actions. Reasoning excellently about each situation to determine all of these "rights" will lead a person to habituating the sort of character that will always act in such ways, or to virtue. In order to reach the level of true virtue, all of these things must be second nature to the individual. Neither of these commits Aristotle to arbitrary definitions of the good or of the excellent. Both are determined by the nature of things — the nature of the good and the human nature.

Having developed these notions of the good and virtue, Aristotle turns the method of collection and division to types or kinds of people. When one is attempting to classify people as virtuous or not, it quickly becomes clear that there is a wide range of human behavior. It is not reflective of human nature to divide people into only two levels — the virtuous and the not virtuous. Aristotle realizes this and demarcates four types of people in regard to virtue. These are the virtuous, the continent, the incontinent, and the vicious.

The virtuous person is one that we have already begun to envision. He does the right thing at the right time in the right way and for the right reasons. His ability to reason is fully developed, and this virtuous behavior is second nature. He does not hesitate in taking action as he knows exactly what he should do. Not surprisingly, the truly virtuous person is rather rare.

The continent person is a bit more common. This person often does the right thing often at the right time usually in the right way, but he has some particular difficulty in the area of right reasons. This person typically does all of these "rights" for external reasons. Perhaps he wants to avoid negative consequences, such as punishment for doing the wrong thing, or maybe he would like to be thought of as a good man. More positively, it is possible that he has simply not developed the second nature that is required for true virtue; thus, he chooses to do these things so that he may one day be virtuous himself. Whatever the case, the actions are ultimately externally, not internally, motivated.

The incontinent person is less hopeful. He sometimes does the right thing, occasionally at the right time, but rarely in the right way and almost never for the right reasons. In this circumstance, doing the right thing is really a matter of simple moral luck. Reason rarely comes into play, and any concept of virtuous behavior is often undercut by incorrect motivation. The incontinent person is also marked by what Aristotle calls *akrasia*, or weakness of will. This person is not irredeemable. He may very well be on the path to virtue, but he must develop his ability to reason, to maintain strict moral discipline, and to strengthen his will so as to control his desires — characteristics that are likely to hold little appeal to this individual.

Our final type is the vicious person. The vicious person may or may not do the right thing at the right time or in the right way, and his reasons are always wrong. It is important, however, to make the distinction between two types of evil people, on Aristotle's view — the malevolent and the ignorant. Recognizing this necessary distinction, Aristotle allows that there are two types of vicious people. The first type fails to do the right thing (and nearly always fails) because of a mistake. Perhaps he mistook the evil for the good but had genuine intentions of doing good. This person is redeemable because a correction of this mistake can allow him the ability to move forward in pursuit of virtue. The move will be difficult because he must first surrender false beliefs about the good; beliefs he does not think are false, obviously. The second type is the truly vicious. This person will often do right things but always for the wrong reasons. He does these right things, however, because he has some greater plan, some evil that could be thwarted by tipping his hand too early in doing things that are obviously wrong in simple or meaningless matters. He is not obviously evil to outside observers, at least initially. However, all of his aims are toward the opposite of the virtuous actions. With full knowledge, and with intellectual excellence, he chooses the wrong thing simply because it is wrong.

The most appealing character to begin our discussion would be Batman. Questions of his virtue as a vigilante have always provided fodder for debate, and Christopher Nolan's Batman is certainly no exception. In the opening scenes of *The Dark Knight*, Batman is asked to explain the difference between himself and others willing to be vigilantes as well. Men dressed as Batman are attempting to disrupt the Scarecrow's mischief; after the attempts fail, the real Batman rushes to their aid, admonishing them for their actions. Angered by his lack of gratitude, the imposters shout: "What gives you the right?! What's the difference between you and me?!" Batman is unable to give any more than the glib reply, "I'm not wearing hockey pads." Oddly enough, Batman is wearing state-of-the-art body armor, or glorified hockey pads. His dismissal of their right to be vigilantes would serve as a dismissal of his own. When pressed for an answer about what makes him virtuous in his actions where others are not, Batman finds himself without an answer. This hesitation, marked by the witty but unsubstantive reply, demonstrates that any virtue Batman has is not yet second nature nor is it completely clear that he is fully aware of what virtue is composed.

Batman's hesitation in action is often apparent to those around him. Even his enemies note his difficulty in determining the right thing to do and the right way to do it. In threatening Maroni, a Falconi crime leader, he realizes that perhaps the only way to get to the Joker is to turn himself in to the authorities. Maroni aptly points out: "...you already know what it is. Just take off that mask and let him come find you. Or, you want to let a couple more people get killed while you make up your mind?"

The climactic scene between Batman and Joker demonstrates Batman's inability, or at least hesitation, in doing the right thing at the right time in the right way and for the right reasons. Batman defeats this enemy in hand-to-hand combat, leaving him dangling over the edge of a building at his mercy. Batman is now faced with a moral dilemma. Should he kill the man who has caused so much harm or should he let him live? After pushing the Joker off of the building, he quickly stops his fall, unsure of his decision. The Joker aptly points out Batman's motivation as well as his own: "You won't kill me out of some misplaced sense of self-righteousness ... and I won't kill you because you're too much fun. We're going to do this forever." Batman cannot make the decision to kill the Joker because he is unable to accept the guilt that his overactive sense of self-righteousness causes. From this, one can determine that Batman is continent rather than virtuous. He is often hesitant in making moral decisions and has not yet developed the ability to act from the right reasons. His actions are almost always motivated by external reasons — he is concerned with how his works will be received by the people of Gotham and strives to avoid emotional conflict. Doing the right thing when motivated by emotion and care for reputation makes one continent, not virtuous. Thus, Batman is certainly on the path to virtue, but he still has much to learn.

But, if Batman needs to learn, who is to teach him virtue? This person is Bruce Wayne's trusted servant, Alfred. Servant is a term of art; Alfred is far more than a servant — he is Bruce's surrogate father, offering wise council on the one hand and stitching his wounds, on the other. Alfred has come to the place where he can be Bruce's guide through hard-won experience of his own, even working with the local governments in Burma to catch a bandit raiding caravans. Alfred does not hesitate when Bruce asks him for advice; he knows the right thing to do. Bruce is conflicted about whether or not he should turn himself in: "People are dying, Alfred. What would you have me do?" Alfred's answer is firm and soundly reasoned: "Endure, Master Wayne. Take it. They'll hate you for it, but that's the point of Batman.... He can be the outcast. He can make the choice no one else can face. The right choice." Alfred's actions demonstrate that he knows what the right thing is, the right way to go about it, and the right reasons for doing so. He encourages Bruce to look beyond his concern for reputation and even his emotional conflict. He must make the choice no one else can face because it is the right thing to do. That is what virtue requires.

The final component to being virtuous is knowing the right time to act, and Alfred demonstrates the ability to make this determination as well. Rachel writes Bruce a letter that tells him that she will marry Harvey. She leaves it in Alfred's care: "You know Bruce best, Alfred.... Give it to him when the time is right." After Rachel's death, Alfred considers giving Bruce the letter, but carefully assesses the situation first. He realizes Bruce's ability to cope hinges on believing that Rachel would have chosen him; thus, he removes the letter from Bruce's view. When Alfred realizes that Harvey will never recover his sanity and that Bruce will always need the comfort of Rachel's supposed choice, he burns the letter. After careful deliberation about the letter's contents, Alfred understands that the time will never be right, so he destroys it. By doing the right thing at the right time in the right way and for the right reasons, all as second nature, Alfred exemplifies the virtuous character.

Thus far, we have examined characters that are upwardly mobile in the path to virtue, but it is important to remember that one can also fall. Harvey Dent is a good example of this possibility. Harvey begins *The Dark Knight* as a continent man. He strives for virtue but has not yet mastered all of the criteria to be virtuous. At first glance, it may seem strange to view Harvey as continent given his apparent reliance on chance for decision-making. However, his lucky coin, we discover some way into the movie, is a useful piece of artistic flair. As a double-headed coin, Harvey is able to "make" his own luck. But, it is not chance that guides his decisions. Rather, the coin hides what Bruce sees — that Harvey Dent is supremely confident in his own decision-making abilities. His confidence is not arrogance, but a seemingly incorruptible sense of understanding of the right thing to do and the right way to do it. For example, in claiming to be the Batman, Harvey rightly judges that Batman will do the right thing: "He'll save my ass."

However, as Aristotle pointed out and as common sense demonstrates, great tragedy can radically affect even the most carefully constructed and confident character. Following Rachel's death, Harvey loses the ability to make rational decisions; his decisions are left solely to chance. Any choice of the right thing is simply because his coin, now characterized by one pristine and one scarred side, tells him to make that choice. He does the right thing occasionally, but only for external reasons — the flip of his coin. Harvey is ultimately motivated by blinding grief and an unquenchable desire for revenge. He confronts a detective in a bar to attempt to find out who betrayed him and Rachel. The detective attempts to mitigate his own guilt: "I swear to God, I didn't know what they were gonna do to you." Harvey responds simply, "Funny, I don't know what's going to happen to you, either." He flips his coin; receiving the verdict of the scarred side, Harvey instantly shoots the man. Murder is obviously not the action that should be taken by a man of virtue, and moral luck is not the hallmark of a continent man. The effect of Rachel's death on Harvey is powerful and destructive of his character — this once continent, and aspiringly virtuous, man has now become incontinent. His moral choices depend solely on luck.

All of which brings us to the Joker. One of the more controversial aspects of Aristotle's division of people into four types is that the truly vicious person, the one who exults in evil, exists. This person at least exists in fiction as Nolan has given us the Joker. He is irredeemable; he consistently does the wrong thing simply because it is wrong. The Joker has been amassing a fortune by robbing mobsters; however, he is not motivated by greed. Standing in front of his large hoard of money, the Joker boldly tells his partners, "All you care about is money. This city deserves a better class of criminal, and I'm going to give it to them." He then sets the money, and the accountant, on fire. When he refers to a better class of criminal, the Joker means a man like himself—a criminal who does the wrong thing simply because he finds fulfillment in making the wrong choice. It is left to the virtuous man to fully describe the nature of the vicious: "some men aren't looking for anything logical, like money.... They can't be bought, bullied, reasoned or negotiated with. Some men just want to watch the world burn." And so we have it—Nolan has demonstrated to the scholar of virtue all four Aristotelian types. Some are inspiring; some are hopeful; and others are quite simply chilling.

Works Cited

Aristotle. *Nichomachean Ethics*. Trans. Joe Sachs. Newburyport, MA: Focus Publishing/R. Pullins Co., 2002. Print.
The Dark Knight. Dir. Christopher Nolan. Warner Bros. 2008. DVD.

2

The Dark Knight Errant
Power and Authority in Frank Miller's Batman: *The Dark Knight Returns*

CHRISTOPHER BUNDRICK

There has been a lot of critical attention directed at Christopher Nolan's revival of the Batman film franchise. Considering the news that his second installment, *The Dark Knight*, topped the $500 million mark within six weeks of its release, it is obviously more than just the critics who are paying attention to Nolan's new take on the character that DC introduced in 1939 (Germain). The popularity of Nolan's new, grittier Batman, however, is a direct result of both how enmeshed Batman has become in the cinematic and how clearly the new films rely on the version of the character that emerged in 1986 when Frank Miller's *The Dark Knight Returns* changed the way we read not just *Batman*, but the entire comic book genre.

In "Cape Fear" Kim Newman points out that *Batman*, "has 'begun' many times," and Nolan's efforts represent only one of many attempts to reframe the origins and character of the Dark Knight (18). Newman clearly privileges the original DC Comics as the authoritative *Batman* texts and spends considerable time explaining the differences between versions of Batman's origins according to the 1939 story arc and Nolan's reimagining in his 2005 *Batman Begins*. Trying to, "give credit where it's due," Newman is especially interested in the contributions of Bill Finger and Jerry Robinson — who created the Joker and Commissioner Gordon, respectively — and who, until they were credited by Frank Miller in *Batman: Year One* (1987), had been essentially forgotten (19). Reconciling issues of continuity between the 1939 comics and the 2005 movie and emphasizing the slow process through which many artists worked to develop the *Batman* mythos that Nolan inherited, Newman seems to be suggesting that there is more to the character than a traumatic childhood memory and an overzealous drive for justice. Highlighting the contributions of Finger and Robinson, in fact, feels like an unambiguous effort to place Batman within a context larger than his own personal experience. Existing somewhere between Jim Gordon's good cop and the Joker's maniacal anarchist, Newman's argument suggests that Batman represents a specific location on the continuum of order and chaos—somewhere between agent of the state and outlaw.

Manohla Dargis, in her *New York Times* review of *Batman Begins* takes an entirely different approach to Nolan's efforts. While it does briefly mention Bob Kane (who created the Batman character), Dargis' review mainly credits Miller, to whom, she writes, Nolan "owes a specific debt" ("Dark Was"). "Like Mr. Miller's Batman," the review continues, "Mr. Nolan's is tormented by demons both physical and psychological [...] this is a hero caught between justice and vengeance, a desire for peace and the will to power" ("Dark was"). Zeroing in on the internal struggle between Batman and Bruce Wayne, Dargis's review suggests that *Batman Begins* is successful for its recognition of the origin story as a kind of coming of age tale in which Bruce Wayne—who she defines by his "air of casual entitlement" and "aristocratic hauteur"—must reconcile himself to the Batman ("Dark Was"). Read this way, the Batman story is essentially an internal psychodrama of identity. But, if we, like Newman (and Miller for that matter), recognize that Batman cannot truly exist outside of the context provided by characters like Gordon and the Joker, we have to understand the character as representing much more than a single figure torn between two identities. Three years after her review of *Batman Begins*, Dargis shows signs of understanding just this. Identifying *The Dark Knight* as a "postheroic superhero movie," Dargis argues that Nolan's sequel to *Begins* has "tension and interest beyond one man's personal struggle" ("Dark Was"). Even more interestingly, she concludes this deservedly glowing review by observing just how closely the Batman we see in *The Dark Night* treads the dark threshold that characters like the Joker or Two-Face have already crossed. "When Batman takes flight in this film," she writes, "it's as if he were trying to possess the world as much as save it" ("Showdown").[1] It's precisely this sort of ambivalence that Miller captures in *Batman: The Dark Knight Returns*. The figure we see in Miller's text isn't conflicted about being Batman so much as he is of two minds about whether to continue serving the woefully inadequate structures of law and order that have so utterly failed Gotham, or simply to strike out on his own self-proclaimed authority and serve his own sense of justice. To some degree, this has always been the essential tension in the Batman story, and Miller's portrayal—subtle and layered as it is—sharpens the primal elements more than it re-imagines. In the process, Miller made

Batman into a cautionary figure whose conflicted relationship to the rules and order he protects has a lot to tell us about the complications surrounding authority and its expression in a modern democracy.

The murder of Bruce Wayne's parents has loomed large in every version of the Batman story. Miller's does not change that at all, but *The Dark Knight Returns* blurs what has, in the past, always been the immediate connection between the murders of Thomas and Martha Wayne and the birth of Batman. Mark Fisher argues that Batman is "a thoroughly Oedipal figure" because of the way the young Bruce Wayne feels responsible for his father's (and mother's) death ("Gothic Oedipus"). Batman is an Oedipal figure, of course, but the most important manner that this aspect of his personality manifests is not in whatever marginal way he might feel he contributed to his parents' death, but in the sense that he is a figure who acts as a bridge to the powerful structures of a patriarchal authority that loom in our past. Oedipus, we must remember, was a sitting king in Sophocles's play and part of his tragedy is the result of his inflexible application of his own law. It was by his own decree that he was blinded and sent into exile at the end of play, after all. Batman represents a similar degree of inflexibility, to say the least. Frank Miller's Batman is perhaps more recognizable by his strict enforcement of and adherence to a personal code of moral righteousness that, while overlapping in places, operates essentially independent of the laws that govern the rest of society.[2]

In *The Dark Knight Returns*, Batman's war on crime has as a backdrop 1980s-style Cold War brinksmanship between a not-at-all veiled President Ronald Regan and the still extant Soviet Union. While certainly more decisive than Gotham's mayor, Regan's cowboy wisdom leads him to bumble his way into a nuclear exchange that ends with the Soviets deploying a special "Coldbringer" missile, designed to generate an electromagnetic pulse (EMP) that will disable most electronics, shut down power grids, and destroy normal climate patterns over its target. Superman tries to stop the missile, but is not fully successful. As it detonates, the entirety of Gotham is plunged into the darkness and cold of a nuclear winter. Pages later, Batman descends on the rioting citizens, restoring order to a city that, in the absence of visible, tangible authority, has immediately fallen into chaos. Of course, the EMP has made automobile travel impossible, so Batman arrives on horseback. On one level, this simply represents the character's resourcefulness, but when we remember (as Miller's title forces us to do) that one of Batman's monikers is the Dark Knight, we have to reconsider the significance of the image of Batman charging across the page like a knight errant in a medieval romance.[3] In "Gotham's Dark Knight: The Postmodern Transformation of the Arthurian Mythos," Jesse Nash develops this aspect of the Batman character beginning with the premise that "Batman comic books [...] exploit traditional Arthuriana" (36). Miller's version of Batman, is postmodern, Nash argues, specifically because of the way it revises those Arthurian myths. "Miller's *Dark Knight* [is] postmodern," Nash explains, because it has "rejected and/or transformed the older Arthurian mythos" (37). Since the Arthur myth, Nash maintains, "*is* the ideology of the American political system," Miller's revision of these myths makes his Dark Knight "revolutionary, if not un–American" (37). Nash understands the central thrust of the Arthur mythology as a belief that "a golden age of politics and culture can be relived, especially when inaugurated by a politician deemed to be an 'outsider' to the political system, but who has 'blood ties' to that system [...] and who because of his uncertain status rejuvenates the system" (38). From a certain perspective, this description seems to be tailor-made for Bruce Wayne/Batman. The sole heir of Gotham's most influential industrialist, Wayne's blood ties are beyond question. At the same time, his playboy act and staged rejection of adult responsibility, combined with the fact that he dresses up like a monster to fight crime certainly demonstrates his outsider status.

Miller, it seems, also recognizes that the real danger Batman represents extends beyond the evil-doers against whom he's declared a personal war to the point that it actually threatens the ordinary structures of authority under which the city generally operates. Obviously, putting the "Dark Knight" on horseback goes a long way toward highlighting the medieval aspects of Batman's word-view, but Miller takes it a step further. The full-page image of Batman charging to the rescue on horseback after the Coldbringer's detonation would seem to further emphasize his Arthurian nature; however, the visual similarity between that image in *The Dark Knight Returns* and Miller's depiction of the first Persian messenger in *300* is so striking that it deserves some further attention. The reader sees both head on, as if they were going to charge straight out of the page.[4] They hunch over their horses' necks, both faces contorted by expressions of grim purpose, long capes flowing out behind them. The problem with this similarity is that if Batman is Arthur, the character from *300* whom he should most resemble is King Leonidas, not a Persian. The messenger, of course, stands in lieu of Xerxes, whose empire (which he inherited from his father, Darius) the narrator of *300* claims represents, "the old, dark, stupid ways" against which the Spartans pit reason, justice, and law (*300* 80, 64). This similarity could simply suggest that Miller's sketchbook has a limited selection of equestrian scenes, but I think it is more likely that it reveals how Batman, on some levels, denies aspects of the reason and law which Leonitas (or Arthur) represents. Always a figure in the shadows, Batman has never really been an agent of the state; however, if Miller's Dark Knight has rejected reason, then what we see when Batman charges in on horseback to restore order is not Arthur restoring a golden age, but a more essentially medieval scene of a lord using his power and authority as blunt instruments to protect and restore the social structures that serve his hegemony. This Batman hasn't arrived to reveal the balance inherent in the system — he has come to compel order by force. The Batman this comparison reveals is a troubling figure. His one unbreakable rule aside, Batman rejects the culture of law, the democratic process, even basic human rights. At times, his violence is shockingly close to that of a Dark Age tyrant. While his ultimate goals might suggest a certain nobility, his methods seem to reject the very way of life that traditional superhero — like Superman — swears to protect.

One of Batman's first tasks during the "Coldbringer" riots is to stop the "Sons of Batman," a vigilante group made up of former members of the Mutant gang (which Batman defeats earlier in the story), who want to use the power failure as an opportunity to raze the city. "No," Batman exclaims on rampart black steed as he takes control of the scene, "Tonight **we** are the law. Tonight, **I** am the law" (Miller 173). Maybe more than any other moment in *The Dark Knight Returns*, this instance truly exposes the nature of the Batman character. He holds himself to be, if not a king, at least a noble in the medieval model. His word is law and his authority unassailable. In this scene, Batman assumes the mantle of his true character — he is a figure out of medieval structures of paternalistic authority. He assumes authority over Gotham during this crisis because he has always assumed authority over Gotham — because, as a scion of the Wayne clan, he has, to one degree or another, always thought of Gotham as a personal fiefdom. Coupled with the gothic persona he adopts after his parents murder, this approach would seem to align Bruce Wayne with something very much like a medieval sensibility. Read through this lens, we can see that Miller's *The Dark Knight Returns* works to develop a Batman whose existence represents a deeply felt ambivalence over constructions of authority in this particular iteration of the United States.

"Alexis de Tocqeville's primary fear, delimited in *Democracy in America*," Tim Blackmore writes, "is that democracy will transmute itself into authoritarianism" (37). Miller's *The Dark Knight Returns*, Blackmore goes on, "depicts this event [...] from the decay of democracy and the birth of the authoritarian state to the loss of individual rights, the rise of the charismatic leader, the mass which follows him, and the future of the 'state'" (37). Blackmore's identification of the anxiety we see in Miller's text is spot on, but it may be that he has incorrectly located the source of that anxiety. In Blackmore's argument, the state which erodes individual rights is actually democratically elected. However, it is the ineptitude — not despotism — of Gotham's duly elected government, particularly, its mayor, that allows criminals to limit the rights of ordinary Gotham dwellers. In this sense, it is the citizens of Gotham who, having voted such spineless do-nothings into office, are to blame. Bruce Wayne sees this first-hand early in the novel when, after sharing a drink celebrating the tenth anniversary of Batman's retirement with Commissioner Gordon, he walks home, thinking to himself, "I walk the streets of this city I'm learning to hate, the city that's given up, like the whole world seems to have" (Miller 12). At the same time Wayne sees himself as "a zombie. A flying Duchman. A dead man, ten years dead" (12). It seems clear that, in Miller's vision, the people of Gotham are at least as much to blame for their predicament as the state.

If anything, Wayne and his Batman alter-ego represent a much greater challenge to democracy and individual rights than the comically ineffective mayor whose responds to almost every question is a frantic "I'm still pooling opinions. I'm still pooling opinions" (Miller 61). Compare this to the scene in which Batman confronts one of Two-Face's henchmen at the arch-criminal's now abandoned hideout: "I got rights," the hood (who is on crutches from injuries sustained during an earlier run-in with Batman) shouts just before Batman shoves him through a window (44). "You've got rights. Lots of rights," Batman agrees, "But right now you've got a piece of glass shoved in a major artery in your arm. Right now you're bleeding to death. Right now I'm the only one in the world who can get you to a hospital in time" (45). About this scene, Blackmore writes, "the word 'rights' changes from the benign idea of individual protection to the Old Testament justice where the frightening reality becomes clear: the man must submit or die. The word becomes a curse in the Batman's mouth" (44). As Andreas Reichstein points out, unlike Don Diego (whose Zorro alter ego was one of Bob Kane's influences while developing the Batman character), Bruce Wayne, as the citizen of a "modern, democratic society" could have chosen to fight crime as part of the system "by joining the police force or using his money to establish a police training center" (344). Reichstein's suggestion here is that Wayne's goals and motives are different from those of the system. After more (or less) than simple justice, Wayne "wants to strike terror" (Reichstein 344). This question of motives is an important one. Bruce Wayne chooses to work outside (and thus, to some degree, against) the system. He consciously rejects the structures of law enforcement and judicial process already in place in order to pursue his personal vendetta against crime. Personalizing crime this way, of course, puts Batman in the position of representing all of Gotham without even having been elected to do so. Whether or not Wayne/Batman draws his authority from his own personal wealth or some sort of divine fiat, isn't as important as the fact that his mandate comes from something other than public consensus, and that makes him dangerously close to the villains he battles who have also, on their own authority, rejected the normal rules of civilized, democratic society. From this perspective, Batman's personal war on crime looks, at its best, like a monarch's inquisition, and at its worst, like a turf war over Gotham City that pits Batman equally against his rogues gallery and the democratically elected officials that represent the city.

In a similar vein, Blackmore connects Batman to Bernard Goetz (whose actions in the New York subway preceded the first issue of *Dark Knight Returns* by only fourteen months). While there are clear similarities, thinking of Batman as a hero of the masses overlooks some fundamental and very troubling aspects of his character. To begin with, the masses that populate Miller's Gotham City are often contemptible. In a series of man-on-the-street style interviews, Gotham-dwellers reveal their own morally problematic nature while discussing Batman: "Yea, I think he's A-Okay," one man proclaims, "He kicking just the right butts — butts the cops ain't kicking, that's for sure. Hope he goes after the homos next" (45). In the next panel, a smug-faced executive says of Batman's approach to crime, "It makes me sick, we must treat the socially misoriented with rehabilitative methods. We must patiently realign their — excuse me —? No, I'd never live in the city..." (45). The most obvious comparison's to Goetz is not Batman, but the tragic Arnold Crimp, who even bears some physical resemblance to Goetz, and whose violence springs from delusional paranoia rather than any sort of righteous indignation or moral imperative. As Bruce Wayne observes in the beginning of the story, the people of Gotham have "given up" to the extent that the only hero who can rise from the masses is the sort we see in Arnold Crimp, whose twisted sense of justice and retribution reveals the people's utter inability to confront the state of their society in any meaningful way. Batman's solution is as elegant as it is authoritarian: he does it for them.

When Batman declares that he is the law, he is essentially acknowledging his long-standing rejection of the actual rules of law that at least ostensibly govern the city: "Sure we're criminal," Superman — clearly frustrated with Wayne — remembers Batman telling an ostensibly Congressional "sub-committee," "We've always been criminals" (Miller 135).[5] Batman was never part of the system because he holds himself to be superior to the system — a kind of *force majeure* who swoops in to dispense, if not justice, then law. At the same time, ironically, Wayne is very much part of the system. The son of Gotham's first citizen and head of Wayne Enterprises, Bruce Wayne is literally at the heart of both Gotham's financial and social networks. Batman's Gotham is a gritty, urban wasteland — Mark Cotta Vaz calls it "a vision of decay and the coming collapse of civilization" (176) — but Wayne Manor, where Bruce Wayne lives, remains a bucolic and sprawling estate complete with the sort of stables and floor to ceiling diamond-paned windows we might expect in an opulent Tutor residence. But where Wayne Manor emphasizes the character's *nobles oblige*, the shape of the Batcave, with its nude stone walls and seemingly hand-hewn stairs locates Batman in a more primitive, more savage, aspect of the Old World. Whether Bruce Wayne or Batman, the threat lying just beneath the surface of this character's personal war on crime is the same; either way it represents an ideology of violent authoritarianism that rejects post–Enlightenment democracy and egalitarianism and harkens directly back to Old World structures of patriarchy, totalitarianism, and monarchy.[6] As much as he emphasizes the Oedipal, Mark Fisher's argument also relies heavily on the idea that the gothic elements of Batman are at the core of his character: "From the start," Fisher writes, "the Batman mythos has been about the pressing of Gothic Fear into the service of heroic justice" ("Gothic Oedipus"). Citing the panel from the November 1939 Detective Comics #33 where a young Bruce Wayne specifies that his crime fighting costume must "strike terror into their [criminals'] hearts," Fisher's argument distinguishes the more noir aspects of Batman's appearance and namesake from what he identifies as the Oedipal aspects ("Gothic Oedipus"). These two are not as incongruous as they might seem, however, and I believe Miller's treatment of Carrie Kelly — the first female Robin — does a wonderful job of illustrating where the gothic and the Oedipal overlap.

Frank Miller uses the death of the Waynes as a short-hand to express the horror Carrie Kelly feels when she realizes the Joker's plans for a mass killing at the county fair: "Half my friends'll be there..." she says, and the next frame flashes an image of the young Bruce Wayne's face showing his horror when his father is shot (136). Connecting her shock at the scope of the Joker's evil to a trauma which is central to Batman's identity develops Carrie Kelly's role as Robin in both predictable and innovative directions. Dick Grayson, the original Robin was orphaned and, in this sense, like Bruce Wayne. This specific trauma — this intimately personal loss — is the first necessary component of the Robin character for both practical and aesthetic reasons. The most prosaic reason Robin must be orphaned is because it simply is not plausible that a teenager could hide such activities from parents. More significant to the nature of the character, however, is the necessity that Robin must feel something like the loss that Wayne experienced in order to identify fully with Batman's gothic sensibilities.

The Dark Knight Returns handles these issues in a very interesting way.

Carrie Kelly is only symbolically orphaned by parents who seem too self-involved (and too high) to raise their daughter. In "The Dark Knight of Democracy," Tim Blackmore argues that Kelly's parents represent "today's 'nostalgic' hippies" (43). "Obviously a fascist. Never heard of Civil Rights," one of her parents — both of whom are always off-frame and thus absent — says in response to news coverage of Batman's crime fighting (45). "Sometimes I despair," the disembodied voice continues, to which the response is "Give me another hit of that, huh?" (45). Later, while Kelly witnesses Batman's startlingly violent fight with the Mutant gang leader who is behind the seemingly random uptick of violence in Gotham, Miller jumps back to the Kelly apartment (readily identifiable by the marijuana smoke wafting through the frame) where one of Carrie's parents — apparently noticing their daughter's absence for the first time — asks, "Hey ... didn't we have a kid?" (76). At about the same time, Carrie is rescuing Batman, who has been terribly injured in his fight with the Mutant leader. "What's ... your name..." he asks and the girl replies, "Carrie. Carrie Kelly. Robin" (85). Just like that Carrie lets go of the parents who seem to have long ago let go of her and allows herself to be "adopted" by Batman. The text tries to imply that Batman will serve as a better parent that Carrie Kelly's biological ones even though it also recognizes the character's more monstrous aspects. Tim Blackmore argues that what we see in Carrie Kelly's parents is how, "Miller is enraged at those who dare live off, and yet criticize, the central authority" (43). The suggestion is that Batman's willingness to act and to do so independent of the anemic structures of civil authority makes him a better parent than superannuated hippies. Blackmore's is an interesting point, but the way it seems to arrange Batman as opposing the counter culture and supporting the "central authority" is problematic. Comparisons to Mayor Daley aside, Miller's Batman is as much at odds with Gotham's police force as he is with Gotham's criminals. Ellen Yindel, James Gordon's replacement, makes this abundantly clear in her first speech as Commissioner, during which she issues an arrest warrant for Batman, including charges of "breaking and entering, assault and battery [and] creating a public menace" (Miller 116). Ultimately, Miller's Batman is a complicated figure in the sense that he occupies the cultural space we generally reserve for superheroes, but he doesn't precisely fit the role. This ambivalence is, however, really just a reflection of the more important contradiction which resides in the Batman character — that is the contradictory figures of the paternal and the patriarchal. On the one hand, Batman is the strong, reliable figure who protects without expecting a reward. On the other, he is a powerful force that circumvents or simply ignores democratic rules and law and exerts an almost parental authority he has assumed for himself.

Behind these Oedipal issues, however, is an important element of the Gothic. In the introduction to her 1999 *Return of the Repressed*, Valdine Clemens argues that although Gothic novels might seem "less socially responsible than the 'realistic' novel, which pays closer attention to the surface textures if daily life," they actually serve a very important social function (4). "Gothic novels," Clemens reminds us a few lines later, "emerged with the development of the urban industrial world" and serve to "stress the fragility of civilized constraints on human behavior and demonstrate that the world is much older and less anthropocentric than we would like to think" (4). In this sense, Batman is the protagonist of his own Gothic narrative. Of course the cape and cowl work to conceal his identity, but the real reason he wears the costume is its capacity to "strike terror." Batman's Gothic story, the story his persona suggests, follows the usual pattern of most cautionary tales: behave, or monsters will come to get you. The fundamental work of the Gothic, Clemens concludes is to expedite the "return of the repressed,"[7] which she defines in this context as the "emergence of whatever has been previously rejected by consciousness" (3). This material is repressed, of course, precisely because it is always something dangerous, something that, as Clemens puts it, "threatens the established order of things" (7). Interestingly, Batman could represent both the act and the object of repression. On the one hand, he serves as the monster that lurks in the shadows, an eerie manifestation of justice ready to pounce on evil-doers all across Gotham. At the same time, however, the values and ideas he represents are mostly ones that had to be repressed in order to allow urban, industrial, and — most importantly — egalitarian society to exist. Gothic landscapes are haunted because they are locations in which the past is especially present. Gotham's buildings abound with gargoyles, spires, and crenellation, but architecture is not the city's most Gothic aspect. The city is most truly Gothic because Batman "haunts" it the same way the memories of his parents' murder haunt Bruce Wayne. In "Psychic Trauma and Its Solutions," Michael Brody argues that "Bruce Wayne's vow to fight crime is a compensating wish," something to assuage the boy's guilt for surviving when he parents did not (174). Clearly the death of his parents is intimately connected to Bruce Wayne's transformation to Batman, but Miller's version of the story in *The Dark Knight Returns* intimates that, in the most important ways, the Batman identity was formed before the Waynes were gunned down. In an early scene, Miller's text shows the young Wayne playing on the manor grounds while his parents watch on. Chasing a rabbit to test his own speed, young Bruce accidentally falls into a hole that drops him into a cave full of bats, where one especially hideous creature responds by "claiming [the boy] as his own" (Miller 19). Miller's implication is that it is the encounter with the monster in what would become the Bat Cave — not the murder of his parents — that essentially forms Batman, and this takes the character in a very interesting new direction.

If "Batman" predates Bruce Wayne's trauma over seeing his mother and father murdered in the street, then he simply cannot be the product of the boy's attempts to sublimate his grief and anger. In fact, the language that Wayne uses to describe the creature from the cave, which he seems to feel is essential to Batman's existence, might offer another, potentially very interesting, explanation of Batman's origins. Wayne's memory of the creature as, "Gliding with ancient grace [...] the *fiercest* survivor [...] the *purest* warrior," of course foreshadows both the survivor and the warrior that he is destined to become, but it also suggests that the creature's power comes from Wayne's sense of it as a figure from an ancient and atavistic past. The implication — and this is vital to Miller's interpretation of the character — is that Batman is who Bruce Wayne has always really been. Batman has been retired for ten years when *The Dark Knight Returns* begins, and without a reason to keep pretending, the Wayne we see in the opening pages is morose, constrained, overwhelmed by the chaos that has poisoned his world — nothing at all like the playboy millionaire we are used to seeing. He wears a mustache, like his father, which seems to suggest a certain acceptance of both his parents' death and the legitimacy of Bruce Wayne as his real identity. The truth, however, is that Wayne is deeply conflicted, and the Batman personality is becoming harder and harder to repress. Wayne clearly must constantly work to make sure that Batman stays retired. Miller does a wonderful job representing this struggle graphically. In the opening pages of the book, we often see Wayne surrounded by chain-link fencing and bars, even the frames of each panel are tight and confining — so much so that Blackmore argues "Miller's unprecedented 16-panel grid works cinematically to produce a dark, claustrophobic world" (43). While these features might indicate the danger of this modern Gotham City, they also point to the barriers that Bruce Wayne must erect to control Batman, or at least keep his alter ego at bay.

These structures of control and repression notwithstanding, Bruce Wayne finds that his nocturnal wanderings lead him to the scene of his parents' murder. "Once again, he's brought me back to show me how little it has changed," Wayne thinks when he realizes where he is. "It could have happened yesterday," he thinks, "It could be happening right now. They could be lying at your feet, twitching, bleeding..." (13). The "he" Wayne refers to is, of course, Batman; retirement does not sit easy with the Dark Knight. In one early scene, Wayne, plagued by memories of his past, drinks too much and wakes up standing in the Bat Cave. Alone in the mothballed hideout, Wayne thinks,

"He [Batman] laughs at me, curses me, calls me a fool. He fills my sleep. He tricks me. Brings me here when the night is long and my will is weak. He struggles relentlessly, hatefully, to be free. I will not let him" (19). When Alfred comes to check on his somnambulant employer, he notices that Wayne has shaved his mustache. If the mustache represented a willingness to be his father's heir, its absence represents a return to the bat — that figure of "ancient grace" that claimed Bruce Wayne even before his parents were dead (19). Wayne's inability to let go of the past is, in many ways, the definitive mark of his character. Frozen in the moment of grief over his parents' murder, Bruce Wayne experiences a kind of past-in-present that is especially Gothic.

The figure of the bat and its "claiming" him represents an interesting departure from the traditional version of Batman's origin. In the original story (told in "The Legends of Batman — Who He Is and How He Came to Be!"), Wayne's parents were already murdered, and he had already vowed to avenge their deaths by becoming a crime fighter when a bat flies into his room, giving him the idea for his disguise. Rather than claiming it as a symbol after he has vowed to fight crime, as the young Bruce Wayne does in Bob Kane's version, the Bruce Wayne we see in *The Dark Knight Returns* does not seem to have a lot of agency. The "ancient" bat in the cave seems to represent or perhaps awaken the potential Batman in Wayne even before his parents are killed. I believe that this is extremely important to Miller's vision of the character as somehow essentially Batman. Many critics read Batman as a coping mechanism that allows Bruce Wayne to go on after his parents' murder. In Miller's story, however, Wayne always was the Batman. Told this way, Wayne becomes Batman not because of the trauma of seeing his parents killed, but because of a quasi-mystical connection to an ancient past. Such an understanding of the character explains the darkness of Miller's vision and also forces us to reconsider our understanding of Batman's motives. If Batman is not simply Bruce Wayne's vehicle for grief or revenge, we have to wonder just what this war on crime is really all about. The dark truth this reveals about Batman is that his war on crime is not really about crime at all, but rather about taking the opportunity to impose his personal sense of order on the world around him. In this sense, Batman is essentially a feudal figure, resurrected out of a past he can neither remember nor escape.

Miller signals this most clearly by pitting Batman against Superman — the classic superhero in the American comics pantheon. Besides representing Truth, Justice, and the American Way, this iteration of Superman is a direct agent of the government to the extent that he seems to actively participate in U.S. military action against the USSR. (Batman, obviously, is not the only hero to have found a darker side in *The Dark Knight Returns*.) What Batman has rather than special powers, however, is an extraordinary discipline and strength of will. Batman fights crime as a way of imposing that will on the world. Superman identifies Batman's activities as a "holy war," and in some ways, this is exactly what they are. U.S. readers tend to understand holy war in the twenty-first century as jihad, but readers from another time might just as readily associate the term more with the Crusades. In the case of Batman's war on crime, both apply. Batman is simultaneously a sort of crowned regent and a guerilla fighter. He constructs an identity for himself that simultaneously occupies both ends of the spectrum. He does this by first dismissing the authority of elected officials and their law so that he can instead obey a higher law he has received in the presence of the monstrous bat — the law he later "becomes" while quelling the Gotham riots. Remembering the bat encounter nearly fifty years later, Bruce Wayne narrates, "unwilling to retreat as his brothers did ... eyes gleaming, untouched by love or joy or sorrow [...] glaring, hating ... claiming me as his own" (19). It is this bat that Wayne uses as the model for the alter ego that, as of the beginning of *The Dark Knight Returns*, he has been suppressing for ten years, and the "creature" in him does not recognize governmental authority. That Wayne appreciates these features enough to incorporate them into his crime-fighting persona later suggests that he believes Batman's goals are both more pure and more ancient that the corrupt society, whose failings have forced the Dark Knight to act.

Essentially, Batman swaps the traditional authority of police chief, mayor, and president for a more "ancient" one. In doing so, he reaches back to more of an Old World authority that matches the sort of crusade upon which he has embarked. As Clark Kent, at the president's order, tells Bruce Wayne why he has to put Batman back into retirement, he explains, "Sooner or later, somebody's going to order me to bring you in, somebody with *authority*" (119). Wayne, who seems to wear an almost feral grin throughout the entire encounter, interrupts, "When that happens, Clark — may the best man win" (119). Turning Kent's official warning into a personal challenge, Bruce Wayne reveals his fundamental dismissal of the legitimate civil authority. Where Superman waits either for permission or command, Batman simply imagines the word he wants and acts. The showdown, of course, is inevitable and, borrowing Batman's theatricality for a moment, Superman issues the challenge by using his heat vision to burn a one word question in the snow before Bruce Wayne, "WHERE?" "Crime alley," Wayne responds and brings the story's end to the place it began.

It is during the final battle with Superman that the two very different ideas about authority that Superman and Batman represent for Miller becomes plain. With most of the narration for the scene coming through Batman's internal monologue, it is clear that Miller thinks of this final fight as the most meaningful in the book. We know from his preparations for the battle that Batman has something up his sleeve, but the plan is unclear. In one frame Bruce Wayne swallows a pill while musing, "At midnight ... a grand death," and in the next, we see him manipulating something in a glove box that glows with a suspicious shade of green. The battles with the Mutant Leader, Two-Face, even the Joker, pale beside the scene of Batman, wearing what looks like a high tech version of a medieval suit of armor, standing at the site of his parents' death, calmly waiting to face Superman. The Man of Steel descends gracefully before him, and Batman thinks, "Now he's talking — trying to *reason* with me. I can't hear him of course..." (191). In much the same way he twists the term "rights" with Two-Face's henchman, Batman's scornful reference to Superman's attempts to "reason" transforms the word's significance. It emphasizes that reason is the wrong tool for Superman to wield in this circumstance. As an avatar of medieval-style authority, Batman has a somewhat less-than-firm relationship with post–Enlightenment reason. He is a self-proclaimed creature of the night, a boogie man who lurks in the shadows and collective subconscious, a mystic incarnation of the spirit of Gothic fear — he represents terror, the opposite of reason. Although it may seem contradictory, his mocking use of "reason" also signifies that Batman understands fully that he has taken things too far and attracted too much official attention to ever be allowed to continue. He understands that the moment Regan ordered Superman to "settle him down ... ride him around the yard a few times if you have to," as the president puts it — it became too late for talking (86). Batman understands this because, more than any other character in *The Dark Knight Returns*, he is comfortable with the relationship between governance and violence. "Keep talking, Clark..." Batman thinks as he attacks Superman with a sonic weapon, "you've always known what to say. 'Yes'— you always say yes — to anyone with a badge — or a flag —" (190). "My parents ... taught me a different lesson," he continues, "they showed me that the world only makes sense when you force it to..." (192). The two grapple in the street until Superman, still weak from attempting to stop the Coldbringer, falters and Batman lands a vicious right cross that knocks the Man of Steel off his feet (190). Batman, however, has known all along that this fight could only end one way. Superman recovers quickly and peels off Batman's helmet. "This is idiotic," he says, pleading with Batman to surrender, "you're just bone and meat — like all the rest" (191). Distracted by this fight with Batman, Superman does not notice Oliver Queen (formerly Green Arrow) whose help Batman has secretly enlisted. Just before Superman can finish off the all but defeated Batman, Queen fires a kryptonite arrow — which Wayne has synthesized for just such an occasion — that robs the Man of Steel of his power. "We could have changed the world..." Wayne says as he pummels the now helpless Superman, "now ... look at us ... I've become a political liability ... and you ... you're a joke" (195). As Batman, hand around Superman's throat, positions him for the *coup de grace*, however, his mysterious pill takes effect. An EKG graph superimposed over Wayne's grimacing face flatlines, and Batman falls — unvanquished but dead — at Superman's side. At the same time, Alfred activates a self-destruct device that demolishes the Manor as well as the Bat Cave. The trusty butler dies of a stroke while the house goes up in flames. All this and the fact that Wayne, reports reveal, has cleared out all his bank accounts, in effect, makes the man disappear like a bad dream whose content completely vanishes by daylight. With nothing more tangible than a grave stone left to mark his existence, Wayne essentially becomes a memory. But in the Gothic sensibility, memories can be very dangerous indeed.

The story should end at Bruce Wayne's funeral, but as a seemingly inconsolable Clark Kent staggers away from the grave the EKG suddenly returns. Looking back, Kent senses that Wayne's death was a ruse, and the nun still hovering over the grave is, in fact, a disguised Carrie Kelly. He grins and winks at her, then walks away. "They'll kill us if they can, Bruce," Superman thinks earlier, imagining what he might say to a more "reasonable" Bruce Wayne (129). "Every year they grow smaller," he goes on, "Every year they hate us more. We must not remind them that giants walk the Earth" (129–30). Symbolically tipping his hat at Batman's elegant solution to the kind of excessive entanglement with petty civil governance that Superman clearly seems to understand as a sort of deal with the devil, Superman is willing to let Wayne drift off into memory and shadows. What he does not appreciate, however, is that Wayne is not any less dangerous as a memory than he was as Batman. In fact, the shadows are where the Gothic is most powerful. On the final page of *The Dark Knight Returns*, we see proof of this as Bruce Wayne — not Batman — leads Carrie (still wearing her Robin costume) and a group of former gang members into deeper, untouched regions of the caves beneath what was Wayne Manor. Ordering his followers to gather around him, Wayne calls out to a straggler, "We haven't got all night, boy," but then thinks to himself, "That's not true ... we have years — as many as we need. Here, in the endless cave, far past the burnt remains of a crimefighter [sic] whose time has passed ... It begins *here*— an army — to bring sense to a world plagued by worse than thieves and murderers..." (199).

In Wayne's resolve we see the full implications of his Gothic nature. Instead of continuing to openly prosecute his personal war, he is going to lay low and spend years training an army of young people who can carry his fight and his sensibility forward. His funeral was a false burial (a common theme in Gothic tales), but in this final scene we see him literally bury himself both in the ground and in the powerful medium of memory. Accepting a fully Gothic identity, the Bruce Wayne we see at the end of *The Dark Knight Returns* finally embodies and embraces the real threat that Batman has always represented. Expressing his will over a world that "only makes sense when you force it to," Batman is a feudal figure, looming out of a dark age, denying the sort of egalitarian freedom that makes the world difficult to control and struggling, not so much against crime, as toward an authoritarian order based on violence and fear (192).

Notes

1. The potential for ambiguity in her use of the verb possess is especially apropos since, Bruce Wayne does, in fact, own huge swaths of the city and the criminals of Gotham see Batman him as a kind of demon who has seized their turf.

2. The traditional reading is that Oedipus suffered from hubris, or overweening pride, a flaw that often manifests in the ways a character might challenge the gods' authority. Frank Miller's Batman — like Oedipus — seems to possess a similarly inflexible sense of the law, one that often finds him at odds with more traditional (if nor higher) civil authority.

3. This might be one more way to understand the ambivalence Miller feels toward the character. Framing Batman as a kind of knight errant might tend to associate him with ideas of honor and chivalry, but considering that "errant" has the same root as "err" might also force us to consider that way that Batman's aristocratic and feudal views have led him to wander astray from some fundamental American principles.

4. Interestingly, in *300* this positions the reader as one of the Spartan heroes while *The Dark Knight Returns* frames the reader as one of Batman's targets.

5. The hearings that Superman remembers are an allusion to the Senate Subcommittee on Juvenile Delinquency, which scrutinized the comic book publishing industry's influence on children in 1954 (this was largely triggered by *Seduction of the Innocent*, Dr. Frederic Wertham's attack on comics published the same year). As a result of these hearings, the industry created the Comic Codes Authority to police the moral valence of its content. It's possible that Miller intends for the agreement Superman refers to later, "I gave them my obedience and my invisibility. They gave me a license," to reflect the way the Authority affected comics (Miller 139).

6. This is something that Andrew Klavan misses altogether in his attempts to shore up George W. Bush's legacy by comparing the president to Batman. "Like W," he claims, "Batman sometimes has to push the boundaries of civil rights to deal with an emergency, certain that he will re-establish those boundaries when the emergency is past" ("Bush and Batman"). The telling problem with this comparison, of course, is that — as is obvious in his joyous brutality — Batman hasn't temporarily suspended anything. He has declared total war on crime and corruption in his city and only nods toward a recognition of civil rights by not killing.

7. Freud originally used this term to describe the actions that revealed a subject's repressed fears or desires. Clemens, however, is using the term to connote a larger, culture-wide repression that might go better with Jungian interpretation of Freud's ideas.

Works Cited

Blackmore, Tim. "The Dark Knight of Democracy: Tocqueville and Miller Cast Some Light on the Subject." *Journal of American Culture*. 14.1 (2004): 37–56.
Brody, Michael. "Batman: Psychic Trauma and its Solution." *Journal of Popular Culture*. 28.4 (1995): 171–178.
Clemens, Valdine. *The Return of the Repressed: Gothic Horror from the Castle of Otranto to Alien*. Albany: SUNY Press, 1999.
Dargis, Manohla. "Dark was the Young Knight Battling His Inner Demons." *The New York Times*. 29, September, 2008. http://movies.nytimes.com/2005/06/15/movies/15batm.html.
_____. "Showdown in Gotham Town." *The New York Times*. 29, September, 2008. http://movies.nytimes.com/2008/07/18/movies/18knig.html.
Fisher, Mark. "Gothic Oedipus: subjectivity and Capitalism in Christopher Nolan's Batman Begins." *ImageTexT: Interdisciplinary Comics Studies*. 2.2 (2006). Dept of English, University of Florida. 30 Sep 2008. http://www.english.ufl.edu/imagetext/archives/v2_2/fisher/.
Germain, David. "'Dark Knight' Swings Past $500 Million Mark." 30, September, 2008 http://ap.google.com/article/ALeqM5gjvsDg9hAnh78d-tj2WmrfcB-d7QD92TSRIO0.
Klavan, Andrew. "What Bush and Batman Have in Common." *The Wall Street Journal*. 25 July 2008: A15.
Miller, Frank, with Klaus Janson and Lynn Varley. *Batman: The Dark Knight Returns*. New York: DC Comics, 2002.
Miller, Frank, and Lynn Varley. *300*. Milwaukie, OR: Dark Horse Books, 1999.
Nash, Jesse W. "Gotham's Dark Knight: The Postmodern Transformation of the Arthurian Mythos." *Popular Arthurian Traditions*. Ed. Sally K. Slocum. Bowling Green, OH: Popular, 1992. 36–45.
Newman, Kim "Cape Fear." *Sights and Sounds* 15, July 2005: 18–21.
Reichstein, Andreas. "Batman — An American Mr. Hyde?" *Amerikastudien /American Studies* 43, no. 2 (1998): 329–50.
Vaz, Mark Cotta. *Tales of the Dark Knight: Batman's First Fifty Years*. New York: Ballantine Books, 1989.

3

Why Adam West Matters
Camp and Classical Virtue
KEVIN K. DURAND

If any of the incarnations of the Batman are singled out for exclusion from the canon of Batman studies, it is George Clooney, his anatomically annoying muscle suit complete with nipples, and *Batman and Robin*. After Clooney's expulsion, though, Adam West's character often comes next to the chopping block. Campy, cartoonish (not used here in a complimentary way), simplistic, prone to hyperbole, and utterly unbelievable are but a few of the epithets hurled at the 1960s Caped Crusader and his equally cloying cartoony cohort, Robin. Indeed, www.imdb.com offers this synopsis of the show: "The ludicrously straight-laced Caped Crusader battles evil in this parody of the comics."

However, in the midst of camp, there is more than a kernel of philosophic import. I argue that in spite of the "KA-POW," Adam West's Batman not only belongs in the canon, but does so because perhaps better than any of the other incarnations, it puts forward an understanding of friendship and virtue rooted in the classics and adapted for a much more sophisticated and fast-paced world. Rather than "ludicrously straight-laced," I think it better to see West's Batman as both closer to a sort of everyman than any other Batman incarnation, and, in virtue of that, a sort of exemplar that serves as a counterpoint to the Aristotelian notion that virtue and goodness of character are reserved for but a few.

Before turning to the substantial portion of the argument, a brief digression into the thematic relations between the 1960s *Batman* and the rest of the canon should make clear that there is a sufficiently strong case to be made for the presence of Adam West's *Batman* in the canon based on its own interplay with the comics of the 1950s. From that interplay, one can discern threads that extend to the franchises that follow. This digression is, on its own, sufficient to argue for at least a limited view of the importance of the television series.

During the first season alone, no fewer than twenty different storylines were directly taken from comic books — *Batman*, *Batman Annual*, and *Detective Comics*. Some of the particularly interesting connections here include the second episode, "Smack in the Middle," the main plotline of which was taken almost directly from *Batman #171*, "Remarkable Ruse of the Riddler." The Penguin makes his debut in "The Penguin's a Jinx," playing the plot from *Batman #169*, "Partners in Plunder." Interestingly enough, it was the Adam West *Batman* in which Mr. Freeze premiers. This is not to say that the character was absent from the comics, for indeed, he was not. But, prior to the television folks deciding that "Mr. Freeze" sounded far more ominous than "Mr. Zero," the icy villain went by the latter moniker. Drawing from *Batman #121*, "The Ice Crimes of Mr. Zero," Mr. Freeze attempts to foil the dynamic duo in "Rats like Cheese." After the change was made in this eighth episode of the television series, the subsequent comic books incorporated it, and Mr. Freeze was born.

Digressions aside, it will be remembered that in the Preface, I argued that Batman is a far more accessible character than almost any other superhero character. He is clearly more accessible than Superman or any of the other superheroes of supernatural origin. Batman does not have the radioactive origin and powers of a Spiderman; he is not born of Atlantis like Aquaman; he is not descended from Greek gods like Wonder Woman or Norse gods like Thor. While these dissimilarities are obvious, what is perhaps less so is that Adam West's Batman is the most accessible of the incarnations of this most accessible of superheroes. A brief examination of West's Wayne is sufficient here.

In the rest of the *Batman* universe, the Dark Knight is far darker and more brooding prior to the addition of a sidekick. One can only speculate about the arc of the Nolan *Batman* franchise as no Robin has yet appeared, but leaving Nolan's Batman aside, every time a frontline, in the trenches crime-fighting companion is introduced, the Dark Knight lightens a bit, sometimes significantly. Let's look first at a particularly obvious example of this.

Michael Keaton's Batman is dark. Depending on the slightly off-kilter reputation of the actor and Keaton's ability to play a tenuously psychologically balanced character always on the edge of becoming an unbalanced one, Keaton's Batman is edgy and potentially volatile. When Jack Nicholson's Joker pays a visit to Vickie Vale, only to discover that Bruce Wayne is there, they spar a bit, matching dark and crazy sides. Bruce reacts much as a mobster might expect trapped prey to act, spinning a yarn to distract the bad guy from his appointed rounds. He begins to tell a story about a kid he once knew. Casting his eyes downward almost constantly giving the Joker an image that could well be interpreted as one trying to use bluff to extricate himself from a hopeless situation, the viewer easily recognizes the barely hidden the suppressed energy beneath the veneer, he tells the Joker in whispered voice, "I know who you are." With a slight pause, Wayne continues, "Lemme tell you about this guy I know, Jack. Mean kid. Bad seed. Hurt people." The Joker interjects, "I like him already." Wayne continues, intensity held in check, "Ya know, the problem was, he got sloppy. Ya know, crazy." He turns from the Joker toward the fireplace. "He started to lose it." As he walks toward the fireplace, the now very intrigued Joker follows him. "He had a head full of bad wiring, I guess. Couldn't keep it straight up here. He was the kinda guy who couldn't hear the train until it was two feet from him." As the Joker nods expectantly, Wayne grips the fireplace poker and continues, "Ya know what happened to this guy, Jack?" Joker shakes his head quickly, intense to hear the end of the story. "Well, he made mistakes." After a big pause, Wayne explodes. He suddenly breaks the vase on the mantel with the poker, then, in a crazed rage of his own that taps something deeper than mere play-acting, he yells, "He had to [vase shatters] his lights out. Now, you wanna get nuts!?! Come on! Let's get nuts!" The viewer is left wondering just how much of Wayne's challenge to the Joker is posturing so that the Joker won't punish Vickie and how much of it is a peek into the psychological state this is always present, but generally repressed behind either a façade of gentility (as Wayne) or the mask of the vigilante.

In *Batman Returns*, Keaton's Batman is just as haunted and repressed, but cast alongside Christopher Walken and Danny DeVito and cast within a dystopian Gotham, the psychological edge seems somehow less part of the character and more part of Tim Burton's self-indulgent direction of a movie that had great promise and yet delivered only at the visual level. Indeed, this Batman is one that is less accessible than the one from the previous film, if for no other reason than the environment he inhabits is so completely fantastical. Skipping ahead, though, one encounters the advent of the sidekick in this particular franchise arc of the story in the sequel, *Batman Forever*.

Val Kilmer's Batman is not the edgy character that Keaton's is, by any measure. He is cool and calmly rational. Even faced with the Sophie's Choice at the end, he assesses the situation dispassionately and renders his answering quip to the frenetic Riddler with a sort of matter-of-factness that borders on the deadpan. Says Batman, "I had to save them both. You see, I'm both Bruce Wayne and Batman, not because I have to be, now, because I choose to be."

One might suppose that because Kilmer is partnered with the hyperenergetic Jim Carrey and the scene-stealing Tommy Lee Jones, he is even less robust a character. It does seem that the humanizing quality of starring opposite such wildly fantastic villains renders Kilmer's Batman all the more identifiable with Bruce Wayne, and thus, with the many viewers of the film. While it is true that Kilmer's Bruce Wayne chooses to be Batman, it is also the case that Kilmer's Batman *chooses* to be Bruce Wayne.

It is not simply the script or the casting that renders Kilmer's Wayne/Batman more human and less edgy. It is also, as I have suggested, the introduction of his sidekick, Wayne's ward, Dick Grayson. It also cannot be ascribed to the presence of a love interest, as Keaton's Batman had Vickie Vale in the first film of this arc. Rather, it is the presence of a friend. As the movie moves to its ultimate encounter, Dick (with Alfred's help) creates his own Robin suit. Bruce does not really have the option of not including Grayson's Robin in the battle against Riddler and Two-Face. The interchange is particularly telling.

> BRUCE: Dick ... Where did you get that suit?
> ALFRED: I ... um ... took the liberty, sir.
> DICK: I thought you could use a friend.
> BRUCE (while staring): Not a friend. (He reaches out for a handshake with Dick)
> (Bruce and Dick clasp hands.)
> BRUCE: A partner.

Bruce has already accepted a friendship with Grayson, but in this interchange, he envisions a partnership—a sort of relationship of relative equals. Bruce Wayne struggles with doubts about himself and about his role as both Batman and Bruce Wayne, but ultimately he integrates both roles through the help not so much of the psychiatrist/love interest as through the presence of the friend/partner.

While the relationship between Batman and Robin is explored a bit further in the final movie of this arc of the franchise, *Batman and Robin*, it is in the 1960s version that the relationship is most fully explored to date. That Adam West's Bruce Wayne/Batman is far more like the common person than the other incarnations is actually rather obvious. However, why West matters may not be. Simply pointing out a difference between West, on the one hand, and Keaton, Kilmer, and Bale, on the other, however interesting that might be, still falls somewhat short of being a compelling reason for watching the 1960s show for more than comic pratfalls and cartoon pugilism. It also falls short of arguing that West matters. It is to that argument that we now turn.

One of the central reasons that Adam West matters is neither Adam West nor Batman. It's Dick Grayson and Robin. Unlike all of the other incarnations of *Batman*, in West's world, Robin is present from the beginning. As a result of this presence, Batman doesn't have time to develop the brooding, tormented character that marks the other series. In one sense, that perhaps prevents the viewer from developing the sympathies for the Wayne character that the origin stories emphasize to one degree or another. At the same time, the presence of a counterpart, partner, and friend from the outset introduces a different sort of pathos to Batman, and a sort of depth that, despite the cartoon feel at times, is more human.

In each of the visual texts that mark the film canon of *Batman*, Robin, where he exists, also clearly has a humanizing character. It would obviously be utter speculation to imagine how Keaton's Batman may have reacted with Chris O'Donnell's Robin, but it is a reasonably clear that Kilmer's Batman's icy reserve is cracked not only by Nicole Kidman's turn as psychologist/love interest, but also by the tragedy of Dick Grayson's family's death; deaths for which Batman feels some measure of responsibility. Wayne is even challenged by Alfred to assume a sort of paternal role with Grayson akin to the role that Alfred has played for Bruce.

Similarly, it is hard to imagine what sort of shape the relationship between a Christian Bale Batman and a Robin might have. However, what seems inevitable is that the inclusion of another person, for whom one is accountable and to whom one is mentor and friend, necessarily eliminates the possibility of the lone wolf vigilantism that marks the Batman character at the outset of all of his incarnations.

So, in one sense, Adam West matters because his Batman is the most human of all. He is contextualized in a set of relationships — with Alfred, with the Commissioner, with Chief O'Hara, and, most especially, with Robin. Theirs is a partnership that is far more fully developed *as a partnership* than any other incarnation of the Batman. While it is clear that Bruce Wayne is the elder partner and Dick Grayson is the ward, nevertheless, their interactions are those of friends and respectful colleagues. Batman not only entertains Robin's insights, he encourages him to play an active role in the investigations. If Batman is somewhat protective of Robin, he is not overly so; he doesn't try to prevent Robin from wading into the fray against villainy; he doesn't restrict him to "sidekick" status. Robin is the junior partner in the relationship, but he is, nevertheless, a partner.

A brief foray into the pages of Aristotle's *Nicomachean Ethics* might well be helpful in our examination of the friendship found between Bruce and Dick. Aristotle approaches the question of friendship in the same way he approaches any question — by applying the distinctively Aristotelian Method of Collection and Division. The Method of Collection and Division is quite simple, in theory, and likely derives much of its analytical power through its very simplicity. It consists, not surprisingly, of two stages. The first is to collect all of the relevant objects into one group. In the case of politics, for example, this may be a collection of all of the various constitutions that one might find or imagine as the governing document of a nation. In the case of friendship, one might collect all of the sorts of relationships that are generally referred to as "friendships." Thus, the nature of the inquiry determines what objects are to be collected for survey. After collecting all of the relevant objects or concepts, one then begins to look for those ways in which they are similar, and more importantly, those ways in which they are different. Like elements will be grouped with like and different with different. Thus, one begins to understand what are the essential and the accidental properties of any particular set of objects. While it is easy enough to call the relationship between Bruce and Dick a friendship, the philosophically interesting question is what sort of friendship is it?

Let's first look at the Aristotelian distinctions that grow out of his application of the method to the question of friendship. On Aristotle's view, there are three general sorts of friendships — friendships based on the good, friendships based on pleasure, and friendships based on utility. For Aristotle, true friendship, or the only sort of friendship that is really worth the name, is the friendship between two people based on the good — that is, each partner in the friendship loves the other because that other is a good person and desires the good for that other. Obviously, a strong reading of Aristotle's view would entail that such a mutual sort of friendship is only possible between social and intellectual equals. Though Bruce Wayne and Dick Grayson meet the main criterion — friendship based on the good — they are not social equals, and while Grayson is bright, it isn't clear that he is Bruce's intellectual equal, either.

It has often been commented that Aristotle's notion of friendship is unduly restrictive, but the *Batman* of West and Ward provides a visual textual rebuttal to Aristotle. Indeed, they fulfill all of the common requirements for friendship, despite the insuperable obstacles that Aristotle supposed would make such impossible. Further, Bruce Wayne and Dick Grayson can be seen as examples of a sort of friendship that is alluded to in Aristotle but not fully developed. Before it can really be argued that Wayne and Grayson illustrate Aristotle's best type of friendship in the way I have suggested, it is necessary to show that their relationship does not fall into the other sorts of friendship described by Aristotle, resulting in the conclusion that the true friendship or the friendship based on the good is the only proper place for it, despite the seeming obstacles.

The friendship based on pleasure and the friendship based on utility are both inferior, or "imperfect" friendships. Aristotle regards each as defective. A brief assessment will demonstrate why. Let us suppose that Riddler befriends Two-Face because he receives pleasure in the relationship. That pleasure could take the form of exhilaration at the robbing of banks or the enjoyment of a crime spree, but the focus of the "friendship" is pleasure. If more pleasure was to be found with Catwoman, for example, then the Riddler would have no problem in abandoning his former friend for the new one.

The friendship based on utility is even more defective than the one based on pleasure. In a "friendship" of this sort, the Joker, for example, would befriend a local thug because the thug could give him something useful — perhaps access to a sector of the city that he didn't yet control. Or, Poison Ivy could "befriend" Dr. Freeze because he gives her greater access to doing in Batman (even if it means that she has to kill Freeze's wife — or attempt to — in order to secure his services). Obviously, this sort of friendship lasts only as long as those involved are useful to each other. When the usefulness has passed, so, too, does the "friendship."

Friendships based in pleasure or utility are transient by their very nature. As transient and unstable, they are not worthy of the good or virtue which, as a stable state of character, is enduring. It seems clear from even a brief survey that the relationship enjoyed by Wayne and Grayson is neither one built on pleasure nor one built on utility. While it doesn't immediately seem to fit the friendship of equals that the best Aristotelian friendship exemplifies, a closer look at the aspects of that sort of friendship leaves some room for expansion.

Strict equality being impractical, at best, and impossible, at worst, means that some further analysis of the nature of that equality is necessary. Perhaps the way to discuss Aristotelian equality with respect to interpersonal relationships is to subdivide that "equality" into three characteristics, the presence of which would be the equivalent of "equality." That said, the best Aristotelian friendship is one that exemplifies three characteristics — benevolence, reciprocity, and mutuality. A person is genuinely benevolent if she wishes for the good of the other. A relationship exhibits reciprocity when both partners are benevolent toward the other. A mutual relationship is one that is marked by a general benefit of each for the other; that is, more than simply wishing for good, each partner acts in ways that result in benefit for the other. Thus, the relationship is not only marked by a sort of fellow-feeling on the part of each partner, but it actually produces some benefit directed toward the good, which, in the case of true friendship, is a product that tends to aiding the partners toward a virtuous life, which is, of course, the highest good.[1]

One feature that is noticeably absent from the Aristotelian account, but which the Batman and Robin of the 1960s demonstrates is an essential feature of a true friendship based on the good is the notion that the friendship produce some benefit beyond the benefit of the two partners. That is, there should be some product of the friendship that serves to benefit society more broadly. For example, the friendship of two chemists could, one might imagine, result in a collaboration through which both partners received benefit personally, but that also produced something that benefited society; that something being a thing that neither was likely to accomplish alone. Or, in another example, imagine two mathematicians, Lord Alfred Whitehead and Bertrand Russell who together collaborated to produce one of the greatest works of mathematics of the past several centuries. Both acknowledged that they were quite dependent on the relationship itself as an essential condition of the development of the work, *Principia Mathematica*. Though both differed from the other in remarkable ways, this was a lifelong friendship that itself helped to shape both men for the good and which contributed beyond themselves to the good of society. One might imagine, as well, a friendship that did not have this productive component could quickly become solipsistic, and thus, while seeming to be a friendship based on the good, is rather one based on either pleasure or utility.

That West and Ward portrayed characters whose friendship exemplified this sort of Aristotelian notion is straightforwardly clear. However, the piece that their characters' friendship demonstrates, and thus provides grist for the philosophical mill, is that character of productivity and concern beyond oneself. Batman and Robin, and Bruce and Dick, are clearly of great benefit to Gotham. It is important, I think, to note that beyond examples themselves of virtue (which I will address shortly), they are providing a direct benefit to the citizens of Gotham. By making the city a safer one, they help to create an environment that is more conducive to the development of individual virtue on the parts of the citizens whom they have protected.

In addition to proposing a philosophically interesting notion of benevolent, reciprocal, and mutual friendship, one is able to see in West's Batman a reasonably clear example of some of the classical virtues, as well; virtues like courage and wisdom and justice. In other words, if Batman and Robin are an example of a friendship based on the good, what is that evidence, beyond their clear concern for each other's well-being, that it is virtue at which they aim? Here, I will examine three virtues that seem particularly relevant — Justice, Courage, and Wisdom.[2]

Justice is the easiest of the group, I suspect. In one sense, it is obvious that Batman and Robin fight for justice — understood as stopping the bad guys and rescuing the citizens of fair Gotham who have been harmed, kidnapped, robbed, frozen, and otherwise put upon by the evildoers. Thwarting the Riddler, Penguin, Joker, and a host of villains each week, the Dynamic Duo make Gotham safe for law-abiding folk. However, the ancients understood justice to be more than a simple law-and-order sort of thing. Justice was conceived, by Plato at least, as each part of the soul of the individual performing its function and not pretending to the function of another. In *Republic*, Plato uses the analogy of a city to an individual to discuss individual virtue — if Justice can be found among the three parts of the city (Rulers, Guardians, Auxilliaries), then its analogue can be found among the parts of the individual soul (Reason, Spirit, Appetites). For Plato, for example, the appetites were not themselves bad, but became problematic if they were allowed to rule the individual rather than reason governing him or her. Similarly, too, if the desire for recognition and honor overwhelmed one's good rational sense, even the pursuit of noble aims could be unjust. Instead, the individual who was just was ruled by his reasoning faculty which kept the motive powers of the appetites and spirit in check.

The Gotham of Adam West's Batman develops along the lines of the analogy as well. Each of the villains can be interpreted as an individual who has been overcome with one appetite or another. Generally, the desire for money or the desire for power or revenge, or some combination of them all, are at the core of the motivations of the villains. One elaborate, Rube Goldbergian plot after another that is supposed to secure some diamond of infinite value, vanish the secret vaults of Gotham National Bank, or eliminate the meddling dynamic duo is developed in ever more comedic ways. These appetites snowball until the villain has become even a comic caricature of the comic villain he or she was at the outset, blustering impotently at the vagaries of fate that have conspired to thwart the evil schemes once more.

As a contrary to the comedic villainy, there is the almost imperturbably calm Batman. While Robin's exclamations are infused with an excitement that at times borders on panic, Batman's calm voice is even calmer in the face of ever greater peril. He, at times, remonstrates Robin — and even the Commissioner and Chief O'Hara — reminding them that justice ultimately will out. Thus, Batman provides an example of the person who, though in the midst of crisis, acts from a confident character and a settled knowledge of the triumph of good over evil. While it seems that Robin is an overly rambunctious youth requiring the energy of the calming influence of West's Batman, this actually serves to point out the distinction between the character who is in control of himself, though inspired by a vision of justice, and his younger colleague whose inspiration for justice might well slip toward a more vengeful vigilantism without the influence of his mentor. Nevertheless, the very presence of a partner, albeit a younger and junior one, renders the Batman a more human character, precisely through the nature of the friendship itself.

The virtue of courage, like that of justice, is fairly straightforward, also. Faced with one perilous situation after another, Batman and Robin place their very lives on the line every episode. Here, again, an Aristotelian model can shed some light on the dynamic duo, though it also serves to demonstrate, contra-Aristotle, the depth of the friendship (or comradeship) that Aristotle would restrict from West and Ward.

Aristotle's notion of courage is particularly restrictive, and the careful Aristotelian scholar might well argue that it is inappropriate to use it here. For Aristotle, courage is the name of that virtue that applies to conduct in the theatre of war. For those wanting to pick nits, it could be argued that Batman and Robin are not properly in the midst of a war, they are not proper combatants (either soldier or police), but rather they are in the midst of a crime spree and are unsupervised vigilantes. While one might also think this rather a strawman example, one need only recall the arguments concerning whether terrorism should be treated as a war or as a police action to discern the relevance of the distinction. All that being said, with proper recognition of the failure of the example to hold for all of the particulars; nevertheless, it is a helpful model, *mutatis mutandis*, or with all the necessary changes being made.

Faced with a dire situation on the battlefield, an individual feels the tug of fear. Fear, and its attendant desire toward self-preservation, can be overwhelming. Those individuals who flee when they should have stayed and fought are labeled "coward." Those individuals who charge forward into battle when they should have retreated to fight another day are labeled "reckless." The courageous person is the one who, feeling fear, nevertheless analyzes the situation properly, and does the right thing at the right time in the right way and for the right reasons. He doesn't stay and fight in hopes of some grand recognition at a later time, as this wouldn't be the proper reason; he doesn't think he should always fight; he doesn't think he should always run; he isn't afraid that in exercising his knowledge and retreating that he will potentially be thought a coward, and he doesn't charge into battle for fear of the label. Rather, in those cases where fighting is appropriate, he fights. In those cases when retreat is appropriate, he retreats. Courage has to do with a sort of intellectual excellence — knowing what to do, when to do it, how to do it, and the proper reasons for doing it — and a sort of moral excellence — the ability to engage in the proper action, regardless of fear.

That Batman and Robin demonstrate versions of the virtue, courage, is clear. If the show has any theme other than justice, it is that of heroic courage.

If it were the case that Batman was always in the position of trying to rescue Robin from some dilemma that his impetuousness and recklessness got him into, then it would perhaps be appropriate to suppose that theirs is not a friendship but a co-dependent sort of relationship. However, while Robin does find himself in the majority of the life-threatening moments, Batman, too, is sometimes captured by the bad guys, hoisted onto some machinery of death, only to find himself rescued at the last minute by the Boy Wonder. It is true that Robin does not demonstrate the advanced level of intellectual excellence or self-control that Batman does, but it is also true that his level is sufficiently advanced that Batman both encourages and depends on his counsel. Thus, the two have a relationship that, while not of equals, is nevertheless one of mutual respect and benefit, to the end that both exemplify courage.

The foregoing discussion of courage, however, does point to a potential difficulty in the argument that Batman and Robin share a friendship that is of a sort that can be commended as a virtue itself. While both are striving for justice and exemplifying courage, they demonstrate differing levels of intellectual excellence. Thus, the virtue of wisdom is perhaps the most difficult, not because Bruce Wayne fails to have wisdom, but because Dick Grayson clearly doesn't. He is at times impetuous, at times reckless, at times rushing in where angels fear to tread. On the strong reading of the Aristotelian model that we have suggested is an overly restrictive reading of Aristotle, if Bruce Wayne is wise (and, virtuous), then he cannot truly be friend to Grayson. He can be mentor and teacher and patron, but not truly friend. If he is friend, gaining from Grayson's insights and benefiting from Grayson's friendship, then he is not truly wise, but something short of it. However, if the only argument is semantic or rationalistic, then the argument must give way to empirical realities. It would be impossible to list all of the instances of the sort of experience that is particularly common among teachers and students. However, one should suffice here. Imagine a professor of mathematics who is known for being among the most demanding, most challenging, and least susceptible to student excuses for settling for less than their very best. Imagine also a young student, bright but perhaps a bit lazy. Initially, the relationship is clearly one of teacher/student, with the professor employing all manner of pedagogical prods to get the best from the student. He has seen the potential of the young student, realized that there is far more that the student can do than even the student thinks possible, and doesn't shrink from pushing the student, even when the student thinks he is being treated unfairly. Imagine also that this relationship develops as the student begins to grasp the horizons possible to him, and that what began as a teacher/student relationship evolved into a mentor/pupil and ultimately into a friendship as the young student grew to become a professor himself. Though not universal in the experience of all teachers and all students — how could it possibly be, after all — the experience is not one that is foreign to all. Indeed, it is an experience that has been replicated again and again, and it is one of the experiences that makes professorial life rewarding. Thus, not only is it possible, it is a relationship that contributes to the flourishing of both the professor and the student who becomes a professorial equal; it is a friendship that began in inequality, but precisely *because* of the virtuous character of the professor, excellent both in his field and in his own character. Thus, it is a mark not of the inferiority of either the relationship or the virtue of the professor, but, in fact, is an indication of the power of such friendship and an affirmation of virtuous character. Thus, one can conclude that wisdom does not preclude friendship in this case, and neither does friendship preclude wisdom.

Thus, Adam West's Batman is more accessible, more human, and, at the same time, a better example of the realities of human life and friendship than any of the other incarnations. West provides examples of friendship that critique the limited views of the Aristotelian classical view of friendship. West's *Batman* is a modern hero tale that, while extolling the classical heroic virtues, at the same time provides an example in which hero and friend are not only compatible, but encouraged as the pinnacle of virtue. Very few people are superheroes, but it is the exceptionally few who cannot be a friend to another. Friendship is, perhaps, the most important of all of the virtues of human life; being an excellent friend is both laudable and difficult. For those who wish to find it, the *Batman* of Adam West is an example of both the nature of such virtuous friendship and of its value. That, simply, is why Adam West matters.

Notes

1. For a more complete discussion of the Aristotelian notion of the Highest Good and the Life of Virtue, see Durand, *Footnotes to Plato* or Durand, *Virtue: Essays in Ancient Philosophy*.

2. For a much more detailed discussion of the nature of these classic virtues, see Durand, *Footnotes to Plato* and *Virtue: Essays in Ancient Philosophy*.

Works Cited

Aristotle. *Nichomachean Ethics*. Trans. Joe Sachs. Newburyport, MA: Focus Publishing/ R. Pullins Co., 2002. Print.

Batman (TV Series 1966–1968). *IMDB.com.* http://www.imdb.com/title/tt0059968/
Batman—Holy Batmania. Image Entertainment, 2004. DVD.
"Batman #121: The Ice Crimes of Mr. Zero." New York: DC Comics, 1959. Print.
"Batman #169: Partners in Plunder." New York: DC Comics, 1965. Print.
"Batman #171: The Remarkable Ruse of the Riddler." New York: DC Comics, 1965. Print.
Batman and Robin—The Complete 1949 Movie Serial Collection. Sony, 2005. DVD.
Batman Begins. Warner Home Video, 2005. DVD.
Batman: The Motion Picture Anthology, 1989–1997. Warner Home Video, 2009. DVD.
The Dark Knight. Warner Home Video, 2008. DVD.
Durand, Kevin. *Footnotes to Plato.* Lanham, MD: University Press of America, 2009. Print.
_____. *Virtue: Essays in Ancient Philosophy.* Lanham, MD: University Press of America, 2001. Print.

4

Dark Knight, White Knight, and the King of Anarchy

Stephanie Carmichael

The Dark Knight, directed by the brilliant and visionary Christopher Nolan, succeeds as an incredibly complex film. Arguably, one of *The Dark Knight*'s most prominent achievements doubles as its strongest downfall, at least for one-time moviegoers. The movie supports so many layers and philosophical insights on top of surges of action and pandemonium that when those elements are combined with the movie's two and a half hour length, it becomes somewhat difficult to digest the first time. Nevertheless, Nolan handles the interweaving parts remarkably well. Despite the claims of the unhappy critics, who seem to be few and far between, *The Dark Knight* does not beat its audience over the head with its own morality and message; viewers are most capable of gauging its depth. *The Dark Knight* stands as a film that keeps revealing more of its secrets the second and even third time through; more pieces fall into place, and subtle threads take on much larger meanings. With so much to be found in the film, this essay does not propose to make the judgments that the audience is capable of making itself. Instead, this essay will serve as a character analysis, allowing the reader the insight necessary to draw his or her own conclusions regarding the film's purpose and overall message.

With the film promising the introduction of the Joker to Nolan's movie franchise, the audience waits from the beginning moments to see the nemesis of Batman. They are not disappointed:

> THUG 1: "So why do they call him the Joker?"
> THUG 2: "I hear he wears make-up."
> THUG 1: "Make-up?"
> THUG 2: "Yeah. To scare people. Like war paint."

In the back heist scene at the beginning of the movie, two of the Joker's clown mask-wearing thugs make those remarks about the mysterious new figure in town, the Joker. Harmless speculation, perhaps? Wrong. The Clown Prince of Crime indeed smears on the war paint and helms an unforgettable battle for the soul of Gotham City, the fictional setting of the movie. Filmed in the gorgeous architectural city of Chicago, *The Dark Knight* embodies some of the strongest moments of over seventy years of Batman comics while bolstering its beautifully written, character-centric story with the conflict of morality and ethics and the rich depths of human nature.

Things have changed in Gotham City over one year's time. A vigilante who calls himself Batman has taken to cleaning up the city's streets, a cesspool of crime and corruption. The Dark Knight has also dressed for war. Bearing a rather expensive "suit of armor" and a car — the Tumbler, known more commonly as the Batmobile — Batman constructed a powerful and dramatic reputation drawn from years of training and living inside the heart of crime itself in order to fully understand it. His extreme dedication began on a fateful night when he was eight years old; his parents, Thomas and Martha Wayne, were shot to death in front of him outside a theater on the cold street of the infamous Crime Alley. When they hit the pavement, so did the innocence of Bruce Wayne, and the soul of Batman rose from the ashes. Now, Bruce revels in luxury as a billionaire playboy by day and spreads order through terror as a masked avenger by night. Batman wields fear to his advantage; he became it after purging his own and turning it "against those who prey on the fearful." As we see in a scene after the bank heist, Gotham's street scum eye the Bat-signal in the foreboding clouds above the rooftop of the Gotham Police Department and think twice about involving themselves in future criminal activities. They fear him, and they are right in doing so.

Batman, however, must both literally and figuratively stick to the shadows. Early in *The Dark Knight*, he endures a thrashing in the scene shared by the Chechen, a Russian crime lord, and the Scarecrow, a.k.a. Jonathan Crane, former psychiatrist at Arkham Asylum. The two's drug talk comes crashing to a halt courtesy of a group of Batman copycats named the Citizens for Batman — loosely based on the Batman copycat gang from Frank Miller's noteworthy graphic novel, *The Dark Knight Returns*. Following this, Bruce returns to the Bat-Bunker — temporarily substituting as the Batcave while Wayne Manor undergoes reconstruction — and his butler, Alfred Pennyworth, comments on his cuts and bruises: "Know your limits, Master Wayne." "Batman has no limits," Bruce answers. "Well, you do, sir," Alfred pushes. "Well, I can't afford to know 'em." "And what happens the day you find out?" Alfred correctly foreshadows that Bruce, even as Batman, bears limits and much to lose, demonstrating a theme that will shape Batman's and, therefore Bruce's, character.

Meanwhile, others are the exact opposite when it comes to limits and having much to lose. In the bank robbery scene, the Joker manages to turn his henchmen against one another by manipulating them into killing each other off for him, consequently leaving the entire money cut to him. When he takes off his clown mask, his first line of dialogue addresses the manager of the mob-owned bank: "I believe that whatever doesn't kill you only makes you ... stranger." Afterwards, Detective Anna Ramirez and then–Lieutenant Jim Gordon are puzzling over footage in the bank vault: "He can't resist showing us his face," observes Ramirez. Likewise, Gordon muses, "What's he hiding under that make-up?" Nothing, they come to learn. Batman has much to lose, despite how hard he tries to protect what, and who, he holds most precious. As the movie progresses, the Joker reveals quite the contrary. He does not fear Batman; he does not fear death; as a result, nothing exists that can be used as leverage against him — neither money nor material possessions. Most importantly, he has no one else to lose. All he is, and all he desires to be, is anarchy incarnate: "An agent of chaos." With nothing to hold him back, the Joker proudly introduces Gotham to such chaos.

Thus far, we have introduced the Dark Knight (Batman) and the King of Anarchy (the Joker), but what about the White Knight? We first meet Harvey Dent, District Attorney and White Knight of Gotham City, in a courtroom with Rachel Dawes, who serves as a love interest for both Harvey and Bruce. As this scene shows, the character of Harvey Dent proves headstrong and smart. When his witness, Al Rossi, pulls out a gun and aims it at Harvey point-blank, Harvey grabs it, pushes it away, and punches Rossi. With ardent determination, he turns around and confronts Sal Maroni, the crime boss who clearly gave the order beforehand. When they start to take Rossi away, Harvey turns to the judge and says calmly, "But your honor, I'm not done." Harvey fosters the willingness to do what it takes to clean up Gotham, just like Batman — but within the confines of the law.

It is also during this scene that we are introduced to something that carries a burden of foreboding much heavier than its literal weight: Harvey's coin. Comic fans understand the depth behind the simple line, "My father's lucky coin," and Nolan pays respect to the source without choosing to go down the road of Harvey's origin — a choice that succeeds in its homage while telling Harvey's story in a fresh way. Harvey tells Rachel, in response to her question of how he could leave such important decisions to the chance flip of a coin, "I make my own luck." Several times throughout the film we are brought back to the coin; the audience sees Harvey using it to influence his decision-making. Those unfamiliar with the character might see Rachel's point about chance; however, Harvey later reveals to Rachel that his coin is a silver dollar, bearing heads on both sides. For most of the film, Harvey indeed makes his own luck. He himself decides, and he only jocularly uses the coin or wields it to a specific advantage. Nevertheless, the White Knight of Gotham falls to darkness near the end of the film, bringing to light the significance of the coin to Harvey Dent as a character. Until his downfall, the audience has come to know Harvey as a good and just man, qualities that influence the audience and the characters in the film to view him in that light even after he fully becomes a tragic hero.

As a way of examining character reactions to Batman and revealing concepts related to the idea of heroism, it is beneficial to explicate the scene of Rachel, Harvey, Bruce and his date Natascha — the prima ballerina for the Moscow Ballet set to perform in Gotham — discussing the mysterious Batman over dinner at a restaurant. Those who have seen Christopher Nolan's prior work, *Batman Begins*, know that Rachel Dawes, a childhood friend of Bruce, has discovered the truth about the billionaire playboy's nightly activities, and this revelation adds much conflict to any possibility of a romantic relationship between the two as well as the tension present in this conversation. While Natascha talks about Batman with disdain, Harvey Dent defends Batman, not knowing that the man seated across from him dons the cape and cowl every night:

> NATASCHA: "I'm talking about the kind of city that idolizes a masked vigilante."
> HARVEY: "Gotham's proud of an ordinary man standing up for what's right."
> NATASCHA (to Harvey): "Gotham needs heroes like you," "Elected officials, not a man who thinks he's above the law."
> BRUCE (playing along for the sake of alibi): "Exactly. Who appointed the Batman?"
> HARVEY: "We did. All of us who stood by and let scum take control of our city."

Then Harvey says something that, through history, explains Batman's presence: "When their enemies were at the gate, the Romans would suspend democracy and appoint one man to protect the city. It wasn't considered an honor. It was considered a public service." Not an honor. We will examine later on just how much Harvey's words ring true. Throughout the entire film, no one understands Batman as well as Harvey Dent does; perhaps even more than Bruce Wayne. As Harvey says, "I guess you either die a hero or you live long enough to see yourself become the villain." Ironically, this statement can be applied to Harvey himself as his character progresses. Before all of that, however, we have Harvey as hero, with the conversation ending in a playful suggestion that Harvey will perhaps take up the mantle that Batman may wish to shed.

Despite Harvey's lack of reluctance toward the idea, he does not need to take up the mantle of the Bat. As Bruce admiringly tells Rachel, "Harvey is that hero. He locked up half the city's criminals, and he did it without wearing a mask. Gotham needs a hero with a face." Once again, Harvey demonstrates his understanding of Batman. Bruce does not want to have to set things right through the force of Batman forever. He wants Gotham to be healthy, and he wants to live a normal life — alongside Rachel. Unfortunately, the events and characters in the film teach him that Batman is a responsibility he started and cannot, *will* not, escape from so easily. The heart of Batman, all he represents and values, exists as too big a part of Bruce Wayne for him to yield the role. It's not Bruce, but Rachel who clearly recognizes and explains this to him, elaborating on her observation from *Batman Begins* where she told Bruce that his "real face is the one that criminals now fear. The man I loved — the man who vanished — he never came back at all." Yet, while Harvey Dent offers a brighter hope for Gotham than what Batman can ever give, darkness equally grows elsewhere: the Joker.

The Joker attempts to make his presence known in the world of organized crime, a move that will allow him to progress his own plans. Crime bosses from throughout Gotham gather in a hotel's kitchen to discuss their money transactions with a Chinese businessman named Lau, the CEO of LSI Holdings. The Joker quickly surfaces in the conversation, but Maroni confidently dismisses him: "He's not the problem — he's a *nobody*." This statement is more apt that it first appears. The Joker has no other alias, no fingerprints, and seemingly emerged from out of thin air — a nobody by definition. However, the position was by choice; the Joker's choice at that, and one that soon proves lethal. The Joker might be a nobody, but everyone in Gotham, including the mob, soon learns that a nobody can be horrendously destructive. Uninvited, the Joker bursts in on the mob meeting, presenting his services for hire to take care of the Batman, the true problem Maroni referenced. They insult the Joker, calling him crazy and a freak, and for the time being, he allows them the authority, his only retort being, "No, I'm not. I'm *not*." It is easy to ascertain, or rather misunderstand, why the mob expresses disinterest and dismisses him so easily. "*A nobody*"—but a nobody who becomes extremely dangerous and powerful in a short period of time.

The initial scene in which the audience experiences fear of the Joker acts as a sharp contrast to the scene in the hotel. A criminal named Gambol puts a high bounty on the Joker's head for whoever brings him the Joker, dead or alive. In a pool hall, someone delivers the Joker to him in a body bag; he is not dead, just snuck in by his own men, thus giving off the dreaded sense that the Joker is already gaining power and allies by buying people's loyalty. Even more frightening, in this scene we hear the Joker's first lie about how he got his scars — channeling Alan Moore's *The Killing Joke*, a highly regarded graphic novel in which the Joker describes his history as "multiple choice," just the way he prefers it (38). More mystery and darkness begin to surround the Joker with the telling of his story, cementing our first look at how ruthless the Joker can be. The Joker is not afraid of anything; nothing matters to him, not even his own life. He brings with him a whole new world of danger and crime, which clearly differs from the demeanor we witnessed in the hotel scene. Then, the audience saw only a raving madman playing at a game that was beyond him. In the bank robbery scene, the manager says with disgust, "Criminals in this town used to believe in things ... Honor. Respect." Just like he promises to the Chechen later in the film, the Joker plans to show Gotham a better class of criminal, beginning with him. Honor and respect disappeared long before the Joker walked into town, but he stands for something entirely different and much worse.

On the other end of the spectrum, Alfred functions as an invaluably insightful character, crucial to Bruce as moral support and a fresh eye. Alfred has known and cared for Bruce ever since he was a boy; he knows him better than anyone else does. Further, Alfred possesses the most objective perspective. He is not uninformed about what is happening around him; in fact, he has the privilege of being much more connected than the majority of Gotham, yet not directly involved, either. Throughout the film, the wisdom he offers Bruce and even Rachel holds incredible worth. In a critical moment of needing insight, Bruce finds clarity only when he consults Alfred about the mob not submitting without a fight and crossing a line by hiring the Joker; as Alfred reminds him, "You crossed it first, sir. You've hammered them, squeezed them to the point of desperation. And now, in their desperation they've turned to a man they don't fully understand." In addition, Alfred does not allow Bruce to reduce the significance of the Joker's anarchy: "Respectfully, Master Wayne, perhaps this is a man you don't fully understand, either." Then, Alfred tells him a story about a bandit that stole precious gems only to throw them away, which resurfaces later in the movie as a highly important metaphor. Bruce, still trapped in the mindset that every criminal has a motivation or an end, questions the logic. It is Alfred that points out that logic and goals are not necessary factors: "[S]ome men aren't looking for anything logical, like money. They can't be bought, bullied, reasoned, or negotiated with. Some men just want to watch the world burn." Men like the Joker, who only wants to bring anarchy in its purest form to Gotham, create a world without rules. Maroni, when later interrogated by Batman, even expands on the concept: "You got rules ... The Joker, he's got no rules. No one's gonna cross him for you."

What Alfred explains, and even what Maroni communicates, shows exactly why the Joker is indeed a problem — despite being a "nobody," as Maroni ignorantly admitted earlier. Such misconception is why the Joker was able to gain power, fear and respect, and reputation so rapidly. Simply, the Joker is untouchable; as he himself explains to Batman, "You have nothing. Nothing to threaten me with. Nothing to do with all your strength." In other words, there is nothing the Joker wants for himself; nothing for him to lose or gain, and there is no fear to latch onto and manipulate. He merely exists. On the other hand, the Joker knows perfectly well how to exploit those around him: The everyday man, like Jim Gordon, who worries about his family; people like Harvey Dent and Bruce Wayne, who hold someone dear to both of them and must protect them. Then, there are those who are greedy and power-hungry like the mob. The Joker eventually lays this out for the Chechen: "I'm a man of simple tastes. I like dynamite ... gunpowder ... and gasoline. And you know what they have in common? They're *cheap*." They are cheap like the mob, whose attention can be so easily bought. The Joker knows how easy the mob makes it for him to manipulate them. In a way, the Joker would agree with the bank manager: Criminals used to believe in things. The Joker used the mob as stepping stones to climb his way to the top of the chain, gaining more power with each stride. Such a task presents no challenge a man who, as Alfred said, "can't be bought, bullied, reasoned, or negotiated with." When all a man wants to do is watch the world burn, he becomes untouchable, and the polar opposite of Batman.

Interestingly, it is Ra's Al Ghul's definition of the vigilante in *Batman Begins* that also applies to the Joker: "A vigilante is just a man lost in the scramble for his own gratification. He can be destroyed, or locked up. But if you make yourself more than just a man, if you devote yourself to an ideal, and if they can't stop you, then you become something else entirely.... A legend." In a twisted way, Al Ghul's advice fits what the Joker represents. The Joker exists as an absolute, and Batman is incorruptible, as the Joker realizes in his last encounter with Batman when he admits, "I guess this is what happens when an unstoppable force meets an immovable object." As a mortal, like Bruce, the Joker can be destroyed or locked up; however, the Joker has successfully devoted himself to his ideal of anarchy. Throughout *The Dark Knight*, no one can stop him because of this. He became something more than just a criminal; in the mythos, the Joker elevates to as much of a legend as his arch-nemesis, Batman.

Similarly, Harvey Dent will become unforgettable to Batman. After the

4. Dark Knight, White Knight, ... King of Anarchy (CARMICHAEL) 61

memorial parade in the streets of Gotham, Harvey notices one of the Joker's thugs wearing a badge titled, "Officer Rachel Dawes." Harvey inconspicuously forces the man to a condemned building, where he interrogates him in a scene that heavily foreshadows Harvey's disgraced fall. His unconventional and illegal means reflect his growing desperation and frustration over the state of Gotham and its cracked legal system. Gotham runs corrupt, mobsters like Sal Maroni walk, and madmen like the Joker wreak chaos on the city Dent continuously tries to save and rebuild. It is worth noting that he believes, as he was intended to, that Gotham's most honest cop, Lieutenant Jim Gordon, was just shot and killed protecting the Mayor. In addition, he now knows that Rachel has become a target of the Joker. Both Harvey's hope and perseverance are faltering. In the run-down building, Harvey endeavors to obtain information from of the Joker's thug by making him think that he would decide whether or not to shoot him based on the flip of a coin. The audience, however, does not yet know that his coin displays heads on both sides, although savvy comic fans do. The thug honestly believes Harvey will kill him, and he begs for mercy, insisting that he knows nothing about the Joker's schemes. Harvey continues to test him until Batman interrupts, stopping the coin from flipping a second time. Batman tells him that the man he is interrogating is Thomas Schiff, a paranoid schizophrenic and former patient at Arkham Asylum. Contrasting the roles the two have to play, Batman genuinely reminds Harvey:

> You're the symbol of hope that I could never be. Your stand against organized crime is the first legitimate ray of light in Gotham for decades. If anyone saw this, everything would be undone — all the criminals you got off the streets would be released. And Jim Gordon will have died for nothing.... Gotham is in your hands, now.

With this charge of responsibility, tragically, and somewhat ironically, Harvey progressively inches closer to reaching his own limit and succumbing to his pain, frustration, and desperation.

Immediately after the scene with Harvey, another deliberate contrast unfolds. Rachel and Bruce converse and she mentions that Harvey called and told her that Batman is going to relinquish his identity. "...I've got enough blood on my hands," Bruce says with a tinge of despair. "I've seen, now, what I would have to become to stop men like him." Bruce understands that he would have to stoop to the Joker's level, breaking his one rule of refusing to take another's life; good or evil, playing God is a line he will not allow himself to cross no matter how tempted he may be. Doing so would tear the city apart; he just witnessed Harvey and everything he stands for begin to erode. He does not wish to see Gotham's shining White Knight turn red from blood — not only his own, but of the blood he might spill if he continues to be pushed closer to an edge from which he cannot return. However, Batman must be the one to push onward, and only he can stop a madman like the Joker. He knows he must endure despite how difficult it is for Batman or for Bruce Wayne; such is the sacrifice he has made and the promise he intends to keep for Gotham's sake as well as in honor of his parents. Like the Joker reminds him, "There's no turning back."

In the Wayne penthouse, Rachel watches on television as Harvey declares himself to be Batman and Bruce watches silently from the back of the room. She expresses fury at how Bruce could stand there and allow Harvey to shoulder the blame. Alfred suggests an alternative: "Perhaps both Bruce and Mr. Dent believe that Batman stands for something more important than a terrorist's whims, Miss Dawes, even if everyone hates him for it. That's the sacrifice he's making — to not be a hero. To be something more." Not a hero. Those words echo back at their most powerful at the end of the film. Batman stands for something greater; he acts as a symbol. He can never kill, and he must always put Gotham first; though he may lose much in the process, he will persevere and continue to protect his city. Batman cannot accept any of the glory attached to heroism, and for that reason, he vanishes before he can be praised for catching criminals. Batman must always act selfishly, and to ensure Gotham's ultimate protection he must also alienate himself. To maintain his reputation, he must be fear incarnate, even to his allies.

Harvey Dent believes this philosophy, as well. As Harvey is escorted to an armored vehicle, he reveals to Rachel his plan to act as bait for the Joker during transportation: "This is the Joker's chance, and when he attacks, Batman will take him down." After Harvey seemingly uses his coin to make the decision to go through with the plan, he shows Rachel it is, in fact, a double-sided coin. At least for the time being, Harvey still has control of his composure and remains confident and level-headed enough to make his own decisions. He remains the White Knight. Nonetheless, all that he stands will soon plunge into jeopardy, and the Joker only exacerbates that degradation.

After having been captured, the Joker demonstrates just how he exacerbates Gotham's degradation. When Gordon accuses the Joker of kidnapping Harvey Dent, the Joker plays on Gordon's sense of responsibility, "Who did you leave him with? Your people? Assuming, of course, that they are your people and not Maroni's.... Does it make you feel responsible for Harvey Dent's current predicament?" Gordon ignores the Joker's question, but the expression on his face, despite how much he tries to conceal it, tells us that the Joker has struck a chord of inner fear and guilt. He feels guilty because the corruption, much like a disease, has even managed to penetrate his Major

Crimes Unit. What is important here is not only Gordon's feelings of guilt but also the power someone wields when he can so easily perturb someone. The Joker possesses sociopathic intelligence, and he intricately comprehends how to manipulate others. He sees beyond people, and beyond masks, as well.

Drawing on the idea that the Joker can see beyond masks is his interaction with Batman during the Joker's interrogation. While it cannot be proven, the tension that quickly escalates as Batman interrogates the Joker alone — added with the diction the Joker chooses and Batman's response to it — hints that the Joker may have determined Batman's identity. The Joker understands Batman on a frightening, twisted level that only a sadistic, misanthropic mind like his could achieve. Batman finally asks, "[W]hy do you want to kill me?" In response to this, the Joker laughs hysterically. "I don't want to kill you," he confesses almost sweetly. "What would I do without you? You. Complete. Me." In the comics, Batman and the Joker reflect each other's existence. Batman's presence causes the escalation that evokes the Joker, and Batman refuses to break his "one rule" that would allow him to conclude the Joker's madness permanently. They are, simply, two forces that are stuck, always in opposition: good and evil.

In a move that decidedly reveals the Joker's commitment to anarchy, the ultimate joke the Joker delivers takes the form of the trick he plays on Batman. The Joker manages to slip past Batman's otherwise sharp defenses and intelligence, overriding the instinct that would have caused him to think through the situation before acting. The Joker preys on the emotions of Bruce Wayne, not the decided Batman. At first, the Joker wanted to know Batman's true identity; he longed to expose it to all of Gotham: "Why don't you take off your little mask and show us all who you really are?" Now, the Joker knows Batman better, and he no longer cares whose face lies underneath the mask. Just like in the comics, Bruce's true face and soul resides in that black mask, for he only experiences true freedom of self when he roams the night as Batman. Bruce Wayne serves as the real mask, the false self. Batman embodies the wealth of Bruce's beliefs and allows him fulfill his promise to his parents. Yet, the Joker is there to upset the order that Batman tries to impose: "Killing is making a choice....You have nothing. Nothing to threaten me with." Batman truly is helpless, for nothing matters to the Joker except anarchy. While no means exist to strike his own core, he can easily figure out how to destroy everyone else. The Joker announces the locations of Dent and Rachel, but he presents Batman with a choice, thus forcing him to indirectly break his own rule. Batman chooses the life of Rachel Dawes over Harvey, leaving one condemned; both Batman and the Joker understand that only he can reach either location in time. However, Batman instead finds Harvey on the other side of the door—and there lies the punch line. The expression on Batman's face when the Joker's sadistic joke registers with him is heartbreaking, for the Joker tricked him by switching the addresses. He already knew that Batman would choose Rachel, and in his cruelty, he ensured the person Batman would find would instead be Harvey Dent. Arguably, the Joker was only able to fool Batman because he ascertained that Batman and Bruce Wayne were one in the same, and Bruce Wayne is nothing more than a mortal man with weaknesses.

In being consoled and encouraged by Alfred, Bruce returns to the story of the bandit—a metaphor which beautifully conveys the battle waging between Batman and the Joker over Gotham. "That bandit," Bruce murmurs, "in the forest in Burma.... Did you catch him?" Alfred confirms. "How?" Softly, Alfred says, "We burned the forest down." To truly stop someone like the Joker, a man who yearns to watch the world burn, Batman would not only have to kill him, but he would have to tear Gotham apart in the process. Everything would lie in ruins. The matter of what Batman is willing to sacrifice to stop the Joker, and how far he will allow himself to go before he treads over a moral line he cannot return from, frontlines the theme of the film. Batman suffers from the overwhelming temptation to break his "one rule." When the Joker stands openly in the middle of a Gotham street after Batman flipped the truck he was driving, he dares Batman to hit him with his Batpod. Batman almost succumbs to the opportunity. After all the Joker has done, and will do, Batman would enjoy nothing more than having it end there and then. However, as he verges on colliding with the Joker, Batman swerves away, losing control of the Batpod and crashing onto the pavement. Batman knows that if he kills his adversary, not only would it betray everything he fights for and believes in, but the Joker would ultimately win. The Joker would prove that Batman is no better than him.

Meanwhile, Harvey Dent is nearly broken under the pressure of his emotional conflict, as well. Lying in the hospital bed, he spots his coin resting on the tray beside him, returned by Batman. Gazing at the untouched side, he fondly remembers Rachel. Turning it over, he sees that the opposite side has been badly burned, or rather scarred, like him. Dent's emotional pain dominates over the physical, letting him use the mortal pain of his burns function as a sort of release. When Harvey forces Gordon during a visit to admit the men used to call him "Harvey Two Face," he is not merely speaking of his newfound disfigurement. Like Harvey's face, the man inside has become mutilated. Pushed too far by the Joker's mutilation of Gotham and its people, and the corruption festering within the city, he also mourns the loss of someone he loved. Harvey has become scarred on both the outside and the inside; he

4. Dark Knight, White Knight, ... King of Anarchy (CARMICHAEL)

does not want people to fool themselves into thinking he can change. By believing this, the damage becomes an unalterable reality.

What is more, the Joker intends to pour salt in that wound. The Joker calls Mike Engel's television show, *Gotham Tonight* on Gotham Cable News, and announces that if Coleman Reese—who worked out Batman's identity and planned to expose him on live television—is not dead within an hour, he will decimate a hospital:

> I had a vision. Of a world without Batman. The mob ground out a little profit and the police tried to shut them down, one block at a time ... and it was so ... boring. I've had a change of heart. I don't want Mr. Reese spoiling everything, but why should I have all the fun? Let's give someone else a chance.

The Joker means to test society, just as he will test Harvey Dent. He manages to sneak into Harvey's hospital room, disguised as a nurse. Harvey grows furious when he sees the Joker, and he tries to worm his way free from his restraints and strike at him; however, the more the Joker tells him, the more Harvey calms down and listens. As the Joker states, "Do I really look like a guy with a plan? ... I'm not a schemer. I try to show the schemers how pathetic their attempts to control things really are." The Joker breathes anarchy. He is completely impulsive—without rules and without concern for anyone or anything. He presses his gun to his temple, giving Harvey full reign in an act that does not discriminate, even when it comes to himself. Nothing matters to the Joker but chaos:

> It's the schemers that put you where you are. You were a schemer. You had plans. And look where that got you. I just did what I do best—I took your little plan, and I turned it on itself. Look what I've done to this city with a few drums of gas and a couple of bullets. You know what I noticed? Nobody panics when things go according to plan, even if the plan is horrifying. If tomorrow I tell the press that a gangbanger will get shot, or a truckload of soldiers will be blown up, nobody panics. Because it's all part of the plan. But when I say that one little old mayor will die ... well then everybody loses their minds! Introduce a little anarchy, upset the established order, and everything becomes chaos. I'm an agent of chaos. Oh, and you know the thing about chaos?

Dent hangs on every word, beginning to view the world in a way that makes perfect and logical sense to his tormented mind: "It's *fair*." Harvey holds up his coin, showing the Joker the good side: "You live." Turning it over to expose the burned side, he finishes, "You die." The Joker grins. "Now we're talkin.'" Harvey, in his pain, has forgotten the truth and nature of justice, and the Joker now offers him a fresh understanding through anarchy—without plans or discrimination: fair.

The Joker's next act of anarchy adopts the form of another "social experiment." He sabotages two ferries, leaving them dead in the water. The Joker claims that both the commuter and prisoner ferries carry a remote to blow up the other boat. He announces that at midnight he will destroy them both, but if one boat presses its button first, he will spare the lives of that ship's passengers. On the side of good, Batman refuses to sit idly. On a rooftop overlooking the Prewitt Building, Batman tells Gordon he wants to infiltrate the building first. After being cruelly tricked by the Joker about Rachel and Harvey and letting his emotions cloud his judgment, Batman learns that with the Joker, there is always a catch. This time, his intuition saves the lives of innocents. It is also in this quick moment on the rooftop that Jim Gordon's guilt over Harvey Dent — like the Joker points out in the interrogation scene at MCU — becomes evident: "Dent's in there with them," he yells at Batman desperately. "We have to save Dent! I have to save Dent!" On the contrary, Gordon soon discovers from a phone call that Harvey has kidnapped his wife and son. "Where's my family?" Jim inquires weakly. "Where my family died," Harvey replies with venom.

After a stunning action scene in the Prewitt Building, Batman and the Joker fight one-on-one, with the Joker quickly taking the upper hand. He succeeds in pinning Batman down, shoving a steel beam against his neck, protected only by Batman's gauntlets. Midnight arrives with the Joker eagerly anticipating the "fireworks" from the ferries. However, both boats refuse to detonate the other. "What were you hoping to prove?" Batman demands, having confidently foreseen the outcome. "That deep down, we're all as ugly as you? You're alone." Similar to when the Joker confronted Gordon earlier, in this scene, the Joker's disappointment is transparent. He asks Batman if he knows how he got the scars spreading out from the corners of his mouth, prepared to tell another lie to reassure his own megalomania, but Batman cuts him off and takes control. The Joker falls over the ledge, but Batman saves him with his grapple and brings him up to eye level. "You just couldn't let me go, could you?" the Joker asks, laughing. "This is what happens when an unstoppable force meets an immovable object. You truly are incorruptible, aren't you?" Batman indeed stands as an incorruptible symbol with no weaknesses to exploit; likewise, the Joker is an absolute — a symbol of anarchy and an agent of chaos. "You won't kill me out of some misplaced sense of self-righteousness ... and I won't kill you because you're just too much fun." He concludes, with an unsettling air, "I think you and I are destined to do this forever." A hair-raisingly perfect foreshadowing, for just like in the comics, the Joker and Batman have been an unstoppable force and an immovable object, respectively, since their beginning.

Even while the Joker acknowledges his loss, he admits his "ace in the hole": Harvey Dent, now Two-Face. At the warehouse where Rachel died, Harvey holds Gordon's family hostage and, gauging the love Gordon has for his son James when he points the gun at his head, chooses to murder him with a flip of a coin: "It's not about what I want. It's about what's fair! You thought we could be decent men in an indecent time," Harvey growls, desperately trying to explain his pain to both Gordon and Batman. Echoing the Joker's mindset, he declares: "You were wrong. The world is cruel, and the only morality in a cruel world is chance. Unbiased. Unprejudiced. Fair." Batman pleads with Harvey, encouraging him to think reasonably. The exchange that follows demonstrates the complex relationship between Harvey and Batman:

> BATMAN: "What happened to Rachel wasn't chance. We decided to act. We three."
> HARVEY: "Then why is it me who is the only one who lost everything?"
> BATMAN: "It wasn't."
> HARVEY: "The Joker chose me!"
> BATMAN: "Because you were the best of us. He wanted to prove that even someone as good as you could fall."
> HARVEY: "And he was right."

Finally, Harvey points the gun at Gordon's son. In an effort to save his son and to admit the guilt that he has already been feeling, Gordon pleads, "Harvey, you're right. Rachel's death was my fault. Punish me." Harvey answers simply, "I'm about to." In mid-flip of the coin that now determines Harvey's actions, Batman tackles him, the coin falling to the floor, good side up. Harvey topples over the ledge, but Batman retains his grip with James in his arms. Harvey became obsessed with the coin as a means of escaping reality, responsibility, and guilt, and he simultaneously lost his sense of whether he should be doing right or wrong. Batman uses this to his advantage, hitting Harvey while distracted by the coin. Batman does not leave things to chance, and like Harvey once said, he makes "his own luck."

Likewise, with the loss of Gotham's White Knight, Batman must take his place, though in a distinctly different manner. On the ground below, Batman and Gordon discuss what Harvey's transformation into Two-Face means for Gotham: "The Joker won. Harvey's prosecution, everything you've worked for — undone. Whatever chance you gave us of fixing our city," Gordon says in sullen despair, "dies with Harvey's reputation. We bet it all on him. The Joker took the best of us and tore him down. People will lose hope." Batman opposes, "They won't. They must never know what he did." Then, "Gotham needs its true hero," turning Dent's head so that the good side of his face is exposed. When the coin fell, it landed with the untainted side revealed. Batman knows that deep down, Harvey still remained behind the torture of Two-Face. Gotham knew Harvey Dent as a good man, and Batman knows that Gotham needs to remember him as their White Knight: "You either die a hero or live long enough to see yourself become the villain. I can do those things because I'm not a hero. Not like Dent. I killed those people. That's what I can be." Despite Gordon's protests, but Batman rationally recognizes, "I'm whatever Gotham needs me to be."

Batman represents a different type of hero. Like he tells Gordon, and like he told Harvey earlier, Harvey is the hero Batman can never be: "Gotham needs a hero with a face." Batman wears a mask when Harvey had no need; the mask Batman wears serves as much more than a means to conceal his true identity. Inevitably, it separates him from the people of Gotham. The city will never truly understand him because there will always be that missing element of trust. They trusted — they *believed* in — Harvey Dent. He made strides in cleaning up Gotham legally, not as a vigilante or operating in the shadows, wielding fear and using methods outside the law, however doing so honorably. Harvey accomplished positive change as District Attorney. People knew his face, and the hardworking, incorruptible person they saw on the outside was the person on the inside, as well. It is only logical and natural, then, that they would gravitate toward Harvey over Batman; even Batman desired such a result. He wanted to see Harvey lead the way in a Gotham that no longer required the aid of Batman. While Batman epitomizes an ordinary person trying to save the city, Harvey embodied the entire city saving itself. That was the difference, and that was what Gotham needed.

However, Batman cannot afford that luxury. He must be whatever the people of Gotham need him to be. In times of crisis, he will be their savior; in times of anger or despair, he will act as their scapegoat so that they do not lose strength or hope. "You'll hunt me," Batman tells Gordon. "You'll condemn me, set the dogs on me ... because it's what needs to happen. Because sometimes the truth isn't good enough ... sometimes people deserve more. Sometimes people deserve to have their faith rewarded." During the voice-over, numerous things occur that provide further insight. Gordon speaks at a memorial for Harvey Dent: "...a hero. Not the hero we deserved, but the hero we needed. Nothing less than a knight. Shining..." It is extremely important, considering what Gordon says about Batman at the end of the film, to note the contrast between how Gordon describes Harvey and how he describes Batman: "...he's the hero Gotham deserves ... but not the one it needs right now. So we'll hunt him, because he can take it. Because he's not our hero ... he's a silent guardian, a watchful protector ... a Dark Knight." Harvey was the hero Gotham needed. They needed a hero without a mask to clean up the city while functioning within the law in order to show everyday citizens that they can accomplish the same good. They should not necessitate a mask, special gadgets, a costume, or a tank-like car. They can instead find the good within themselves and restore their city together. On the other hand, Batman is the hero the city deserves, but because Gotham and the good people remaining within it deserve someone willing to act selflessly for them, that reality in turn requires that specific individual to tend to what the city needs, as well as deserves. By the end of the film, they need a scapegoat. Like Harvey said earlier when comparing Batman to the Romans, what Batman does is not an honor, but rather a public service. It is not heroic, as Alfred told Rachel, but something more. Batman must take the fall for the lives Harvey took, because otherwise the hope the people of Gotham saw in someone like them would be crushed. Not only would they believe all the good they saw in Harvey and done by him was a lie, but they would also believe that Gotham is beyond saving. They must be allowed to persevere despite the loss.

Depending on what Gotham needs, Batman will either let the city see him as a hero and symbol of hope, or a villain, giving them strength and courage to fight. Gotham must come first, and Batman has to be willing to make whatever sacrifices necessary to uphold that promise. He will always be there, as Alfred said, "even if they hate him for it." He will continue to watch over them and protect them, despite their anger and hate and how much they outcast him: "He can make the choice no one else can face. The right choice."

Works Cited

Batman Begins. Dir. Christopher Nolan. Perf. Christian Bale, Michael Caine, Liam Neeson, Katie Holmes, and Gary Oldman. Warner Bros. Pictures, 2005.
The Dark Knight. Dir. Christopher Nolan. Perf. Christian Bale, Heath Ledger, Aaron Eckhart, Michael Kane, Maggie Gyllenhaal, and Gary Oldman. Warner Bros. Pictures, 2008.
Miller, Frank. *Batman: The Dark Knight Returns.* New York: DC Comics, 1997.
Moore, Alan. *Batman: The Killing Joke.* New York: DC Comics, 2008.

5

Introducing a Little Anarchy
The Dark Knight and Power Structures on the Verge of a Nervous Breakdown

SUDIPTO SANYAL

Chaos, it seems, comes in different shapes, sizes and hair color, and sometimes it even wears face paint. "Do I really look like a guy with a plan?" asks the Joker of a hospitalized Harvey Dent, thus articulating his position as a radically alienated subject within the finely balanced governmental system that operates within Gotham City. The Joker refuses to fit into the scheme of things, constantly challenging the stability of Gotham's power structures and perpetually threatening to superimpose an entirely different structure of power — one that functions arbitrarily, in other words, chaos — onto the one that exists at the moment. In this respect, the Joker appears to be the ultimate agent of chaos, situated on the margins of a profoundly disturbed panoptic order.

"Inspection," says Michel Foucault, "functions ceaselessly. The gaze is alert everywhere."[1] The concept of government becomes intimately connected to the idea of knowledge from the Enlightenment onwards. Governmentality at the level of the state functions in a tension of directionalities — "state centralization, on the one hand, and ... dispersion and religious dissidence, on the other. It is ... at the intersection of these two tendencies" that the central problematic of government, as questions of who rules whom and how, is posed.[2] This power-knowledge structure, expressed through the lens of governmentality, is an essential tool in the formation of the modern subject; in Colin Lucas's words, it "defines and indeed creates ... the individual."[3]

Surveillance becomes important in this context of knowing, and, indeed, this is the central concept of Foucault's history of the prison — *Surveiller et punir* (1975) — usually translated as *Discipline and Punish,* although, technically, "*Observe* and Punish." The rise of surveillance in society today — seen, for instance, in the gradual and steady increase in the penetration of surveillance in our social order from the nineteenth century, from peepshows and optical tricks, through illustrated journals and the "visual maps" of Benjamin's "flaneur,"[4] to our current hyper-televised, visually-supersaturated world so obsessed with surfaces (and surfaces are easily discernable) — is closely connected to the need to know and thereby mould conduct. The dominant system (governmental, political, cultural, call it what you will) needs to function through and within a framework of constant knowledge, a panoptic order.

A minor digression, then: the Panopticon is an architectural concept, first developed by the late-18th century English philosopher Jeremy Bentham as a plan for a model prison. "At its heart is a system of blinds which ensure that the individuals at the peripheral cells can be observed by a central inspector whom they cannot see. The Panopticon is a machine for sustaining a power relation," one working on the idea of domination through surveillance.[5] Power, therefore, exists relationally, and it always inscribes within itself the possibility of resistance.[6] The oppositional impulses that manifest themselves in the desperate attempts to (re)present the growing absence of the self in postmodern art, for example, are expressive of the technological creation of the modern subject through modes of governmentality that are constantly resisted. Thus, there is always an attempted inversion of the panoptic order, which is the governmental mode that becomes increasingly dominant over the course of the twentieth century and into the twenty-first century, because resistance is now intrinsic to the antithetical strains of postmodern behaviour. The Foucauldian way of perceiving such resistances as essential components of certain forms of conduct seems to be a remarkably lucid way of understanding the implications of binaries in the conduct of conduct.[7]

The concepts of surveillance and the Foucauldian Panopticon are especially relevant in attempting to analyze *The Dark Knight* as a sublime cultural artifact. The excessive grimness of a film that is at its structural core essentially nothing more than a comic book on celluloid is a fascinating condition. (Nothing more? The essentializing expectations of genre that comic art creates are themselves challenged by a lot of comic book writers, from George Herriman and Will Eisner to Neil Gaiman and Alan Moore. But that's a separate issue altogether). The thematic darkness of the film is inextricably connected to the teetering governmental system of Gotham City, a system that has slowly-widening fissures in the modes of its citizens' conduct.

History, for Foucault, is not a smooth continuity. "It is a series of radical discontinuities, ruptures, breaks, each of which involves a wholly novel mutation in the possibilities for human observation, thought, and action," says

Clifford Geertz in "Stir Crazy."[8] I think one of the reasons for the uncomfortable mood of *The Dark Knight* can be attributed to the evident unfolding, in the present, of the presence of these discontinuities in "human observation, thought, and action." The Joker's actions in the film create a very visible sense of a rupture in governmentality — he begins to draw attention to the conduct of the state on the conduct of the population, and then gradually, and visibly, begins to exert his own actions on the actions of others. It seems the Joker slowly starts taking over the function of the state, thereby severely disrupting the panoptic order. Again, it is *his* presence that taps into the anarchic potential present in any power relation and draws attention to the continuing presence of the Batman as, first, a policing and therefore possibly dangerous/tyrannical super-empowered agent of governmental order, and second, necessary for the continued existence of supervillains like the Joker — when the Joker points to the Batman as being responsible for the former's existence ("There's no going back," he says, "*You've* changed things. You complete me." [emphasis added]), he creates a severe rift in the panoptic order that is based on the observing and disciplining of abnormality, because he exposes the "system's" ruthless efficiency in fostering resistance in a controlled manner. The panoptic order collapses because the Joker is an uncontrollable force of resistance.

In fact, the act of exposure assumes particular urgency in the context of an upsetting of the established order. The Joker renders a certain "faciality" to his machinations, and the Aristotelian concept of anagnorisis, or recognition of a true self, is often his avowed aim — "I try to *show* the schemers how pathetic their attempts to control things really are," he tells Dent. In an interesting chronological inversion of the Foucauldian formulation that states that, from being once concerned with the Body as the location of power, we are now more concerned with an abstract conceptual entity, a subject position, Gotham's visible power structures are constructed within a "body-head system," while the Joker attempts an "absolute deterritorialization" by articulating a discourse of the face that seeks visibility, but seemingly comes out of nowhere.[9] The Joker's discourse, therefore, has no identifiable origin, and his repeated mythmaking actually makes the attempt to track down an origin meaningless. His is a discursive body, then, without organs. This is why he targets the *bodies* of the Mayor, the Batman, the District Attorney, the police and the citizenry because they are visible. *The Dark Knight* offers a clear image of the Foucauldian modern state in the fact that Gotham, like any other modern state, while possessing a superficial body-head system, ultimately functions on the principle of an absent locus of power, because "one never deterritorializes alone; there are always at least two terms ... and each of the two terms reterritorializes on the other."[10] The various fragmented selves that compose

Gotham's structure are visible in themselves, but they cannot see — they are objects "of information ... never of communication."[11]

"Invisibility is a guarantee of order," and the Panoptic system induces in it subjects, in this case, all of Gotham, what Foucault calls "a state of conscious and permanent visibility that assures the automatic functioning of power."[12] Without a permanent locus of power, all resistance is subsumed by the power structure, and systems are created in such a way that they have modes of resistance/subversion built into them. The "system" relieves large-scale tension by allowing local resistances. The Joker's many localized resistances, such as the attack on the Mayor, are attempts at upsetting the established order, but these acts themselves do very little to destabilize the greater system of power at work in Gotham. This is why he ultimately graduates to creating a form of resistance that truly threatens to impose a veil of chaos over the present power structure when he rigs the two ferryboats to explode and tries to make people blow each other up. This act in effect effaces the Joker's agency — he *almost* manages to create his own alternative system of power with its very own absent locus. Here, a face is given to an otherwise abstract, complicated power relation. The internal is made external; the workings of power as a relational entity are made visible. The "conscious and permanent visibility" of the subject that Foucault mentioned is subverted precisely because selective invisibility comes into play, i.e., while power is *visibly* in the hands of the people on board the two boats, the decision-making process that will or will not result in detonation is not visible outside each boat. The subject, accustomed to being permanently visible, is suddenly made to occupy not the cell, but the tower of the Panopticon, and it looks like he or she is completely confounded. Invisibility, far from guaranteeing order, creates a chaotic framework in this case. "Our society is one not of spectacle, but of surveillance," says Foucault. The Joker's final act of disobedience is deeply unsettling because it transgresses the discourse of modernity to appeal to a discourse of antiquity, which "had been a civilization of spectacle."[13]

The series of oppositions working within the power relations in Gotham are "anarchistic struggles."[14] As the Joker points out, because soldiers being blown up is "part of the plan," no matter how horrifying the plan is, it does not induce panic because the system anticipates this resistance — "...the question of the right of the state to ask an individual to die in a war. This question, without having lost any of its acuteness, has been integrated perfectly, through long historical developments, into the consciousness of people, so that soldiers have in effect agreed to be killed."[15] The system needs to function through a panoptic order, where overseeing everything becomes increasingly important. In this context, if Gotham must work through a superpowered secret agent like the Batman, it obviously has a failing/failed panoptic order. The Batman, therefore, occupies much the same status as the Joker — they are both outside the established order of things, and they both introduce chaos into an apparent order that is being manufactured by various forms of governmentality. The implication is that when normative things, like soldiers dying or gangbangers being killed, happen, the system works. When criminals challenge the system, they operate within the mode of anticipated resistance. The system thus *needs* the Joker to resist and the Batman to quell his resistance so that both cancel each other out and re-establish some kind of panoptic order — agents of chaos are required to validate the existence of order.

Herein lies the uniqueness of the Joker. His speech to Harvey Dent on the introduction of anarchy belies an intuitive grasp of the inner working of power structures. The only way resistance can actually negate existing power relations is if it leads to the creation of a completely different order of things, or, in the Joker's case, a disorder of things. This is why chaos is the only viable form of resistance — what could a dog chasing an ambulance hope to achieve in anything other than chaos? It is also interesting that this conversation takes place in a hospital, that, after all, is another variant of a carceral institution that houses, classifies, observes. And it is symbolic of the Joker's threatened destruction of the panoptic order that he blows the hospital up in a proleptic rehearsal of the more cosmic chaos he attempts to unleash on Gotham's structures of power.

Is chaos decentralised antipower, then? If it is, then the Joker is essential to the narrative, because he seems to be the only supervillain in the Batman Gallery of Grotesques with any chance of actually rupturing the discourses of power that flow in Gotham City. So, in an important respect, he is essential to the Batman's *continued* existence as an agent of order. As opposed to the Batman's fixed origin, the Joker's foundational myths are fluid, constantly morphing in and out of cruelty and black humour. In a lecture delivered in 1980, Foucault traces the intricate connections between subjectivity and technology in the formulation of what he calls the "technology of the self."[16] Foucault's "technology" implies the original Greek *techne,* an act of constructing reality. It is in this context that he constructs a genealogy of self-construction, whereby "individuals ... effect, by their own means, a certain number of operations on their own bodies ... souls ... thoughts ... conduct ... so as to transform themselves." Any subjugated knowledge is bound to be suppressed, and by refusing to disclose such knowledge, or by supplying multiple versions of it, the Joker makes sure it cannot be assimilated into discourse. The Joker's self-technologizing constructs many realities and forms agency — any knowledge that does not have an author, or cannot be validated legally, is subversive. The many origins of the Joker's scars are a unique subversion of the theatrical confession, the exomologesis — there is no component of penitence or acknowledgement of sin here, but the more Stoic technologizing of the self or "*akesis, not a disclosure of the self but a remembering*,"[17] and this is how a resistance to hierarchies is created. If, as Foucault believes, "one of the primary objects of discipline is to fix; it is an anti-nomadic technique,"[18] the Joker refuses to be pinned down, fixed. However, the Joker, like the Batman, should not exist at all for all official purposes. A stable narrative of the origin of his scars would have been subversive in itself, because it would have validated the existence of agents of nondisciplinary excesses, so the Joker sinks below normative criminals, the Batman rises above normative governmental agents. This, therefore, leads to an even greater complication — when the Joker tries to destabilize this subversive identity, what he does is not mere resistance to normative governmental structures; he destabilizes a possible mode of resistance as well. The modern state, with its obsessive classificatory and taxonomic impulses, has no space for an individual like the Joker who refuses to integrate himself within the pre-existing power structure. The integrated delinquent is one "not outside the law.... The delinquent is an institutional product."[19] Not so is the Joker, whose criminality cannot be specified. In this context, when he says something like "Why so serious?" he is contemptuous of both order and resistance to order.

The Joker, of course, also enunciates the contradictory, and perhaps schizophrenic, nature of the Batman's existence as evidence of the malfunctioning of the system of governmental surveillance. There's obviously something rotten in the city of Gotham, or the Batman would not need to exist. The conduct of the state seems to have failed in directing completely the conduct of its citizens, thereby destabilizing "normal" relations of power. Therefore, Gotham's political technology comes under threat, not only from the Joker, but from the very existence of the Batman. And now that the Batman *does* exist, he is the most effective form of a policing apparatus (consider the sonar Panopticon he uses to keep track of "the social field through knowledge of the tiniest detail"[20]); his is, in Geertz's description of the apparatus of the Panopticon, "the tireless gaze alert to the least irregularities."[21] Thus, the public call for the removal of the superhero exposes the extent to which the prevailing power structures are in danger of collapsing. Anarchy works on two levels in Gotham — within the existing power structure, as evidenced, for instance, in the Joker's blowing up a hospital, and outside it, in a sort of chaotic space. *The Dark Knight* repeatedly explores the possibility of these two levels colliding through the agency of the Joker, who operates within a register of subjugated knowledges by experimenting with multiple subversions of authority and resistance.

The apparent irregularities in the governing of bodies in the film create a very interesting problem in *The Dark Knight*. On the boats, the dialogic barrier between prisoner and civilian blurs. There occurs some sort of communication in the imaginative realm between the occupants of the two boats; the decision on either boat to not blow the other up is emblematic of the shift from "objects of information" to those "of communication."[22] Already, one sees a shift towards an older, pre-panoptic system, a shift that is intensified by the emphasis in the text on the Body. Cracks are opened up in the fabric of Gotham's care of the self— Gotham City itself looms large as a metonymic body under threat of disease (in the form of crime that cannot be contained within the usual domination-resistance binary structure), existing in a perpetual state of "abnormality" that seeks "normalization." The text's obsession with the scrutiny of the Joker's physical scars is symptomatic of Gotham's fear of contamination. It is the Joker's physical "abnormality" that provides an entry into his self-technologizing. The Batman exists as a postmodern schizophrenic consciousness, both normalizing agent and disruptive presence (and thereby an example of one of those inversions Foucault himself seems to have been so fond of).[23] The Joker, through various technologies of the self, acts on the action of others, operating on the borderlands of Gotham's panoptic structure, rejecting the usual relations of power that the functioning of governmentality implies by himself attempting to dominate the body politic, as well as simultaneously rejecting the resistance to the overarching modes of state governmentality. He is, by creating a completely alternative relation of power among himself, the citizenry and the state, fulfilling his role as the ultimate agent of chaos. The Joker is beyond classification and beyond integration into an existing structure of power. Perhaps this is also why his origin and end need to be indeterminate, constantly restructured. He drops into Gotham, and he drops out of it.

Notes

1. Michel Foucault, *Discipline and Punish: The Birth of the Prison*, trans. Alan Sheridan (New York: Vintage, 1995), 195.
2. Foucault, "Governmentality," in *The Essential Foucault*, ed. Paul Rabinow and Nikolas Rose (New York: The New Press, 2003), 230.
3. Colin Lucas, "Power and the Panopticon," in *Critical essays on Michel Foucault*, ed. Peter Burke (England: Scolar Press, 1992), 137.
4. Soumik Datta, "Approaching Technological Thresholds for a Panoptic Order: A Brief Note on *Natural Born Killers*" (Unpublished research paper).
5. Felix Driver, "Geography and Power: The Work of Michel Foucault," in *Critical essays on Michel Foucault*, 149.

6. "There is no power without potential refusal or revolt." Foucault, "*Omnes et Singulatim,*" *The Essential Foucault,* 201.

7. For a lucid description of the Panopticon, see Ray Land and Siân Bayne, "Screen or Monitor? Surveillance and disciplinary power in online learning environments," http://www.malts.ed.ac.uk/staff/sian/surveillancepaper.htm (accessed April 5, 2009). "In 1791, the English utilitarian philosopher Jeremy Bentham conceived of the architectural innovation of the panopticon as a way of achieving conformity and order within a 'humane' prison system (see Bentham 1962). The panopticon is a circular building, in which the cells of the prisoners occupy the circumference. The cells are divided from each other in such a way as to prevent any communication between prisoners. At the centre is the 'inspector's lodge' or observation tower from within which prison guards can see into every cell, without themselves being visible. The goal is the achievement of control through both isolation and the possibility of constant (invisible) surveillance. For Foucault (Foucault 1979a) the panopticon encapsulates in its form the shift in the nature of power relations which took place during the seventeenth and eighteenth centuries. Where previously what Foucault refers to as sovereign power had exercised dominion through punishment of the physical body (physical torture, public execution), during this time a different, less visible, power mechanism emerged which Foucault calls disciplinary power. Disciplinary power is exercised over individual and collective bodies 'through surveillance and via a grid or network of material coercions which effected an efficient and controlled increase (minimum expenditure, maximum return) in the utility of the subjected body'" (Smart 1985, p.80).

8. Clifford Geertz, "Stir Crazy," in *Critical essays on Michel Foucault,* 139.

9. Gilles Deleuze and Felix Guattari, *A Thousand Plateaus: Capitalism and Schizophrenia,* trans. Brian Massumi (London: Continuum, 2004 (1988)), 190–1. Deleuze and Guattari talk about the body-head system and faciality as an absolute deterritorialization and a symptom of the body without organs throughout the book.

10. Ibid., 193.

11. *Discipline and Punish,* 200.

12. Ibid., 201.

13. *Discipline and Punish,* 216–7.

14. "The Subject and Power," in *The Essential Foucault,* 129.

15. "The Risks of Security," in *The Essential Foucault,* 75.

16. Michel Foucault, "About the beginning of the hermeneutics of the self" (two lectures delivered at Dartmouth College, Hanover, New Hampshire, USA, 17 and 24 November, 1980). Transcribed by Thomas Keenan and Mark Blasius. Originally published in *Political Theory,* vol. 21, no. 2, May 1993, pp. 198–227.

17. "Technologies of the Self," in *The Essential Foucault,* 145–69.

18. *Discipline and Punish,* 218.

19. Ibid., 301.

20. This is how Bratich, Packer and McCarthy define Foucault's conception of the "police"—"a form of governance [in charge of] total administration of the social field through knowledge of the tiniest detail." Jack Z. Bratich, Jeremy Packer, and Cameron McCarthy, "Governing the Present," in *Foucault, Cultural Studies, and Governmentality,* ed. Jack Z. Bratich, Jeremy Packer, and Cameron McCarthy (New York: State University of New York Press, Albany, 2003), 8.

21. Geertz, 144.
22. See 5.
23. Foucault, says Lucas, had "an acute sense of paradox and ambiguity; a fondness for inversion." Lucas, 135.

Works Cited

Datta, Soumik. "Approaching Technological Thresholds for a Panoptic Order: A Brief Note on *Natural Born Killers"* (Unpublished research paper)

Deleuze, Gilles and Felix Guattari. *A Thousand Plateaus: Capitalism and Schizophrenia*, trans. Brian Massumi (London: Continuum, 2004)

Driver, Felix. "Geography and Power: The Work of Michel Foucault," in *Critical essays on Michel Foucault*, ed. Peter Burke (England: Scholar Press, 1992)

Foucault, Michel. *Discipline and Punish: The Birth of the Prison*, trans. Alan Sheridan (New York: Vintage, 1995)

_____. "Governmentality," in *The Essential Foucault*, ed. Paul Rabinow and Nikolas Rose (New York: The New Press, 2003)

_____. "The Subject and Power," in *The Essential Foucault*, ed. Paul Rabinow and Nikolas Rose (New York: The New Press, 2003)

_____. "Technologies of the Self," in *The Essential Foucault*, ed. Paul Rabinow and Nikolas Rose (New York: The New Press, 2003)

Geertz, Clifford. "Stir Crazy," in *Critical essays on Michel Foucault*, ed. Peter Burke (England: Scholar Press, 1992)

Lucas, Colin. "Power and the Panopticon," in *Critical essays on Michel Foucault*, ed. Peter Burke (England: Scholar Press, 1992)

Part Two

Batman and Literary Theory

6

Batman's *Canon*
Hybridity and the Interpretation of the Superhero

KEVIN K. DURAND

Is there a defining Batman? Is it Christian Bale? Michael Keaton? Adam West? Lego Batman? George Clooney? Okay, so it isn't Clooney. But how would we decide? *Can* we decide? Is there any measure by which we can separate the aesthetic enjoyment of a particular incarnation of the Batman from the discussion of not only which is the best, but which is the truest? And what does it even mean to be the best or truest Batman? The Batman universe is likely unique in the exceptional difficulty it presents to the scholar trying to formulate answers to those questions. All of these are questions of *canon*, of what is the authoritative Batman. And, they are deceptively tricky, some might say, devilishly tricky questions. Indeed, rather than wade into the Batman thicket unarmed without theoretical frameworks, it might be helpful to examine what we mean by *canon* and what controversies surround establishing and maintaining one. Along the way, I will actually argue that the Batman universe is perhaps the most telling example of a hybrid canon, and that, painful though it may be to do so, we have to include the vast majority of Batman incarnations into a canon in flux.

With a canon in flux, it is particularly difficult to sift through it and apply some theoretical framework to making sense of it. Generally, we come to canons that are already fixed or mostly so, and nibbling around at the edges is all that is left to be done. More and more, though, this phenomenon of the fixed canon is coming under greater scrutiny, and once almost sacrosanct literary canons are being reformulated, or being evaluated for reformulation. Increasingly, writers like Kate Chopin and Zora Neale Hurston are being added to the basic canon of 20th century American literature, for example, alongside staples like Hemingway and Fitzgerald. Within the realm of popular culture, canons of particular universes are always in a bit of flux — the *Buffy* canon is more nearly closed now than it has been with the completion of the televised series and the departure of Whedon from the direct control in the graphic novel. The canon of *The Wizard of Oz* universe is mostly closed, even with the advent of Gregory Maguire and *Wicked*. The 1939 movie so thoroughly dominates the landscape that nothing stands much chance of dislodging it from its place of canonical authority. *Batman*, however, is quite dissimilar from these, though. As such, it is necessary that we step back from the survey of the various incarnations of the Batman and develop a bit of a framework with which to deal with a canon that has no Colossus. It will first be helpful to look at the nature of canon and canon formation. We'll then turn to a discussion of some controversies within discussions of the canon, and use examples from scholarship relatively familiar to most readers — namely, scholarship of Christian scripture. Ultimately, the phenomenon of the popular culture event within the culture that popularizes it will be most helpful in understanding *Batman*'s hybrid and fluid canon.

Canon Construction and Controversies

Let's start with an example; one that is notable both for the attempt to establish a canon and for the controversies that were spawned by the attempt. As the twentieth century came to a close, The Modern Library, a division of Random House Publishing, put forward a list of the top one hundred American novels of the century. Leading the list was James Joyce's *Ulysses*. Bringing up the rear was Booth Tarkington's *The Magnificent Ambersons*. Needless to say, the list spawned controversy. There was hue and cry; there was weeping and gnashing of teeth; there were blogs aplenty, even before blogs were that popular. Other lists sprang up. The credentials of the judges at The Modern Library were called into question that's putting it mildly). The credentials of those putting together other lists were similarly met with question. *Ad hominem* abounded. Finally, The Modern Library held a sort of readers' poll and collected a top one hundred books as put forward by and voted on by the reading public. Four of the top eight on the readers' list turned out to be novels by Ayn Rand. Rand is a novelist of some repute whose works didn't crack the professionals' Top Hundred but whose legions of fans and public relations machine are a daunting duo, and rumors of ballot-box stuffing abound. *Ulysses*, a far tougher read and infinitely better novel, slid down to eleven; *Finnigan's Wake* dropped out altogether. And, as a fairly bemused graduate student observer, I found it all rather humorous.

As it turns out, one of the most controversial topics in any scholarly discussion is that of canon. The controversy often takes one of two avenues; sometimes, both. The first question, touched on by the Top Hundred Novels controversy, is the question of which books should be included in a canon of literature. Or, in other words, what are the best examples of a particular genre broadly conceived). This is a question that vexes scholars on many fronts. One of the more popular of late has been the reconsideration of the canon of Christian scripture that has been sparked, at least in part, by both the millennial conclusion and the Dan Brown novel, *The Da Vinci Code*. That controversy is quite heated and will be revisited shortly. For ease of reference, let's refer to this as the Canon Construction Controversy.

The other avenue of controversy has to do not so much with what texts are included in a canon, but how that canon is used as the authoritative standard by which all newer texts are judged, or by which even pieces of the canon are seen as somehow secondary to the central canon, or the canon within a canon. Here, too, Christian scripture provides an intriguing example. For ease of reference, let's refer to this as the Canonical Authority Controversy.

The canon of Christian scripture is a good example of both controversies. As a matter of the Canon Construction Controversy, one needs only survey the inclusion and exclusion of texts with the Christian scriptures. Such a survey will quickly reveal that it is a complicated matter to describe, precisely, what the Christian canon is. Indeed, it is not so much a single canon as it is a set of them. Of course, certain books are in immediately — Matthew, Mark, Luke, John — and the like, but the *Apocrypha*, for example, is commonly included as canonical, if not of the same weight, within the Roman Catholic Church, while within the Protestant traditions, those books written during the Inter-testamental period of roughly 300 B.C.E. to the mid-first century C.E. are rejected. Obviously, there were canonical feuds within the earliest church, and a great number of episcopal epistles listed one set of texts as central to the faith while decrying others as secondary, or worse, heretical. For a very nice discussion of this particular canonical controversy, one couldn't do better than reading Bart Ehrman's *Lost Scriptures*. This is an overly quick synopsis, but it serves to show that the analogy is apt.

In a related matter, there are those churches that explicitly claim the primacy of the New Testament over the Old Testament, and those churches that explicitly reject the claim, arguing instead that all of scripture, Old and New Testament are equally part of the revelation of God. Whatever the official stance of the particular church, it is also the case that when interpreting the text, through sermon, hymn, prayers, and the like, a smaller canon within the canon becomes the lens by which the rest of the canon is seen. For example,

Martin Luther argued that canonical authority rested first in the gospels and the Letter to the Romans, and that, in virtue of the views expressed there, the Letter to the Hebrews and the Letter of James were much less important. Indeed, he labeled them as "straw" and "more straw." John Wesley, the early pioneer of the Methodist movement, preached over half of his sermons drawing as his text the Gospel of Matthew. Even more impressive, perhaps, half of those sermons were drawn from but three chapters — 5, 6, and 7: the Sermon on the Mount. This problem of Canonical Authority accounts for a great many arguments within the Church.

Before turning to what any of this conversation about American novels and Christian scripture has to do with *Batman*, there is one other canonical sort of controversy that grows out of the first two, and that is particularly relevant to *Batman*. What do we do with a text that comes along after the canon is established and is thought, at least by some, to be as important as any of those already included. Let's call this the Open/Closed Canon Controversy.

Obviously, in the course of the development of the Christian movement, there have been those situations which involve a new text being included in an otherwise established canon. One prime example of such a text would be The Book of Mormon. While those of the Church of Jesus Christ of Latter Day Saints have no problem whatsoever with placing the Book of Mormon alongside the Old and New Testaments, those within the Catholic and Protestant traditions very clearly do. One of the issues here, though not the only one, is whether or not new texts can be added after a canon has been officially established. In those traditions that contend that the canon is complete and admits no new additions, we say the canon is closed. In those traditions that permit some degree of leeway with regard to the admission of new texts, we say the canon is open. And, while there is not much open in the way of the Christian canon, there are religious traditions — Hinduism, for example — that have considerably more open canons.

Canon and the Batman

Having touched on some of the traditional canon controversies, the question remains, "How does this apply to Batman?" In some ways, the comparison is more obvious than the solution. The arguments that go on within the hallowed halls of the church are direct analogues, in many ways, to the arguments that take place in the coffee shop, the comic book store, the classroom, and dining room. Indeed, in the two-word title of the first movie of the revitalized Batman franchise, all of these controversies are crystallized, and a position is taken. *Batman Begins* does not suggest that all of the Batman incarnations before it were of equal worth. Nor is it suggesting that the franchise is being revitalized. Intentionally or not, the title straightforwardly rejects much of the work that had gone before it as a failure to capture the Batman mythos. Then, having seemingly solidified a position as authoritative, the next movie, with its own spare title, *The Dark Knight*, serves to broaden the canonical net ever so slightly, now including Frank Miller's 1986 four graphic novel set, *The Dark Knight Returns*. The newcomer to the *Batman* universe strides like a Colossus, and the generally received view is that it has not only revitalized the franchise, but saved it from the cartoonishness of Clooney and West. Thus, if we set out to give an accounting of the texts that comprise the *Batman* canon, one could not possibly exclude Christopher Nolan's movies or Frank Miller's graphic novels.

Despite the relative popularity of those pieces of the *Batman* universe, it does not seem quite proper to limit the canon to only these late-coming works. Indeed, using this sort of bit-by-bit inclusion could well be a sort of slippery slope of comparisons to gradually expand the canon to include all of the incarnations of the Batman, including Clooney's. For example, having included the Miller 1986 graphic novels, it is not a stretch to include Keaton's Batman, nor to include the cartoon, *Batman: The New Adventures*. However, that smacks of informal fallacy, and even though, in this context, I suspect it is innocent of the charge, it is perhaps safer to judge works more individually where possible.

The Canonical Tool

There is a canonical issue that is particularly relevant to our investigations of Batman. In a quick and uncritical way, it can be called the Popularity Test. The incredible popularity of the Batman prior to *Batman Begins* tells against limiting the canon in such a fashion. Whatever cartoony-ness there might be attached to Adam West's Batman, it remains amazingly popular. In 2004 and 2005, it received TV Land awards for Favorite Crimefighter and Favorite Crimefighting Duo. Cheesy though TV Land awards may be, they do capture something important — namely the enduring popularity of the beloved 60s Caped Crusader. Popularity, especially without the perspective of time, can distract the viewer by enfolding him in the crush of the popularity itself. Popularity, on the other hand, is a fickle friend, and one that, on its own, should not be used as a measuring stick of scholarly importance or of canonical primacy. Dan Brown's Robert Langdon novels, for example, are in many ways far more popular than, say, the book of Habakkuk, but no amount of popularity for *Angels and Demons* could supplant the minor prophet from its canonical place.

At the same time, there is an intriguing feature of the Batman universe of texts that makes that universe and the relative popularity of its pieces particularly instructive. It is not the popularity itself, but what we can discern as at least partly *causal* of the popularity that can provide us with an understanding of the variety within the canon. The Batman, unlike almost every other superhero, carries the load that the cultural setting within which it is incarnated places upon him. That is, the Batman event is very much a product of the time. In many ways, it is the culture that creates that generation's *Batman*. Before turning to a brief survey of *Batman* in its cultural contexts, there is another feature of the Batman that sets him apart from the other superheroes. Simply put, Batman isn't Superman, and the difference makes Batman and Bruce Wayne much more accessible than Superman and Clark Kent. Let's analyze why.

To discuss the difference between Superman and Batman, it is best to start with Superman. Superman is not human. He looks human. He can pass for human. But, he is not human; and his alienness alienates him from the possibility of even being considered a proper sort of role model for human behavior. While one might very well ask, "What would Commissioner Gordon do?" in some situation or other and use the answer as something of a guide to one's own ethical reflections and moral actions, one cannot ask "What would Superman do?" and hope to arrive at anything realistic. For example, if one were traveling along a country road and saw a train about to run off a train bridge where the bridge was out and plunge into the waters hundreds of feet below, asking "What would Superman do?" would be wholly useless.

While it is odd to speak of any superhero as accessible or as serious role model, it is particularly so of Superman. His experience of the world is so unlike any human's experience could even *possibly* be that it makes it impossible to identify with the Man of Steel. While it is true that Bruce Wayne is wealthy beyond imagination, he is a human character capable of pain, bleeding, and death in the same ways any human is. While Superman is faster than a speeding bullet, that same bullet could mortally wound Batman. It is difficult, then, to empathize with the one, and entirely possible to identify, at least insofar as it is possible to identify with a fantasy creation, with the other.

Even the attempts to humanize Superman do little but serve to point out his differences. As Lex Luthor pointed out in *Lois and Clark*, was Lois colossally stupid to not recognize Clark Kent for who he really was? Was just a pair of simple glasses enough to deflect her attention from his super alter-ego. Only, Superman isn't Clark Kent's alter-ego; Clark Kent is Superman's alter-ego. At the beginning and end of the day, Bruce Wayne is Bruce Wayne, multi-billionaire with a dark past, a vigilante streak, and a penchant for dressing up in a Halloween outfit and driving a souped-up hotrod. At the beginning and end of the day, Superman is not Clark Kent, mild-mannered reporter for the Daily Planet. He's Kal-el, a powerful alien with a sense of justice and a penchant for dressing up like a reporter and pretending to have to drive. His name even contains the suffix that denotes deity. The "el" is a suffix meaning "god." Thus, the name Bethel means "house of God." Superman is not a man; he's a sort of god.

Philosophically speaking, Superman plays another role, as well, that Batman does not. For Friedrich Nietzsche, the truly free man was the uberman, sometimes translated "over-man" as a way of demonstrating his transcendence from the human condition of being bound by the morality and structures of a society that sought to keep people from maximizing their individual potentials and subvert those gifts to the betterment of the whole (which, necessarily consisted of those less worthy of the benefit of those gifts than the one who possessed the gift to start with). But, another common translation that captures that nuance without making it seem as if the over-man is also necessarily overlord is Superman. The Nietzschean Superman is one who lives as a law unto himself. His actions are deeply self-interested, and he promotes his own well-being as the highest good, expecting others to do the same, and finding them lesser when they cannot. He resembles the Machiavellian prince or the "just" man of Thrasymachus who holds that justice is merely the will of the stronger, or that might makes right. As a thought experiment, one might see the Nietzschean Superman as one whose own interests are supreme. This is obviously completely contrary to the notion of the Superman of values, the one who puts his powers to use for the goal of "truth, justice, and the American way." The Superman of Clark Kent is the one who, though possessing great power and near invincibility, acts on behalf of those who are far weaker and more vulnerable than he. He, thus, stands as a thought experiment rejection of the uberman.

Batman, on the other hand, is without a clear philosophical foil. Instead of imagining him atop a hillside, sun shining in the distance, wind whipping his cape, chest and chin held high, hands on hips as a gesture of greatness, one imagines the Batman lurking in the shadows, dropping down into the alleyways, fighting the good fight and going home black and blue at the end of the day. One sees in Batman the vigilante, the hunger for justice that has a tinge of vengeance, of righteous indignation. One sees in Batman his humanness, foibles and all. And, one can almost imagine that, given a huge trust fund, a butler, and an empire that seems designed to manufacture the very toys one needs to fight crime, one might be the Batman. Farfetched though it be, it is a far cry further to imagine being Superman.

This sort of accessibility evokes a different response in the reader and viewer. Because Bruce Wayne is quintessentially human, individuals can identify with him. That possibility of identification is one of the key features that distinguishes the Batman canon and that makes it unique. The Batman universe is reflective of the society from which it springs. Indeed, even the Batman text itself communicates that connection. Batman's origin story, when told, is always a version of the killing of his parents by a thug in the gritty and darkened streets of Gotham. Gotham is a city struggling with itself and with its own survival. The criminal element is never far from the heart of the city, and it is that cultural milieu that literally gives rise to the Batman. In witnessing his parents' deaths, he is marked and shaped. He becomes not only a Dark Knight, but a Dark Avenger, an Angel of Justice whose Justice is swift, violent, and thorough. He is as much the creation of the textual culture in which he moves as the Batman popular culture event is a product of the culture in which it is developed. A brief survey of the arc of the Batman will serve to demonstrate this.

The Hybrid Batman

The earliest of the Batman screen appearances is not, as many might guess, the Adam West of the 1960s. Indeed, the first screen appearance of the Caped Crusader was 1943. It consisted of fifteen screen episodes of low-budget camp and wartime angst. Shown mainly in the theater, it was not nearly as campy as West's, but Lewis Wilson's Batman (envisioned by Bob Kane and Victor McLeod) was, in many ways, a predecessor to the fantastical worlds of James Bond. In one story arc that is particularly indicative of the way in which the Batman reflects the culture from which it springs, our hero must try to foil the plot of a Japanese superspy who has hatched a plot to turn every scientist in America into a zombie. It is not hard to see the concerns of a nation at war, particularly a war in which science was playing such a pivotal role, played out on the screen, along with the assurance that, as the hero wins the day, America will survive.

Turning to the 1960s, one finds a very different cultural climate. *Batman* premiered in 1966 with Adam West and Burt Ward as Batman and Robin, along with a cast of memorable character actors like Frank Gorshin, Julie

Newmar, and Meredith Burgess chewing up the scenery as over-the-top villains. It is very easy to dismiss this incarnation of the Batman. However, dismissing West's Batman misses something very important. It is as much a product of its period as the 1943 version.

The 1960s, especially in the early years, were a time of great prosperity, hope, and expectation. The death of John F. Kennedy was a terrible blow, but things like the Civil Rights Act, the scientific successes that put televisions in more homes than ever and that would soon put men on the moon were captivating. It was a heady time of hope. Even in the midst of the Cold War and the early years of the Vietnam conflict, expectations for a better world in the near future were high. One need only look at one of *Batman*'s contemporaries, *Star Trek*.

A quick tour of the Enterprise bridge is all one really needs to do to see Gene Roddenberry's hopeful vision of the future. In the midst of the Cold War, a Russian — Chekov — sits at the helm of the ship. Right beside him is a Japanese man, Sulu, less than thirty years after Pearl Harbor. At the communications desk is Lt. Uhuru, played by Nichele Nichols, an African-American woman. Nichols even thought of turning down the role as it was only for a communications officer, but on the advice of Dr. Martin Luther King, Jr., she took it and excelled. At the science desk, an alien, Mr. Spock. Scottie and McCoy round out the central crew — a Scot, obviously, and an American doctor of Scottish descent, which is to say, a Scot and the product of immigrants at some level, respectively. And, of course, James Tiberius Kirk is in the center. Yet, though Kirk is the clear leader, he is not the tyrant his middle name might suggest. The Enterprise is collaborative, and its vision of the future is profoundly hopeful.

In a similar way, the 1966–68 *Batman* expresses similar hopes. Batman and Robin, though clearly of differing gifts, are closer to a friendship than one might suspect of a multi-millionaire at the time) and his ward. Commissioner Gordon and Chief O'Hara are competent, if a little clueless at times. The villains are rather inept, and Gotham City is not the hive of villainy that it is made out to be in later incarnations. All things considered, the world is getting better, and it is doing so with the help of the Caped Crusader and his trusty sidekick.

One thing that is particularly interesting about this incarnation of the Batman is that even though its on-air run was reasonably brief (and so, too, was *Star Trek*'s), it continued to have an incredible following in re-runs. Not only that, despite the turn in attitude and morale of the nation after the devastating events of 1968 — the deaths of Robert Kennedy and Dr. King and the realization that Vietnam was neither World War II nor Korea — the show continued to gather a following. In part, I suspect it was because even though the hope of progress was shown to be a bit naïve, perhaps, the vision of the future was still one that was grasped and grasped for. It was a vision for which parents hoped for their children, for example. The West/Ward Dynamic Duo reprised their roles as cartoons in Scooby-Doo, connecting Saturday morning cartoons with the best of the vision of the 60s. And, whether in cartoon or live-action cartoon, the tone and message were consistent — Crime doesn't pay, working together solves far more problems than segregating into different groups all fussed about their own turf, and friendship and loyalty are to be prized above all else. Whether these are reflective of contemporary values, and one would be hard pressed to suggest that they are not to at least some degree or other, they were definitely expressions of the cultural tenor of their day.

Batman was mainly consigned to reruns and the comic world in the 1970s and early 1980s, and, apart from more relatively small groups of enthusiasts, the world looked elsewhere. However, in 1986, Frank Miller's *The Dark Knight Returns*, a dark vision with an older and more reflective Batman, revitalized the franchise and popular attention. Indeed, it can be argued that Miller's Batman was indirectly responsible (and perhaps, directly so) for both of the film adaptations that followed — the Michael Keaton Batman of 1989 and 1992 and the Christian Bale Batman of 2006 and 2008.

Deep into roughly forty years of Cold War, having the experience of Vietnam, economic crises, outlandish inflation and high unemployment, the Iranian hostage affair, and with a sort of world-weariness pervading the public, Miller's Batman reflects much of the emotional tenor of the American populace. There is no question that Batman is still exceptional — a phenomenally wealthy Wayne, a social position of some standing — but, it is also clear that the years of being Batman have taken an enormous toll. There is considerably more adult reflection in the eyes of the Caped Crusader, and a hardened practicality born of years of a fight that was not over nearly so quickly as one would have hoped or expected. Crime is not something that is easily or quickly (or, perhaps, ever) remedied. And, the Batman is carrying not only that realization but the realization that his younger idealism has foundered on the rocks of reality and *realpolitik*.

In this way, Miller's Batman is a nice analogue to the mood of the nation, and a nice counterpart to West's Batman. Indeed, one can argue that without the idealism of the 1960s Batman, the world-weariness of the Miller Batman is a bit less affecting. Idealism, without realism, is, perhaps, naïve. Realism, without idealism, can trend toward hopelessness. And, realism, without an idealist past that has not been fulfilled, is a highly impersonal practical cynicism that cannot connect with the angst or realization of the ultimate failure to attain those high ideals—not only because of personal failures, which are surely a part, but because of events outside our control. Such a character has no warmth, no shared pain with which the audience can identify.

It many ways, the screen Batman of the 1980s, reflects much of that as well. Prior to the release of *Batman*, many critics and fans expressed great dismay at the casting of Michael Keaton as the titular character. After all, the man known for *Beetlejuice*, *The Dream Team* and *Johnny Dangerously* seemed an odd choice. He was not an imposing physical specimen, he had a penchant for playing odd and oddball characters, and it was not at all clear to many that he could properly fill the role or the suit. The choice of Jack Nicholson to play the Joker, on the other hand, had no detractors. And, until Heath Ledger's performance in *The Dark Knight*, it was thought by many that the role had been done so well that it could not possibly be reprised without paling in comparison to Nicholson's brilliant performance. Indeed, in many ways, Nicholson's Joker overshadows Keaton's Batman. At the same time, Keaton plays the role, without the sidekick Robin, with the same sort of weariness and emptiness that one sees in Miller. The aloneness of the hero, his isolation from the world that he seeks to protect, and his increasing alienation from the hopes that his efforts do more than stem an unstemmable tide is all a part of the Keaton Batman.

The origin story in *Batman*, in which the Joker appears as a young thug who kills Bruce's parents, is a moment that ultimately supports the argument presented here. As culture produces a Batman that reflects both its hopes and dreams but also its suspicions, fears, and, at times, cynicism, so, too, the culture of Gotham creates the Batman. Buried within him are the hopes and dreams of a civilized Gotham, and buried within those are the psychological structures that issue in his later manifestation as a man dressed like a bat. This same structure is repeated in *Batman Begins*, although without the Joker as the original assassin. In a sense, this serves to heighten the sense that Batman is ultimately a product of the culture that gave rise to him—it was not some chance encounter between two adversaries fated to wage eternal war with one another, but rather a punk killing a kid's parents, a situation that had, of its own, no grand importance, but was one of a myriad instances of petty crime representing a sort of banality of evil.

The Hybrid Canon

The canon of the Batman is not closed. It is not limited to the Nolan/Bale vision and representation. *Batman Begins* and *The Dark Knight* come from somewhere. That somewhere is the long line of Batman incarnations that preceded them, and those incarnations are the product of the society from which they sprang. While this seems a sort of reader-response or viewer-response form of critical analysis, I hasten to add that my view is not that Batman means whatever it means to the reader or viewer, but that the Batman has become an archetypal template for which a vision for and an experience of the world provides content. Thus, each incarnation is an artifact of its culture, but it is also an artifact in which each successive incarnation of the Batman is in conversation with the others.

This reading of the Batman either solves or avoids many of the problems that attend canon construction and interpretation. It avoids the Canonical Authority question because each piece of the canon is both time-bound and timeless. It is time-bound in the sense that it arises from a particular place and embodies an era's experiences; it is timeless in that, as a literary successor to all of the previous incarnations, it incorporates them, either positively or negatively, into itself. The primary canonical creation and critique question left to the critic of any particular incarnation of the Batman is whether or not this particular instance reflects the culture, time, ethos, and pathos of the moment into which it is incarnate.

With respect to the question of canonical authority, the strength (and weakness) of any hybrid canon is that no particular instance can claim with much authority that status of authority. This is particularly true with *Batman*. The canon is so diverse that no particular franchise can claim canonical primacy; while, at the same time, the major moments of which there are many) can all lay claim to primacy. Thus, for these reasons, we must answer the opening question of this essay with a resounding, "No, there isn't *a* definitive Batman; there are, in fact, several."

Works Cited

Batman—Holy Batmania. Image Entertainment, 2004. DVD.
Batman and Robin—The Complete 1949 Movie Serial Collection. Sony, 2005. DVD.
Batman Begins. Warner Home Video, 2005. DVD.
Batman: The Motion Picture Anthology, 1989–1997. Warner Home Video, 2009. DVD.
The Dark Knight. Warner Home Video, 2008. DVD.
Nietzsche, Friedrich. *Thus Spoke Zarathustra: A Book for All and None*. New York: The Modern Library, Random House, 1995. Print.
Star Trek: The Original Series. Writ. Gene Roddenberry. Paramount, 2008. DVD.

7

Seminar on the Purloined Batarang
Batman and Lacan

MITCH FRYE

For the past three years, the Batman comics franchise has been controlled in large part by a writer many fans consider a madman. Eager to bring real change to the stagnating Bat-titles, Dan DiDio, Executive Editor at DC Comics, tapped Grant Morrison to write for *Batman*, the franchise's flagship magazine. Morrison's previous works — stints on established titles like *Animal Man* and *Doom Patrol* as well as independent properties like *Seaguy* and *We3* — had been both lauded and derided for their experimentalism. Only a few years earlier, Marvel had hired him to reboot their flagging X-Men franchise with mixed results. While readers were clearly pleased with the chic aesthetic he envisioned for the mutant team, many were less than thrilled with the plodding conspiracy theory story he allowed to unfold over the course of several years. By the time he left the title, he had killed off fan favorite characters Magneto and Jean Gray, victims of skullduggery effected by a sentient strand of bacteria obsessed with ending intelligent life on Earth. So, one assumes DC's editorial staff acknowledged the risks inherent in bringing Morrison on board.

But despite his occasionally off-putting cleverness, Morrison was no Bat-amateur. He had already written a well-received story for the *Legends of the Dark Knight* series and scripted the deeply Jungian *Arkham Asylum* graphic novel. The latter work in particular had been concerned with the deconstruction of the Batman character. Its plot found him wandering the halls of the madhouse, tormented by the very criminals he put away, endlessly troubled by the possibility that his own damaged mental state might be indistinguishable from theirs. The more recent publication of Morrison's newer Batman stories made it clear that he would be retreading this familiar terrain — with a few novel inflections. The first story, "Building a Better Batmobile," begins with Batman's realization that he has inadvertently undermined his own *raison d'être*. The first seven pages show him capturing the Joker, the last of Gotham's criminals to hold out against Batman's "crime blitz," an initiative designed to jail the city's costumed villains (655.12). For a lesser writer, this scene would be implemented only at the end of a *pow-biff-wham* tale spanning several issues; in Morrison's capable hands, it is merely the beginning of something greater, a clear indication that the writer will not demean himself with run-of-the-mill crime-fighting plots.

With no more major villains to apprehend, Batman must invent new ways to divert himself. He attends fundraisers as Bruce Wayne. He falls in love with an international celebrity. He learns that he has a son and that it will be his responsibility to raise him. And then, with the usual suspects safely tucked away in Arkham Asylum and Blackgate Prison, Batman discovers that the biggest remaining threat to Gotham City may be the fallout from his own mythos. A government project he participated in years ago — an effort to psychologically prepare replacements to assume the role of Batman in the event of his demise — has gone awry, and the alternate Batmen have become homicidal maniacs. At the heart of the problem is a psychiatrist named Dr. Simon Hurt, who worked with Batman on the project and seems to have tinkered with the minds of all parties involved, including the Caped Crusader's.

Batman in Conflict

Morrison's story is unique because it involves Batman's history rising up against him. In true postmodern fashion, his story arcs for the title are essentially pastiches. Most of the scenes and characters are cleverly recycled from the long-forgotten Batman stories of the Fifties and Sixties, re-deployed here in a new context. These are presented via a plot device called the Black Casebook, a bound volume of notes Batman has taken on his paranormal cases — the ones that have left him questioning his sanity. Weird tales of space travel, ghosts, and doppelgangers, these are Batman's recollections of the mid-century stories purged from the canon by modern editors eager to maintain a modicum of realism in Batman's adventures. There is subversion in these forbidden reiterations for the simple reason that they break with the Bat-status quo. Batman is supposedly immune to mental breakdown, but Morrison seems determined to shatter his mind and, by connection, the impossible manhood that has been attributed to him. Ever since writer Frank Miller introduced the hyper-masculine, indefatigable version of the Batman character in the 1980s, the vigilante has remained burly and hardboiled, as unstoppable as he is unemotional. Beginning with *The Dark Knight Returns* in 1986, Miller helped establish the gritty Batman we see perpetuated in the films of Tim Burton and Christopher Nolan. Prior to Miller's work, the sillier, paunchier Batman portrayed by Adam West in the 1960s television series was a fairly accurate representation of the comics character. Only in the late Sixties and early Seventies did he begin to evolve into the masked Sam Spade we know today — and it was not until Miller arrived on the scene that the Dark Knight reached the peak of his masculine evolution.

Per Miller's take on Batman, the character's toughness results from his brutal singularity of purpose. He exists to stomp criminals into the dirt, and he harbors no doubts about the virtue of his crusade. While Miller's work concedes that the character has been subjected to considerable trauma, the fiction always indicates that Batman is eminently rational, perhaps the last truly sane man in an increasingly mad world. As he thrashes a lawbreaker in *The Dark Knight Returns*, Batman responds to the criminal's assertion of his rights by lamenting, "You've got rights. Lots of rights. Sometimes I count them just to make myself feel crazy" (1.45). The idea is that the modern world is bonkers for being soft on crime, and Batman — being the uncompromising moral force that he is — serves as the sole voice of reason. The question of sanity is neatly elided, for Miller focuses almost exclusively on the ethics of vigilantism. But Grant Morrison's later insertion of the Black Casebook into the Batman mythos — and his dredging up of embarrassing stories excised from the canon — demonstrates that Miller's hardboiled Dark Knight functions only through psychological and editorial repression. The hyper-masculine Batman can only exist in a world in which he never went to space or tripped into alternate dimensions. A character who did these things (as, indeed, Batman did in the wackier plots of Bob Kane and his ghostwriters) who would risk appearing insane or silly. In the era of gritty storytelling inaugurated by Frank Miller, DC editors were only too willing to accommodate the newly hardboiled Batman by ignoring the unpopular science fiction stories of the past. Even prior to Miller's tenure, DC creators had sought to clean up the unbelievably weird world of Batman. With the "New Look" initiative of the late Sixties and early Seventies, Editor Julius Schwartz asked his staff to wipe out the strangest characters and plots. These excised stories stayed buried until the late 2000s when Grant Morrison and the new editorial staff forced them to resurface like repressed memories.

As a result, we witness the fracturing of Batman's identity. He fluctuates between dominant "alpha male plus" (a term he applies to himself early in Morrison's run) and unstable crack-up (665.12). When Hurt's goons drug him with methamphetamines, he loses his already tenuous grip on the Batman identity to become, first, a baffled homeless man and, subsequently, a cartoonish version of his superhero self he calls "The Batman of Zur En Arrh." This new identity is Morrison's nod to a 1958 space story in which the Batman character meets an alternate version of himself from the parallel dimension of Zur En Arrh; here, it is recycled as evidence of Batman's psychotic break and generally weakened mental state. In his Zur En Arrh persona, Batman emerges as a nearly unrecognizable character. He speaks aloud to himself, believing that he is chatting with an ephemeral imp named Bat-Mite. He is poor, homeless, and filthy, deprived of the wealth Bruce Wayne was capable of funneling to his alter ego. He also eschews the standard black Batman costume for a gaudy hand-stitched purple, gold, and red affair. And, though he proves himself capable of fighting criminals, his masculinity is no longer virile and enviable. Instead, he is a violent madman: unstable, unpredictable, undesirable. One feels inclined to agree with Hurt's cronies, who exclaim upon seeing the "imposter" Dark Knight, "Nonsense! That's not Batman!" and "Batman is cool! Batman wears black!" (680.14)

So, we observe a Batman who both is and is not himself. The standard trappings of the character (his costume, his mission, his history) fall away to reveal a mass of contradictions and complexities. And perhaps the most radical element of the story is its implicit suggestion that this state of confused identity is not the exception but the norm — for Batman as well as for ourselves. Morrison's deconstruction of Batman via the resurrection of old bad plots encourages us to think about the hero through the lens of postmodern identity theory. The writer himself seems to be plotting from the perspective of the psychoanalyst, working the Caped Crusader's case history from his mid-century crack-ups to his current manly overcompensations. Morrison has Batman on the proverbial couch in an attempt to diagnose and treat the character's various disorders. The titles of the various stories, from "Building a Better Batmobile" to "Batman RIP," imply that the character will be analyzed and reinvented as the larger plot progresses. Since Morrison is functioning as *de facto* psychiatrist in the *Batman* title, it seems necessary to bring authentic psychoanalysis into the mix. The author's portrayal of Batman's identity in flux suggests, above all else, that the psychoanalytic work of Jacques Lacan may prove useful in parsing out what Morrison has to say about the roles of repression and resurgence in the character's editorial and emotional histories.

Lacan and the Symbolic Order

Superheroes aren't the only ones to have compelling origin stories; schools of theory and philosophy have them too. The cultural phenomenon of instability and self-reference we think of today as "postmodernism" has its roots in poststructuralist theories of language, and these can trace their beginnings in part to the psychoanalytic theories of Jacques Lacan. Lacan was interested in the relationship between language and identity. He invented a three-tiered system to describe how people try to establish personal identity in the impersonal world. On the most basic level, there exists the order of the Real — the way things actually are outside of language and representation — but this order is rather difficult to talk about since its stark real-ness defies the arbitrary labels of description. A more discussable part of the human experience is the Imaginary order. Human development of the self as ideal ego begins in what Lacan calls the "mirror" stage (*Fundamental Concepts* 257). A young child in this phase begins to conceive of himself or herself as a coherent entity — a self-sufficient body with an independent mind. Prior to this, the child's experiences had been fragmented, devoid of true individuality. For Lacan, this pre-ego confusion is actually a truer experience of the human condition than the fiction sustained by the burgeoning ego. No person in society is ever a truly private, coherent, self-sufficient individual. Ourselves incomplete, we are complemented by our peers and our environment. Thus, Lacan tied idealizations of selfhood to the Imaginary order, which describes the development of the ego through images that support the fantasy of self-sufficiency and utter individuality.

Lacan posited that we are not individuals but subjects, and he articulated his theory of the Symbolic order as a means of explaining the difference. As subjects, we exist in relation to one another in societal interplay. We are from birth subjected to language and society, rendering our identities fragmented and dispersed. The simple necessity of having to put our thoughts and experiences into words reveals that we are not self-sufficient but symbolic creatures — we must reach outside ourselves into a world populated by others for the tools to explain ourselves (*Fundamental Concepts* 244). The thrust of this is that we do not have complete control over who we want to be, no matter how much we imagine that we do. Moreover, the vocabulary we use for self-identification is subject to change, further indicating that our Imaginary selves do not suffice for representing our various roles. If, for example, a man loses his job or his looks or even a body part, his ego may be wounded because his self-image has been altered, but what happens in actuality is that the terms applied to him in the Symbolic order are being rearranged to accommodate his changing role in the society of others. According to Lacan, many psychological problems emerge from conflicts between the Imaginary and the Symbolic: our images and ideals frequently butt up against the language used to express them and us.

Like his predecessor Sigmund Freud, Lacan enjoyed explaining his theories through works of literature, and he managed to eloquently summarize his theory of the Symbolic order in his "Seminar on 'The Purloined Letter,'" a lecture on Poe's famous detective story, the plot of which concerns a politician who wishes to use a stolen letter to blackmail a queen. In his reading of the work, Lacan pinpoints a set number of possible identities for the characters, and he demonstrates that they occupy different subjective positions at certain points in the plot. For instance, the villainous Minister D occupies a position of power early in the story, since he possesses dangerous knowledge that he may make public to shame the Queen. Yet by the end of "The Purloined Letter," Minister D has been tricked by Poe's protagonist, the amateur detective Dupin, and thus has become subject to humiliating exposure himself. The shifting of identities leaves Dupin occupying the position of power formerly held by Minister D, while D has slid down to the undesirable position the Queen was previously in. The argument — how this ties to Lacan's psychoanalytic practice — is that actual life is filled with similar destabilizations of identity, which play out in the Symbolic order and reveal themselves through language. These movements further demonstrate that the private realm of Imaginary, home to the ego, is in constant conflict with the external symbols of culture, language, and society. Self-image struggles to coexist with public subjectivity, but it often finds itself overwhelmed by the many cultural forces at work. As Lacan writes in the "Seminar," man generally exists in a "state of blindness ... in relation to the letters on the wall that dictate his destiny."

One of Lacan's most provocative claims was that the unconscious functions like a language. Forerunners Carl Jung and Sigmund Freud had envisioned the unconscious as a mental region dominated by primal images: archetypes, phalluses, and the like. But Lacan argued for an unconscious modeled on — and influenced by — the symbols of language. He believed that psychoanalysts had erred in becoming fixated on images and abstractions. Per his analysis, they were attempting to fix problems at the Imaginary level, when in truth the mental anxieties over which psychoanalysts could exert control manifested on the level of the Symbolic, in the language of the mind. The goal, he felt, was not to ask patients to retreat into their minds but to have them reach outside themselves, and language functioned as the means for making this leap. A good psychoanalyst could, through extensive dialogue, help a patient identify, understand, and even alter his or her subject position in the society of others.

Paging Doctors Hurt and Lacan

Batman serves as Grant Morrison's patient throughout the stories that culminate in the "Batman RIP" event. Morrison, comic book clinician, walks the character through his identity conflicts and seeks to resolve the tension between his past silliness and present austerity. But to rebuild the hero, Morrison will first need to break him down, and he employs the character of Dr. Hurt to this end. Hurt is a sort of anti–Lacan, an evil genius with the desire to apply his intelligence toward the detriment of his patients. Operating in a semi–Lacanian mode, Hurt seeks to dislodge individuals from their Imaginary conceptions of self-identification — we see this in the effort to prove to the Dark Knight that he is not his own man — but the bad doctor has no intention of leading his patients on to new realizations of Symbolic identity. That second step is an integral one in Lacanian psychoanalysis, which is as much an exercise in reconstruction as deconstruction. Hurt's approach, however, is entirely deconstructive, even destructive. He can demonstrate to Batman that he is not merely the manly crime-fighter that his recent history suggests him to be, but Hurt will not help the hero paste together a workable identity from the shattered fragments of his Imaginary conceits. Hurt is there to destroy the Dark Knight's false self-image. Morrison returns to piece the fragments back together, recovering the lost space oddities of the 1950s and 60s in the process.

The plight through which Batman stumbles is the same suffering experienced by many real people (sans superheroic mental agility, vast wealth, and ninja training) who grapple with questions of identity. And the trauma Batman suffers has the same effect on him as it does on many individuals trudging through relentlessly stressful situations: he goes mad. His symptoms — the reversion into the Zur En Arrh persona, the paranoia, the hallucination of Bat-Mite — indicate a number of potential psychoses, including schizophrenia and delusion. Dr. Hurt exploits these as weaknesses, usurping control of the Bat-Cave and Arkham Asylum. But the works of the good Dr. Lacan allow us and, arguably, Morrison to treat the symptoms as part of a larger syndrome plaguing the modern Batman character. In his lectures on psychosis, Lacan argued that delusions and hallucinations are related to problems of the ego. Such problems manifest in how the subject engages with the outside world and with his peers. In conversation, all of us must mentally position ourselves in dialogue with the persons to whom we are talking. Before we began conversing with any person, we must contextualize our relationship to him or her, imagining how we expect to treat the person, how we expect him or her to treat us, and what we expect to talk about. In effect, we create a simulacrum of the second party in our minds, a mental projection that allows us to relate to him or her. For a sane person, this is a concession to the outside world, proof that we are not self-determining beings and that we must recognize the existence of others outside ourselves. We calibrate our minds to the external symbol systems of society and language before we open our mouths.

But a madman begins a conversation with a solipsistic calibration that focuses primarily on the self, reflecting his ego almost entirely onto the other, frequently substituting what he *imagines* has been said for what has *actually* been said. For instance, Lacan treated a patient under the paranoid delusion that that her neighbor's boyfriend was openly hostile to her, so she imagined that, in a conversation they shared about the local butcher, he called her a "sow. In actuality, he had said nothing of the sort, but her mind gave life to her persecution fantasy" (*Psychoses* 50). Lacan explained that in such cases mad persons are actually in dialogue with themselves and not the outside world. A sane person seeks to engage the world by coming to terms with the other people in it; a mad person populates his or her world entirely with inventions of the ego, imaginary others that are simply functions of the self. This is especially evident in cases that present neologisms (made-up words) and hallucinations (unreal images presumed by the mad to be real).

Batman eventually presents both of these symptoms in Morrison's stories. In several instances, we see him talking to Bat-Mite, the hallucinated imp who floats around his head and offers advice. The Dark Knight first assumes the creature is real, though he later comes to understand that Bat-Mite cannot possibly belong to the empirical world. When he finally asks, "Are you really a hyper-imp from the fifth dimension ... or just a figment of my imagination," Bat-Mite replies provocatively, "Imagination *is* the fifth dimension" (680.12). Indeed, Bat-Mite is best read as a figment of the Lacanian Imaginary — the caricature of a *Batman* that presumes itself to be whole despite its fractured editorial history. His appearance as a hallucination is symptomatic of the Bat-Ego trying to unify a fractured comic book life but finding it impossible to do so. The Bat-Mite character (whose history dates back to his first appearance in 1959) is representative of the weirdest elements of the Batman canon, the far-out mid-century tales that cannot mesh with the hardboiled stories that have popularized Batman today. The trauma he embodies is metafictional, as Bat-Mite signifies the difficult task of reconciling Batman's slapstick sci-fi past with his serious brawler present.

The "Zur En Arrh" neologism is the symptom of a different kind of trauma, the raw emotional pain tied to the character's classic origin (which, despite years of editorial intervention elsewhere has remained unchanged). As even the most casual Batman fan knows, Bruce Wayne's parents were gunned down in a mugging, leaving the young boy an orphan and later inspiring his vigilante war on crime. Though the wild "Batman of Zur En Arrh" alter-ego initially appears to be unrelated to these events, Morrison ties them together in the flashback sequence that concludes the "Batman RIP" story arc. A series of panels depicts the Wayne family walking from the fateful showing of *Mask of Zorro* that will result in the parents' demise. They discuss the merits of Zorro's vigilantism, and Dr. Thomas Wayne observes, "The sad thing is they'd probably throw someone like Zorro in Arkham." Young Bruce doesn't quite catch what his father said, so he inquires, "What?" (681.39) In the background we see the fateful mugger approaching, ensuring the answer will be forever deferred. The final panel in the sequence displays the words "Zur En Arrh" backwards. The implication is that Dr. Wayne's last words, garbled and misunderstood, have lurked in the back of his son's mind for decades, manifesting at last in the form of the "Zur En Arrh" persona. Even prior to this present breakdown, a repetition automatism has forced him to relive the event by habitually dressing up as a Zorro-like masked avenger. The Batman alter-ego has always been symptomatic of deep mental distress. But in reliving the event night by night on the streets of Gotham, the older Bruce Wayne has shifted his subject position, much as Lacan observed in the characters of "The Purloined Letter." Wayne the child experienced the primal trauma from the perspective as victim, with the mugger serving as aggressor; through Batman's crusade on crime, the hero has reversed the dynamic, becoming the aggressor himself.

The "Zur En Arrh" psychosis exemplifies Lacan's point about the three-way relationship between language, identity, and madness. The resurgence of the "Zorro in Arkham" phrase as "Zur En Arrh" parallels Lacan's assertion that the unconscious functions like a language. It is especially telling that Morrison chose to represent the psychotic trigger with a series of words despite the story's appearance in a medium best known for pictures. For Batman, it isn't the powerful image of his parents' death that sets him off—it is the language of it. Lacan argued that virtually all psychotic symptoms—even visual phenomena like hallucinations—spring from "the subject's history in the symbolic" (*Psychoses* 13). He believed that many psychoses result from the displacement of language into the perception of reality. Again, the case of the "sow" patient suggests that a troubled person is capable of hearing and seeing things that exist nowhere else but in the language running through the mind.

In chronicling these symptoms and correlating them to Batman's case history, Morrison's stint on *Batman* reveals itself to be an essentially Lacanian project, with the author offering a psychoanalysis of Batman's editorial history and identity crisis. This is not a particularly surprising evolution for Morrison considering the Jungian inclinations of his earlier *Arkham Asylum* graphic novel, but these newer stories prove to be more mature efforts, able to strike a balance between heady postmodern reflexivity and classical pathos. Such a balancing act is especially evident in the split focus between Batman's two predominant psychoses, the one rooted in his editorial history and the other tied to his troubled emotional past. In one respect, this is a story about the evolving comics medium and one character's ever-changing role in its history; in another, it is the tragedy of a young man who never recovered from a traumatic experience. If the entirety of the Batman character results from the repetition automatism of a traumatized Bruce Wayne, we would do well to remember Lacan's comment on the trappings of repetition: "Whatever, in repetition, is varied, modulated, is merely alienation of its meaning" (*Fundamental Concepts* 61). The silly costumes, the space adventures, the hallucinations, the gadgets, and the gruffness are distracting mutations of the initial trauma being repeated and relived. Cut these away, and one sees that the Batman character is the perpetual signification of a damaged boy who rages against his victimization.

Morrison's overall project entails the creation of a holistic Batman capable of embracing the entirety of his seventy-year publication history as well as the emotional baggage that accompanies it. He allows the character's most outlandish escapades to reenter the modern canon as symptoms of Batman's psychological breakdown. This holistic Batman functions *because* it ruptures; just as the character's editorial history will not support the admixture of the opposing silly and serious elements, so too his mind cannot support the multitude of identities that assault his Imaginary conceit of a reasonable, coherent self. These *Batman* issues arrived at a pivotal moment in the character's history, as Morrison began writing for the title in September 2006, approximately one year after Christopher Nolan had "reinvented" the Batman movie franchise with the Miller-inspired *Batman Begins*. During Morrison's tenure on the work, Nolan's *The Dark Knight* sequel hit theaters, giving moviegoers another dose of the hyper-masculine Miller Batman and reinforcing the false notion that this was the accurate — nay, the only — version of the character.

Morrison's concurrent psychoanalysis of the character serves as a reminder that the character's identity is as fractured, complex, and disparate as any real person's. Despite the Dark Knight's manly swagger, he will always be burdened with a case history of psychedelic space trips, hallucinated imps, and silly costumes. This is not to suggest that the Miller-inflected popular vision of Batman is somehow inferior to its zanier predecessors — few people indeed would prefer the horrid hack scripts of the 1960s to the pleasurable misanthropy of *The Dark Knight Returns*— but Morrison's work insists that, like any facet of actual identity, these elements cannot be merely disregarded, repressed by embarrassed modern editors. Rather, they will necessarily come surging to the surface, demonstrating to the modern fan that the notion of a wholly coherent Batman belies the fact that there have only ever been Batmen, different flavors of fictional personae locked in competition for the approval of the comics reader and moviegoer.

Works Cited

Lacan, Jacques. *The Four Fundamental Concepts of Psychoanalysis*. Ed. Jacques-Alain Miller. Trans. Alan Sheridan. New York: WW Norton, 1978. Print.

_____. *The Seminar of Jacques Lacan, Book III: The Psychoses (1955–1956)*. Ed. Jacques-Alain Miller. Trans. Russell Grigg. New York: WW Norton, 1993. Print.

_____. "Seminar on 'The Purloined Letter.'" *Breaking the (Post)Code*. Emory University Libraries, n.d. Web. 29 September 2009.

Miller, Frank (w, p), Klaus Janson (i), and Lynn Varley (c). *The Dark Knight Returns*. New York: DC Comics, 1987.

Morrison, Grant (w) and Andy Kubert (p). "Building a Better Batmobile." *Batman* 655 (Sep 2006), DC Comics.

Morrison, Grant (w), Andy Kubert (p), and Jesse Delperdang (i). "The Black Casebook." *Batman* 665 (Jun 2007), DC Comics.

Morrison, Grant (w), Tony Daniel (p), and Sandu Florea (i). "The Thin White Duke of Death." *Batman* 680 (Oct 2008), DC Comics.

_____. "Hearts in Darkness." *Batman* 681 (Dec 2008), DC Comics.

8

Queer Matters in The Dark Knight Returns
Why We Insist on a Sexual Identity for Batman

JENÉE WILDE

The Batman made his first public appearance in the May 1939 issue of *Detective Comics.* To provide a point of identification for young readers, Robin was introduced in the April 1940 issue of *Detective,* while a spinoff comic book, *Batman,* debuted the same month. In the nearly seventy years since Batman first hit newsstand racks, the Caped Crusader has become one of the most popular and recognizable comic book superheroes. With more than 150 graphic novel and trade paperback titles in print, the sheer quantity of Batman stories outstrips those of any other superhero character (Goldstein). But as many critics have pointed out, the relationship between Batman and Robin has always been "a bit of a worry" for comics and graphic novel fans: "After all, what are readers to make of an older man who is often described as a socialite, a confirmed bachelor, or a millionaire playboy with a propensity for adopting young boys as his 'wards?' Eccentric? Definitely. Dangerous? Probably. Homosexual? Arguably, though not proven conclusively" (Tipton 321).

In this essay, I propose that the relevant question is not whether or not Batman is gay; rather, the more interesting and important question is why comic book fans and pop culture at large insist on nailing down a sexual identity for Batman at all — be it straight, gay, or asexually repressed? To explore this question, I will examine the history of gay readings of Batman and propose that the appropriation of Batman as a gay-identification figure by gay culture can be supported by the comic book texts; further, I propose that this appropriation troubles the separation of the homosocial and the homosexual necessitated by our society's patriarchal structures. Using Frank Miller's graphic novel *Batman: The Dark Knight Returns* as an example, I will argue that Batman, as a location in popular culture for both gay and straight discourse, allows for *all* readers to experience "moments of queerness" and may thus provide an opportunity for the integration of sexual identity beyond hetero-homo binaries.

The Queering of Batman

In 1949, amateur psychologist Gershon Legman, in his self-published polemic *Love and Death*, was the first writer to suggest a gay subtext in the superhero genre. An erstwhile assistant to sex researcher Alfred Kinsey and advocate of sexual liberation credited with coining the phrase "make love not war," Legman argued in his book that many comic books had "an undercurrent of homosexuality and sado-masochism" that went deeper than the obvious "transvestists [sic] scenes in every kind of comic-book" or the "explicit Samurai subservience of the inevitable little-boy helpers" or the "fainting adulation of thick necks, ham fists, and well-filled jock-straps; the draggy capes and costumes, the shamanic talismans and superstitions that turn a sissified clerk into a one-man flying lynch-mob with biceps bigger than his brain" (qtd. in Heer). But it wasn't until 1954 that the interpretation of a homoerotic relationship between Batman and Robin first entered the cultural awareness as a result of Dr. Fredric Wertham's publication of *Seduction of the Innocent*, a psychological analysis of the negative effects of comic books on children. Although primarily an attack on crime comics, the book became notorious for its argument that Batman and Robin's relationship has homoerotic overtones. This "gay reading" of Batman did not originate with Wertham, however. He notes that a "California psychiatrist" had pointed out "several years ago ... that the Batman stories are psychologically homosexual" and, more significantly, that he based his analysis on the testimonials of "overt homosexuals" who had constructed their own fantasies from Batman comics (189, 191).

Wertham's four pages of writing on "the Batman type of comic book" (190) had a marked effect on discourses around the character in following decades. Often, whenever the question of Batman's sexual identity arises in critical or popular writings, Wertham's interpretation is frequently referenced and generally boiled down to a single oft-quoted paragraph:

> Sometimes Batman ends up in bed injured and young Robin is shown sitting next to him. At home they lead an idyllic life. They are Bruce Wayne and "Dick" Grayson. Bruce Wayne is described as a "socialite" and the official rela-

> tionship is that Dick is Bruce's ward. They live in sumptuous quarters, with beautiful flowers in large vases, and have a butler, Alfred. Batman is sometimes shown in a dressing gown. As they sit by the fireplace the young boy sometimes worries about his partner.... [I]t is like a wish dream of two homosexuals living together [190].

For this reason, Wertham says, "Only someone ignorant of the fundaments of psychiatry and of the psychopathology of sex can fail to realize a subtle atmosphere of homoeroticism which pervades the adventures of the mature 'Batman' and his younger friend 'Robin'" (189–190).

In his critical study *Batman Unmasked*, Will Brooker documents the reactions to Wertham's gay reading of Batman as "almost universally negative" in subsequent decades and as coming from "two very distinct camps: the homophobic criticism of presumably heterosexual commentators [including fans], and the equally vicious mockery from critics who locate themselves within the approach of 'queer' reading and therefore attack Wertham for his own supposed homophobia" (102). On one side of this public reaction, the emphatic denial of the "gay Batman" reading is a constant in both fan response and "in virtually every history of comics I have come across," Brooker says. In addition, Wertham's description of the Batman and Robin household as "a wish dream of two homosexuals living together" has become "a recurring motif to be heavily repressed whenever it raises its head" (105). On the other side, Wertham has been "ridiculed and lambasted ... for his supposedly rampant homophobia" (107) by queer critics such as Andy Medhurst. In his 1991 essay "Batman, Deviance and Camp," Medhurst not only offers a "gay reading of the whole Bat-business" but also decries *Seduction of the Innocent* as "a gripping, flamboyant melodrama masquerading as social psychology" (150). Still others profess that the real issue is Batman's lack of sex drive, such as Michael Brody in the essay "Batman: Psychic Trauma and Its Solution." Brody criticizes Wertham not for his homophobia but for his diagnosis: "The issue of Batman is not one of sexual orientation, but more of a question of balance. There is a lack of sexual interest, all sublimated into his rage and crime-fighting" (176).

Rather than further documenting here the many popular and critical reactions to the gay reading of Batman (see instead Brooker's excellent discussion pp. 103–110), it is more within the purpose of this essay to examine *why* such a reading would have come about to begin with. Brooker notes that it is not unrealistic to read the relationship between Batman and Robin as treading a fine line between the homosocial and the homosexual: "While there is no 'correct' way to see this relationship, it can feasibly be read as 'gay'" (110). This is particularly true when examining Batman comics from the perspective of gay culture in the 1950s. During that homophobic era, mainstream culture circulated a number of stereotyped cues for "spotting" homosexuality: passivity and a dislike for women; an effeminate manner and appearance, including clothing and color choices; and engaging in feminine occupations such as cooking, hairdressing, or interior design (128–29). At the same time, gay culture — seeking alternative images with which to identify — read novels and movies for a gay "subtext," whether intended by the creators or not (129–30). Richard Dyer in *Gays & Film* suggests that gay interpretations of texts came out of the isolation and despair gay men felt within the homophobic culture of the period:

> This isolation (and the feelings of self-hate that much of the imagery we learnt in the cinema instilled in us) perhaps also made the need for escape more keen for us than for some other social groups — so, once again, we went to the pictures. Once there, however, we could use the films — especially those *not* directly offering us images of ourselves — as we chose. We could practice on movie images what Claude Lévi-Strauss has termed *bricolage*, that is, playing around with the elements available to us in such a way as to bend their meanings to our own purposes. We could pilfer from straight society's images on the screen such that would help us build up a subculture, or ... a "gay sensibility" [qtd. in Brooker 131].

Medhurst points out that this is exactly what Wertham's patients seem to have done with Batman: "What is at stake here is the question of reading, of what readers do with the raw material that they are given." Denied the possibility of supportive images from within dominant heterosexual culture, "gay people have had to fashion what we could out of the imageries of dominance, to snatch illicit meanings from the fabric of normalcy, to undertake a corrupt decoding for the purposes of satisfying marginalized desires" (152–53). As a gay man, Medhurst says that he finds the description of gay reading by Wertham's patients as "rather moving and also highly recognizable" (152), noting the following passage from *Seduction of the Innocent*:

> One young homosexual during psychotherapy brought us a copy of *Detective* comic, with a Batman story. He pointed out a picture of "The Home of Bruce and Dick," a house beautifully landscaped, warmly lighted and showing the devoted pair side by side, looking out a picture window. When he was eight this boy had realized from fantasies about comic-book pictures that he was aroused by men. At the age of ten or eleven, "I found my liking, my sexual desires, in comic books. I think I put myself in the position of Robin. I did want to have relations with Batman.... I remember the first time I came across the page mentioning the 'secret bat cave.' The thought of Batman and Robin living together and possibly having sex relations came to my mind" [Wertham 192].

Returning to the original 1950s Batman comics, Brooker points out many of the subtle dress, linguistic, and color codes to gay identity upon which a gay reading could have been based at the time. For example, Batman's alternate identity name, Bruce, has strong gay associations dating back to the 1940s (132). The content of many stories also contained gay signifiers, such as a 1957 story called "The Rainbow Batman." The cover featured Batman standing with Robin in a section of the bat cave housing several brightly colored costumes, not just the usual blue and gray. Donning a pink bodysuit topped with magenta cape and trunks, Batman says, "I must, Robin — I must wear a different-colored Batman costume each night!" Although playing upon a homophobic stereotype, Brooker says, "[t]o the boy wondering about 'Batman and Robin living together and possibly having sex relations,' this colour cue could well have confirmed his pleasurable fantasy that the two were lovers" (129). Along with these "gay" markers, the comics feature story after story of two men who "exhibit a love and trust for each other which often extends beyond the generic conventions of the adventure ... narrative." In addition to constantly rescuing each other from danger, Batman and Robin are frequently shown sharing intimate moments. Booker concludes that these elements provided ample material by which Wertham — and the boys whose testimonies informed his reading — could recognize a "love-relationship" and "subtle atmosphere of homoeroticism" between Batman and Robin (133).

In the spring of 1954, Wertham played a key role in Senate Subcommittee hearings held to investigate the relation of comic books to juvenile delinquency. In order to avoid censorship legislation, the comics industry opted to provide self-regulation and instituted a Comics Code by the end of that year. This marked a turning point in the comics industry; within a few years of the hearings and publication of *Seduction of the Innocent*, twenty-four out of twenty-nine crime comics publishers went out of business, and with the exceptions of Superman, Batman, and Wonder Woman, the superhero vanished entirely for several years (Boichel 13). While the costumed crime fighters at DC Comics were not direct targets of the Code, the publisher introduced several changes to Batman perhaps in response to the Code's directives on "Marriage and Sex," which included the following: "Illicit sex relations are neither to be hinted at nor portrayed"; "The treatment of love-romance stories shall emphasize the value of the home and the sanctity of marriage"; "Passion or romantic interest shall never be treated in such a way as to stimulate the lower and baser emotions"; "Sex perversion or any inference to same is strictly forbidden" (qtd. in Brooker 144). Critic Bill Boichel reports that *Detective Comics* in July of 1956 introduced the character of Batwoman to function as a female presence and potential love interest "perhaps intended to ward off further charges of homosexuality." In May 1961, "[d]etermined to establish Batman and Robin's heterosexuality," the writers of *Batman* added Batwoman's niece as a possible girlfriend for the Boy Wonder (13). These changes, along with a general lack of focus for Batman's character, brought about a decline in the comic's popularity until 1964, when a revamping of the DC property coincided with the emergence of the pop art and camp movements. By 1965, Boichel says, the pop/camp movement had "repositioned and revalued comic books as central to its aesthetic. As a result, the previously unthinkable thought of a television series based on a comic book character emerged" (14).

Despite efforts of the comic industry to normalize Batman's sexual identity, the association of TV's *Batman* with the camp aesthetic ensured that gay readings of the caped crusader would continue. In her 1964 essay "Notes on 'Camp,'" Susan Sontag describes the "essence of Camp" as a "love of the unnatural: of artifice and exaggeration" that "converts the serious into the frivolous." In her fifty-eight remarks on the nature of camp, Sontag points out that "the Camp sensibility is one that is alive to a double sense in which some things can be taken." She also notes a "peculiar affinity and overlap" between camp taste and homosexuality. As a pioneering force for "homosexual aestheticism and irony" in modern sensibility, "homosexuals, by and large, constitute the vanguard — and the most articulate audience — of Camp." Brooker states that the 1966 television show *Batman* fits neatly into Sontag's template "by virtue of its failed seriousness, its dual meanings, its extravagance, its playfulness and even its source material in comic books" (221). Building on Sontag's ideas, Medhurst notes that the Batman comics "had, unwittingly, always been camp — it was serious (the tone, the moral homilies) about the frivolous (a man in a stupid suit)." What the popular television series did was "to overlay this 'innocent' camp with a thick layer of ironic distance, the self-mockery version of camp," Medhurst says. "And given the long associations of camp with the homosexual male subculture, Batman was a particular gift on the grounds of his relationship with Robin" (156). Brooker confirms that "insider" gay readings of the TV Batman were in circulation in the late 1960s, referring to George Melly's remarks in his 1970 *Revolt Into Style*: "We all knew Robin and Batman were pouves ... over the children's heads we winked and nudged, but in the end what were we laughing at? The fact they didn't know Batman had it off with Robin" (qtd. in Brooker 162).

Gay readings of Batman continued into the eighties and nineties, as well, despite the return to a dark, gritty Batman in the 1986 graphic novel *Batman: The Dark Knight Returns* and in the 1989 film *Batman*. A 1996 article in *Gay Times* quotes Wertham as the source for "legendary" rumors about Batman and Robin, using his analysis for the purpose of further gay reading rather than denial. "The most famous and popular comic book characters have definite parallels with a gay lifestyle," suggests the author:

> [They] all lead dual lives. If they do reveal their alternative personae to anyone ... it is usually to their closets friends and their family. They fight a continual battle against prejudice ... some support the underdog. The parallels with gay experience go further. Superman and a majority of the X-Men were born with their mutant powers ... but many don't realize they possess such powers until they reach their early teens. Some try to resist the change and deny the urge. Others (take the Boy Wonder for example) embrace the new culture and lifestyle with relish, creating gaudy, vivid apparel and an arrogant attitude [qtd. in Brooker 163].

The rumor of a gay relationship between Batman and Robin persists up to this day. In a 2008 article in *The Journal of Popular Culture*, critic Nathan G. Tipton notes the persistence of Batman and Robin's "continuing homoerotic legacy," while a July blog by internet writer Heet Jeer traces the history of the rumor in anticipation of the 2008 summer release of *The Dark Knight* in theaters. In the following section, I argue that the question of Batman's sexual identity, far from being a pop culture curiosity, reveals something much more significant about the nature of male homosocial bonds and their potential threat to patriarchal structures in our society. When viewed through the lens of queer reading practices, Batman offers a significant opportunity for the integration of binary views of sexual identity in our culture.

The Significance of Queer Reading

As we have seen, the question of Batman's sexual identity has permeated discourse surrounding the character since the 1950s. Since that time, the dissemination of gay readings of Batman and Robin's relationship has been met by implicit denial and attempted containment by the comics industry and by outright and emphatic rejection from fandom. However, the very pervasiveness and tenacity of the debate suggests that the question of Batman's sexual identity goes much deeper. In other words, why do so many people care? Why do we, the consumers of pop culture — as well as pop culture at large — insist on nailing down a sexual identity for Batman, be it heterosexual, homosexual, or asexually repressed? This level of attention has not been paid to Superman's sexual identity; his devotion to Lois Lane reassures us of his heterosexually normative desires. Likewise, Spiderman has his schoolboy crushes and long-term girlfriends. Public debate is not held on whether Captain America and his sidekick Bucky are erotically involved. And although Wonder Woman's lesbianism has often been assumed, despite her romantic liaison with Captain Steve Trevor, still, no one is righteously defending her heterosexuality. So, why Batman?

I would argue that the answer begins with the attractiveness of the Batman mythos. Not only is he one of the most popular and recognizable of superheroes — the sheer number of Batman graphic novel titles far outstrips those of any other comic book superhero, and the most recent Batman film is one of the highest grossing movies of all time — he is also one of the few superheroes who has no super powers. Without his high-tech gadgetry and special training, he's just like us: traumatized by his past. As Brody has pointed out, Batman's appeal lies in its realism, which is both plausible and human: "Batman successfully plugs into the unconscious of its vast audience because its psychology remains credible. Batman's symptoms, personality fragmenting, and recovery, are all consistent with the psychiatric trauma literature." Plus, his traumatic childhood serves to make him a "true myth" in that his isolation and trials, as well as his metaphorical transcendence, help "[to shed] light on all our stories" (177). As a model of masculinity, the Batman mythos also reinforces cultural ideologies of man-making in that he suppresses his complex feelings (and, some would argue, his sexuality as well) to become a fighter for public good (Leverenz 40). And for fans, Batman's obsessive-compulsive crime fighting — which, in Freudian terms, is an unconscious attempt to undo the original trauma of his parents' murders — offers a satisfying revenge fantasy; who wouldn't like to see their own bullies and bad guys punished?

However, what troubles the (straight) reader's identification with Batman's ideological manhood and literal kick-ass approach to personal problems is the ambiguous relationship between him and Robin. Eve Sedgwick has noted that "male bonding" activities in our society may be characterized by "intense homophobia" due to the "obligatory heterosexuality" that is built into patriarchal structures (1, 3). So, once Dr. Wertham identified the "subtle atmosphere of homoeroticism" between Batman and Robin and the possibility of their "love-relationship" entered public discourse, Batman's potential homosexuality was necessarily suppressed by patriarchal institutions and readers who identify with masculine ideologies, while simultaneously celebrated by readers who feel marginalized by those same institutions and who identify with the subversive potential of a gay Batman-Robin relationship.

Yet, the gay Batman debate *itself* appears to be symptomatic of a much greater and more deeply divisive issue: the dialectical tensions in our culture between normative heterosexuality and its perceived antithesis, homosexuality. Batman, as a cultural icon, carries perceived notions of masculinity that are seen (by some) to be at odds with his ambiguous sexuality; in other words, Batman cannot be both a "real" man and "gay" man.

Sedgwick has argued that the "diacritical opposition" between the "homosocial"— a term describing the social bonds between persons of the same sex — and the "homosexual" in our society is much more dichotomous for men than for women. Political and social acceptance notwithstanding, Sedgwick says that at this point in history there is a common-sense unity to the continuum between "women loving women" and "women promoting the interests of women." This is in striking contrast to the arrangement among males, in which "men loving men" is sharply divided from "men promoting the interests of men" due to the "obligatory heterosexuality" built into patriarchal systems, such as marriage and military service. Because of this, Sedgwick says, "it has apparently been impossible to imagine a form of patriarchy that was not homophobic" (3).

In fact, even the most sanctioned forms of male homosocial bonding are troubled by a double bind analogous to that of women who are victims of sexual abuse (i.e. to dress and behave "attractively" is also to be "asking for it"); with only a slight shift in perspective, what goes on at football games, in fraternities, and in other all-male activities can be seen as "quite startlingly 'homosexual.'" As Sedgwick puts it, "For a man to be a man's man is separated only by an invisible, carefully blurred, always-already-crossed line from being 'interested in men'" (89). Tipton refers to this conflict as "the anxiety of potentiality": in male-male homosocial bonds, such as the hero/sidekick pairings in comic books, "there is already the possibility for an eruption of desire that, ultimately, culminates in two problematic endings: the disruption and/or destruction of the 'bond,' or the deepening of the bond into homoeroticism and/or homosexuality" (323). Because of this homophobic anxiety, Paul Morrison says that to openly "declare one's heterosexual credentials" or to question the sexuality of another "is already to protest too much." At the same time, silence itself is enough to "invoke the specter of homosexuality without ever once risking the word" (2). For these reasons, for the comics or film industry to declare Batman once-and-for-all as "straight" would be to damn him forever as "gay."

Yet Sedgwick has also shown that, even though most patriarchies structurally include homophobia, it has yet to be demonstrated that they structurally *require* homophobia (4). She cites K.J. Dover's study of ancient Greek homosexuality as a strong counterexample: "Male homosexuality, according to Dover's evidence, was a widespread, licit, and very influential part of the [Greek] culture." This demonstrates that "while heterosexuality is necessary for the maintenance of any patriarchy, homophobia ... is not" (4). So as with the continuum of "women loving women" and "women promoting the interests of women," there remains for our culture a possibility, however slight, of a likewise continuum between male homosocial and homosexual desire. Sedgwick says, "To draw the 'homosocial' back into the orbit of 'desire,' of the potentially erotic, is to hypothesize the potential unbrokenness of a continuum between homosocial and homosexual" (1). Despite the disruptions caused by homophobia, the structure of men's relations with other men in our society can be located on the entire continuum, which Sedgwick names "male homosocial desire" (2).

This continuum can be seen as analogous to the Kinsey scale, developed by sex researcher Alfred Kinsey after thousands of interviews with men and women in the 1940s and 1950s. Kinsey himself avoided and disapproved of using terms like "homosexual" or "heterosexual" to describe individuals: "Male do not represent two discrete populations, heterosexual and homosexual," Kinsey said in his controversial 1942 study *Sexual Behavior in the Human Male*. "The world is not to be divided into sheep and goats. It is a fundamental of taxonomy that nature rarely deals with discrete categories.... The living world is a continuum in each and every one of its aspects" (qtd. in "Kinsey"). He asserts that sexuality is prone to change over time and that sexual behavior can be understood in terms of physical contact as well as purely psychological phenomena, such as desire, sexual attraction, and fantasy. The Kinsey scale replaces the common categories of human sexual behavior (hetero, homo, and bi) with a seven point continuum that ranks sexual behavior from) to 6, with 0 being completely heterosexual and 6 completely homosexual ("Kinsey").

In my view, the potential in our culture to experience a unified continuum of homosocial desire as described by Sedgwick — or, at minimum, to recognize the artificialness of the hetero-homo divide as illustrated by Kinsey — can be found within the practice of queer reading. Alexander Doty uses the term "queer" to describe "a range of nonstraight expression in, or in response to, mass culture." While including gay, lesbian, and bisexual expressions, this range also includes "all other potential (and potentially unclassifiable) nonstraight positions" (xvi). Much like the fluidity of Kinsey's sexual continuum, Doty recognizes the possibility that "various and fluctuating queer positions might be occupied whenever *anyone* produces or responds to culture" (3). This is because, unless a text is specifically *about* queers, Doty views the "queerness" of mass culture texts as "less an essential, waiting-to-be-discovered property than the result of acts of production and reception" (xi). He points out that mainstream cultural readings of queerness as "*sub*-textual, *sub*-cultural, *alternative* readings, or pathetic and delusional attempts to see something that isn't there" are actually the result of thinking within "conventional heterocentrist paradigms" that see mass culture texts as made for "the 'average' (straight, white, middle-class, usually male) person." To this assumption, Doty responds, "I've got news for straight culture: your readings of texts are usually 'alternative' ones for me, and they often seem like desperate attempts to deny the queerness that is so clearly a part of mass culture" (xii).

What is radical about Doty's position is his implication that "straight" and "queer" are two sides of the same erotic coin. He recognizes that "queer erotics are already a part of culture's erotic center" as a means by which to define heterosexuality and as a position that can be occupied by straight-identifying people. Because straight and queer are inseparable, he proposes that "basically heterocentrist texts can contain queer elements, and basically heterosexual, straight-identifying people can experience queer moments" (3–4). In other words, we *all* can have moments of emotional and erotic identification outside of what we normally perceive as our sexual identities, and we can recognize and experience these "queer moments" in any text.

Doty's theory of queer reading and its implications are supported by Stuart Hall's theoretical work on cultural production and reception. Hall proposes that the encoding and decoding of meaning structures depends upon the "frameworks of knowledge" used by the encoder-producer and the decoder-receiver. "The codes of encoding and decoding may not be perfectly symmetrical" due to a "*lack of equivalence* between the two sides in the communicative exchange" (94). Referring to the encoding of messages in television broadcasts, Hall points out that signs organized in a discourse will very rarely only signify their "literal" or "near-universally consensualized" meaning; in actual discourse, most signs will also include connotative aspects, where meanings are not fixed or "naturalized" but rather have a "fluidity of meaning and association [that] can be more fully exploited and transformed." It is at the connotative level that "*already coded* signs intersect with the deep semantic codes of a culture and take on additional, more active ideological dimensions" (97). Hall notes that, through the connotative level of signs, different areas of social life are "mapped out into discursive domains, hierarchically organized into *dominant or preferred meanings*." These domains have "the whole social order embedded in them as a set of meanings, practices and beliefs: the everyday knowledge of social structures, of 'how things work for practical purposes in this culture,' the rank order of power and interest and the structure of legitimations, limits and sanctions." However, due to the lack of equivalence in the frameworks of knowledge between the encoder-producer and decoder-receiver, the dominant meanings of signs, while limiting, are also "subject to active *transformations*, which exploit its polysemic values. Any such already constituted sign is potentially transformable into more than one connotative configuration" (98). In other words, "there is no necessary correspondence between encoding and decoding[;] the former can attempt to 'pre-fer' but cannot prescribe or guarantee the latter" (100).

Hall concludes that there are three hypothetical positions from which decodings of a discourse may be constructed: first, the "dominant-hegemonic position," in which the television viewer is operating inside the dominant code, decoding the message in the same terms in which it had been originally encoded; second, the "negotiated code," in which the viewer "acknowledges the legitimacy of the hegemonic definitions" in order to make abstract significations, while at the situational level "reserving the right to make a more negotiated application to 'local conditions,'" which often results in contradictions to the dominant ideology; and third, the "oppositional code," in which the viewer decodes the message in a "*globally* contrary way ... detotaliz[ing] the message in the preferred code in order to retotalize the message within some alternative framework of reference" (100–103).

Hall's theory of encoding and decoding messages illustrates how through "active transformations" queer reading is accomplished and how, as Doty said, straight-identifying readers of "basically heterocentrist texts" can oppositionally decode its "queer" elements and experience the queerness inherent in certain moments. In the context of Batman, the popularity of the superhero's all-too-human mythos coupled with his ambiguous sexual identity provide an ideal opening for *all* readers to identify with the character and, through "active transformations" of image and linguistics signs, to oppositionally decode "queer moments" between Batman and Robin that non-straight readers have recognized for decades. Thus, the process of queer reading *itself* opens the potential for individuals and culture at large to experience an unbrokenness in the continuum between homosocial and homosexual.

The following section examines a sequence in the graphic novel *Batman: The Dark Knight Returns* in order to illustrate how — through a close reading of the book's content and formal structure — a queer oppositional reading is possible despite attempts by its creator to remove "the anxiety of potentiality" present in the story's male-male homosocial bonds.

What Troubles the Dark Knight

Comic book writer Frank Miller is without question the man most associated with the transformation of Batman from the sixties camp figure to a brooding antihero. Miller's 1986 graphic novel *Batman: The Dark Knight Returns* portrays a troubled Bruce Wayne in his mid-fifties who gave up the Batman mantle ten years earlier out of guilt when Robin/Jason Todd died. However, in the face of a Gotham beset by rampant corruption, unchecked crime, and a savage anarchistic gang who call themselves "mutants," Wayne is compelled to become the vigilante crime fighter once again. As interviewer Christopher Sharrett points out, Miller's influential work was part of "a general reevaluation of hero worship in comic book narrative" during the 1980s. Works like Miller's *The Dark Knight Returns* and a follow-up, *Batman: Year One*, as well as Alan Moore's *Watchmen, Miracleman,* and *V for Vendetta*, "use the superhero as a vehicle for challenging received notions of charismatic authority and leadership" (33). And yet, while Miller succeeds in radically recasting Batman as an "obsessed and brooding personality infinitely more three-dimensional than the type generally offered by the narrow moral universe of the comics industry" (33), the Dark Knight of Miller's world remains troubled by the question of sexual identity that has permeated discourse surrounding the character since *Seduction of the Innocent*. Despite the graphic novel's gender-defying inclusion of Carrie Kelly, a smart twelve-year-old gymnast who takes it upon herself to become Robin, Miller fails to drain his Batman story of homoerotic tensions present in the homosocial bonds of its characters.

Miller himself is impatient with the suggestion of a gay relationship between Batman and Robin. "Batman isn't gay," he said in a 1991 interview. "His sexual urges are so drastically sublimated into crime-fighting that there's no *room* for any other emotional activity." Miller has hotly denounced, as well, the implication that Carrie's gender allows Batman, finally, to express his sexual feelings for Robin: "Come on. It's a father/child relationship. It's clearly defined as such. This is where this stuff gets preposterous" (Sharrett 38). As Tipton has observed, the change in Robin's gender suggests that Miller, "along with many comics business-people and aficionados alike, was troubled by Batman and Robin's continuing homoerotic legacy" (324). When Carrie puts on her Robin costume in Book Two, she becomes "Miller's connection to heteronormativity, and her appearances begin to coincide more and more frequently within scenes of overt homoeroticism" (331), such as hand-to-hand combat scenes between Batman and the mutant gang leader or between him and Superman; "Thus she is able to distract from and disrupt scenarios that threaten to 'cross the line' into homoeroticism" (331). Despite this intention, however, a close reading of *The Dark Knight Returns* reveals that Miller cannot entirely shake himself free of oppositional readings that have queered the character since the comic book's early years.

In Book One, before Carrie becomes Robin, the Dark Knight leaves retirement and returns as the mysterious, terrifying vigilante. Repressing the Batman persona had made Bruce Wayne suicidal and alcoholic, but abandoning himself to his alternate identity gives him a profound psychological renewal despite his advancing years. On a stormy night in Gotham, a shadowy figure terrorizes criminals as he delivers his own violent brand of justice. He also unknowingly encounters his future Robin, saving Carrie and a friend from being murdered by mutant gang members. "This should be agony," Batman says on the graphic novel's first splash page, after more than thirty pages of cramped, claustrophobic panels. "I should be a mass of aching muscle — broken, spent, unable to move. And were I an older man, I surely would." Jumping Superman-esque through the air over Gotham skyscrapers, Batman experiences his rebirth. "But I'm a man of thirty — of twenty again. The rain on my chest is a baptism — I'm born again" (34).

Batman's "rebirth" is accompanied by the release of one of his oldest enemies — Harvey Dent. A former district attorney, Dent became Two-Face when half of his face was scarred by acid. Believing his disfigurement revealed a hidden, evil part of himself, Dent used a defaced dollar coin to decide the fate of his victims (Miller 16). "Two-Face is identical to Batman in that he's controlled by savage urges, which he keeps in check, in his case, with the flip of a coin," Miller has said. "He's very much like Batman" (Sharrett 36). Indeed, it is this psychological "doubling" that gives the violent encounter between the two enemies at the end of Book One its strange intimacy and emotional potency. Before Robin even enters the story, the text offers up a psychologically revealing scene that can easily be read as a "queer moment" for Batman, where the homosocial bonds between him and Dent are stretched into the realm of the homoerotic.

After three years of psychological treatment and extensive plastic surgery sponsored by Bruce Wayne, Dent is declared "cured" by Dr. Bartholomew Wolper and released from Arkham Home for the Emotionally Troubled. But Dent disappears after leaving a phone message for Wayne: "I just want to *thank* you.... You've done so *much*. I feel so *whole*, so *free*. I want you to know that, someday — I'll find a way to repay you" (Miller 26). Tormented by a split personality, Dent is both sincere and ironic in this message, which anticipates the bond revealed between the two men in the culminating battle of Book One.

Having returned to a life of crime, Harvey Dent threatens to blow up Gotham Towers if the city does not pay him five million dollars. On pages 50–51, Dent has landed two helicopters on the towers carrying bombs capable of leveling the buildings. What Dent doesn't know is that the bombs — provided by The Joker — are already set to detonate. Batman disables one bomb; then, as he crosses a cable to the second tower, a gunshot sends him plummeting off the high wire. This high-tension action is calmly narrated by Batman's own interior voice. "In ten years I've never felt so calm. So right," Batman says in small, gray blocks of text. "A fine death. But there are the thousands to think of." He saves himself by harpooning the helicopter that carries Dent and the other bomb. "And Harvey ... I have to know" (51). Dent, his surgically corrected face wrapped in white bandages, leans out of the helicopter as he attempts to shoot Batman swinging below. Dent falls (or is pushed by his henchmen) and Batman grabs him; in a fall from that height, Batman knows there would "not [be] much of a corpse left" and "I have to know" (53). What does Batman have to know? That despite the money spent by millionaire Bruce Wayne to "cure" Two Face, Harvey Dent has returned to a life of crime? But he already knows that — the doubly defaced dollar coin he found earlier on a bank-robbing henchman told him that. So, what does Batman really need to know? The final two pages of Book One reveal the answer to this question and, in the process, confirm Alexander Doty's proposition that "basically heterocentrist texts can contain queer elements."

Swinging on Batman's cable, the two enemies crash into the window of a dark office building in the wide top panel on page 54. Drawn in shadows and shades of gray, the next eight small panels show the helicopter flying away interspersed back and forth with Batman knocking away Dent's gun and literally punching the obscuring bandages from his enemy's face. As each of the helicopter panels gets smaller, so do the sound effect words "whup whup" as the machine gets farther away. The cuts from the retreating helicopter to the tight close-ups of Batman's punches give the fight action a swift pacing. In a very short time — three small frames — Batman has disarmed and subdued Dent. The last two of the eight small panels show the helicopter getting smaller and smaller, emphasized by shrinking frames and increasing white space. The wide bottom panel of the page shows a red fireball — the only color on the page — from the exploding bomb that obliterates the helicopter. Where the pacing seemed short and quick in the panels above, this wide fireball seems to suspend the action as the flames expand and hover in midair, allowing time for the confrontation between Batman and Harvey Dent to unfold on the final page.

Before this confrontation, however, the sequence on page 54 deserves a closer look, as its rhetorical device shifts this homosocial conflict in the direction of the erotic. The action images tell the story easily, without need for additional dialogue bubbles or narration. However, narration is included once again in the first-person voice of Batman. Framed in small, gray boxes, his observations add nothing to the plot sequence, which is aptly conveyed by the images and sound words. What they do add is the shading of Batman's inner state during this climactic battle. As breaking glass shatters the silence of panel one, Batman drops his first observation: "We tumble like lovers." This strangely intimate description of his crash into the office building with Dent is followed by three more unadorned statements in panels two, four, and ten: "The air is cold." "The night is silent." "Leaving the world no poorer ... four men die." Linguistically, these four sentences are all descriptive declarations, even though the first and last sentences include judgments: "like lovers" and "leaving the world no poorer." But because these phrases are connected through parallelism to simple declarative statements ("we tumble," "the air is cold," "the night is silent," "four men die"), the judgments carry the linguistic weight of declarations as well. This rhetorical structure has various effects. First, we can assume that for Batman these equal declarative statements also carry equal emotional weight; that four criminals die means no more to him than the air is cold or that he and his enemy are as intimate as lovers. Also, because of this rhetorical equivalence, what we might usually expect to elicit an emotional response — homoerotic intimacy and death — is instead emotionally flattened; the coldness Batman observes is matched by the coldness of his thoughts. And yet, despite the use of a rhetorical device to drain emotional content from his words, the words *themselves*, "We tumble like lovers," can be seen as "queering" the moment, à la Doty. But *why* does Batman feel as intimate as a lover with his enemy? And *what* does he need to "know"? The answers are revealed on the final page of the sequence.

The first thing one notices about page 55 is that the layout mirrors the previous facing page: ten panels beginning with a page-wide panel on the top followed by eight small frames (four stacked over four) against a white background and ending with a page-wide panel on the bottom. Viewed as a two-page spread, pages 54 and 55 reflect a symmetry that visually reinforces the revelation that is about to come. In the first panel on page 55, the stark glare of the explosion outside reveals Batman crouched menacingly over Dent, who leans defeated on one arm in the dark office. In one word, Batman conveys his anger and disappointment at the revealed face of his enemy: "Harvey." Dent replies, "What are you so mad about, Bats? I've ... been a sport..." In the first set of four small panels, the point of view shifts to show Harvey's face close up for the first time: "Take a look ... Have your laugh. I'm fixed all right. At least both sides match." His heavily ironic words are reinforced by the revealing panel images: Dent's face appears "normal" in panels two, three, and five, but in panel four his face is wholly disfigured: "Have your laugh, Batman — take a look!" Panel four is the moment that Batman sees Dent as he truly is: "I close my eyes and listen," Batman narrates in his characteristic gray boxes below Dent's dialogue. "Not fooled by sight, I see him ... as he is." The plastic surgery "fix" only hides his true inner disfigurement. Outwardly "normal" but inwardly maimed, Dent's personality remains split; redemption is not possible for Two Face.

In the second set of small panels, the point of view shifts to Batman's face. Mirroring the previous four panels, we see Batman's face close up in panels six, seven, and nine, but panel eight reveals the demonic bat spirit that has haunted Bruce Wayne since he fell into the bat cave as a child. This mirrored panel sequence reinforces the point that, as Batman sees Dent as he truly is in panel four, the Dark Knight simultaneously sees himself as he truly is in panel eight: "I see ... a reflection, Harvey," he says aloud. "A reflection." Looking into the face of Dent — his perfect visage masking the grotesque scars beneath — Batman learns what he needs to "know": "The scars go deep, too deep," he thinks in panel two. Situating the two sets of panels in the same sequence on the page so that they literally mirror Dent's and Batman's public masks and inner disfigurement allows the two deeply wounded men to face each other as they are — psychically scarred and unable to change, despite Bruce Wayne's efforts to rehabilitate Dent and, by proxy, himself. By using formal elements that mimic the mirroring of interior emotions and exterior appearances, Batman's revelatory insight is made clear: redemption is not possible for the Dark Knight.

Sedgwick points out that homosocial desire is a kind of "affective or social force, the glue" that shapes an important male-male relationship "even when its manifestation is hostility or hatred" (2). When that relationship is shaped by an erotic triangle, the homosocial bond "that links the two rivals is as intense and potent as the bond that links either of the rivals to the beloved" (21). While Batman and Dent do not battle for the love of a woman in this final scene, their triangle is a battle over Gotham City itself: one for its safety, the other for its destruction. This is consistent with René Girard's observation that *any* relation of rivalry — no matter who or what occupies the three corners — is structured by a complicated play of desire and identification that originates in the Oedipal triangle as schematized by Freud (Sedgwick 22–23). The intensity of the rivalry between Batman and Dent mirrors the structure of an erotic triangle, which draws their homosocial bond into what Sedgwick called "the orbit of 'desire,'" or the "potentially erotic." In addition, the mirrored structure of the pages themselves suggests that Dent is more than a rival; he is also Batman's "double," a literary motif used to show an external manifestation of one's shadow side. This "doubling" of Batman coupled with their potentially erotic rivalry lend a strange intimacy to the scene and make the final panel of page 55 all the more poignant.

Panel ten shifts the point of view to a wide shot of the dark office after the glow of the explosion has faded. From Batman's silhouetted head in panel nine, the eye drops straight down to the right side of panel ten where the bright moon shines like a target behind the broken window. Reversing the eye's typical left-to-right travel in panel ten delays the final, starkly revealing image contained in the left side of the panel: before the window, the two men kneel together, heads bent to each other. In silhouette, the two enemies are one, for no light is visible between them. Just as the top panel of the previous page proclaimed, they huddle now like lovers. No dialogue or narrative interprets for the reader this final moment of Book One. Rather, we are left with a set of conflicting impressions from these two pages: of reflection inextricably tied to recognition, of mortal enemies locked in an emotional embrace, of violence coupled with tenderness. As the final image of Book One, these dark ambiguities queer the moment — opening the text, as Doty would say, to *all* potential non-straight interpretations and thereby leaving its homoerotic charge intact.

Conclusion: Batman and Sexual Identity

In the world of comic books, the conventions of superheroes offer readers the security of the known quantity. The superhero will always prevail; good will triumph over evil, and we can rest easy in our fantasy of chaos returned to (patriarchal) order. In this predictable world, heterosexuality is the presumed norm; Batman provides a model of masculinity while Robin gives young readers a place of identification. However, this normative view is challenged by perceived ambiguities in their relationship; just what Batman and Robin are up to between the frames is never precisely clear.

But the lack of a definitive answer *itself* reveals an opportunity present in Batman's character — a potential for the cultural "queering" of sexual identity. The question of whether Batman is straight or gay is ultimately a question about the nature of our own sexual identities; we insist that there is a *real* answer in an attempt to contain (or promote) queer moments that threaten or challenge the easy binaries of heterosexual and homosexual. As Marjorie Garber puts it, "The question of whether someone [is] 'really' straight or 'really' gay misrecognizes the nature of sexuality, which is fluid, not fixed, a narrative that changes over time rather than a fixed identity, however complex" (66). The real challenge of Batman, then, is that his sexual ambiguity forces the reader to see sexuality as "a process of growth, transformation, and surprise, not a knowable state of being" (66). In this way, what can be read as the "queerness" of Batman reveals the "queerness" possible within all of us.

Works Cited

Boichel, Bill. "Batman: Commodity as Myth." *The Many lives of the Batman: Critical Approaches to a Superhero and his Media.* Ed. Roberta E. Pearson and William Uricchio. New York: BFI Pub., 1991. 4–17.

Brody, Michael. "Batman: Psychic Trauma and Its Solution." *Journal of Popular Culture* 28.4 (1995): 171–178. *Academic Search Premier*. EBSCO. University of Oregon Knight Lib. 8 Nov. 2008.

Brooker, Will. *Batman Unmasked: Analysing a Cultural Icon*. New York: Continuum, 2000.

Doty, Alexander. *Making Things Perfectly Queer: Interpreting Mass Culture*. Minneapolis: Universtiy of Minnesota Press, 1993.

Fingeroth, Danny. *Superman on the Couch: What Superheroes Really Tell Us About Ourselves and Our Society*. New York: Continuum, 2004.

Garber, Marjorie. *Vice Versa: Bisexuality and the Eroticism of Everyday Life*. New York: Simon & Schuster, 1995.

Goldstein, Hilary. "The 25 Greatest Batman Graphic Novels." *IGN*. 13 June 2005. 8 Nov. 2008 http://comics.ign.com/articles/624/624619p1.html.

Hall, Stuart. "Encoding, Decoding." *The Cultural Studies Reader*. Ed. Simon During. New York: Routledge, 1993. 90–103.

Heer, Jeet. "Batman and Robin: Just Friends?" *Sans Everything*. 15 July 2008. 18 Oct. 2008 http://sanseverything.wordpress.com.

"Kinsey Reports." *The Kinsey Institute*. 28 Nov. 2008 www.iub.edu/~kinsey/indexhtml.

Leverenz, David. "The Last Real Man in America: From Natty Bumppo to Batman." *Fictions Of Masculinity: Crossing Cultures, Crossing Sexualities*. Ed. Peter Francis Murphy. New York: New York University Press, 1994. 21–56.

Medhurst, Andy. "Batman, Deviance and Camp." *The Many Lives of the Batman: Critical Approaches to a Superhero and his Media*. Ed. Roberta E. Pearson and William Uricchio. New York: BFI Pub., 1991. 149–163.

Miller, Frank with Klaus Janson and Lynn Varley. *Batman: The Dark Knight Returns*. New York: DC Comics, 1986.

Morrison, Paul. *The Explanation for Everything: Essays on Sexual Subjectivity*. New York: New York UP, 2001.

Rank, Otto. *The Double: A Psychoanalytic Study*. Chapel Hill: University of North Carolina Press, 1971.

Rizzo, Johnna. "ZAP! POW! BAM! When Dire Times Called for New Heroes." *Humanities* 27.4 (2006): 28–29. *Academic Search Premier*. EBSCO. Universtiy of Oregon Knight Lib. 18 Oct. 2008.

Sedgwick, Eve Kosofsky. *Between Men: English Literature and Male Homosocial Desire*. New York: Columbia University Press, 1985.

Sharrett, Christopher. "Batman and the Twilight of the Idols: An Interview with Frank Miller." *The Many lives of the Batman: Critical Approaches to a Superhero and his Media*. Ed. Roberta E. Pearson and William Uricchio. New York: BFI Pub., 1991. 33–46.

Sontag, Susan. "Notes on 'Camp.'" *Partisan Review* 31:4 (1964): 515–30. University of Oregon Web Reserve Readings. http://libweb.uoregon.edu/eres/karlyn695/sontag.html.

Terrill, Robert E. "Put on a Happy Face: Batman as a Schizophrenic Savior." *Quarterly Journal of Speech* 79.3 (1993): 319–335. *Communication & Mass Media Complete*. EBSCO. Universtiy of Oregon Knight Lib. 3 Nov. 2008.

Terrill, Robert E. "Spectacular Repression: Sanitizing the Batman." *Critical Studies in Media Communication* 17.4 (2000): 493–509. *Communication & Mass Media Complete*. EBSCO. University of Oregon Knight Lib. 8 Nov. 2008.

Tipton, Nathan G. "Gender Trouble: Frank Miller's Revision of Robin in the *Batman: Dark Knight* Series." *Journal of Popular Culture* 41.2 (2008): 321–336. *Academic Search Premier*. EBSCO. Universtiy of Oregon Knight Lib. 8 Nov. 2008.

Wandtke, Terrence R. "Frank Miller Strikes Again and Batman Becomes a Postmodern Anti-Hero: The Tragi(Comic) Reformulation of the Dark Knight." *The Amazing Transforming Superhero! Essays on the Revision of Characters in Comic Books, Film and Television*. Ed. Wandtke. Jefferson, NC: McFarland, 2007. 87–111.

Wertham, Fredric. *Seduction of the Innocent*. Toronto: Clarke, Irwin, & Co., 1954.

Williamson, Catherine. "'Draped Crusaders': Disrobing Gender in 'The Mark of Zorro.'" *Cinema Journal* 36.2 (1997): 3–16. JSTOR. University of Oregon Knight Lib. 1 Nov. 2008.

9

The Hero We Read
The Dark Knight, Popular Allegoresis, and Blockbuster Ideology

ANDREA COMISKEY

Upon the July 2008 release of *The Dark Knight* (director Christopher Nolan), many questioned whether it could live up to the hype and garner the earnings of its predecessor, the franchise-rebooting *Batman Begins* (Nolan, 2005), especially given the sequel's markedly grim, unsettling content — i.e., its unremitting "darkness."[1] In fact, *The Dark Knight* exceeded all expectations. In fewer than five weeks, it became the second-highest grossing film of all time in North America and, in a qualitative coup for a superhero franchise film, earned near-universal critical acclaim. The film also spawned vigorous, high-profile debates in the English-language press and the blogosphere regarding its underlying political message — specifically, about its standing as an allegory of post–9/11 America, the George W. Bush administration, and the "War on Terror." The debate, and the film's high profile, continue as of this writing. Upon the July 2010 release of Nolan's subsequent film, *Inception*, New *York Times* critic A.O. Scott noted its *de facto* status as the summer's "most anticipated movie": "Mr. Nolan, after all, was responsible for "The Dark Knight," the most widely viewed, intensely debated, passionately embraced movie of the summer of 2008, and the spell that the movie cast over that season has proven remarkably durable. People are still fighting about its stature and its allegorical meanings."[2]

This essay explores and attempts to account for both the proliferation of and wide variety among allegorical interpretations of *The Dark Knight* by journalists, film critics, and bloggers. The quasi-mythic structures and urban crimefighting subjects that are axiomatic of superhero narratives frequently lend themselves to loose readings in terms of a sociocultural "zeitgeist." So, what was it about this particular film that opened the gates to a deluge of allegoresis? I argue that a particular set of textual cues established, or authorized, the War on Terror as an allegorical pretext. However, the film's carefully structured narrative and ultimately incoherent (or, more charitably, ambivalent) thematic elements ensure that, beyond these intersubjectively agreed-upon cues, the film can accommodate a wide range of suggested allegorical relationships and political readings. Granted, these readings are *all* strained to varying degrees, and many collapse under even casual scrutiny. However, simply to write them off for their "wrongness" misses the broader significance of their proliferation.

With enough semantic wrangling, allegorical readings, however weak, *can* be mapped onto almost any text. But allegoresis is by no means the norm in popular film criticism or film blogging. So, again, why was there such a sustained and impassioned debate over the allegorical meaning of *The Dark Knight*? And what is the relationship between this phenomenon and the film's popularity? To answer the former question, I turn to the work of literary scholar Sayre N. Greenfield, who posits a model of allegory in which readers match structured sets of textual cues with analogically structured sets of real-world or other extra-textual elements. I argue that *The Dark Knight*, unlike most blockbusters, encourages this mode of reading. And to answer the latter question, I argue that the wide, but nonetheless observably circumscribed, range of allegorical readings accommodated by *The Dark Knight*'s narrative both results from and demonstrates the utility of polysemy and ambiguity in blockbuster filmmaking. In sum, *The Dark Knight* is special in the clarity and forcefulness with which it clearly authorizes a specific, and crucially, a *topical* allegorical pretext, thus accruing the cultural and critical capital typically associated with "relevant" films. But, at the same time, it safeguards its potential economic capital by remaining thoroughly and constitutively ambiguous, thus leaving ample room for vigorous debate, which, upon the film's release, only increased its public salience.

To develop these arguments, I first provide overviews of *The Dark Knight*'s plot and the film's reception as political allegory. I will then explain Greenfield's model of allegory and identify the textual cues that provide a relatively stable framework for interpretation of *The Dark Knight* as an allegory of the War on Terror. Following this is an examination of the many narrative and other elements that complicate and allow for divergence among such interpretations of the film. I then contextualize *The Dark Knight* and its reception as allegory in relation to the transmedia Batman universe from which the film draws, Hollywood's well documented history of strategic ambiguity, and, more broadly, the imperatives of the popular media text.

The Dark Knight *and Its Readers*

As established in the ending of the franchise reboot *Batman Begins*, Batman's highly effective vigilante crusade against organized crime in Gotham has encouraged a new kind of criminal — the Joker — who, we learn, has forged an uneasy alliance with the beleaguered mob. *The Dark Knight*'s opening sequence features an elaborately choreographed and viscerally disturbing heist organized by the Joker, during which it quickly becomes clear that he obeys no ethical code, including any sense of "honor among thieves." He has told each of his accomplices that he is to kill one of the others and take his share; the one not so eliminated by the time the getaway vehicle arrives, the Joker kills. The early portion of the film also establishes the opposing yet complementary forms of justice (vigilantism versus legal methods) practiced, respectively, by Batman and Harvey Dent, Gotham's new District Attorney and "White Knight." Mediating the two is soon-to-be Police Commissioner Gordon, whose department liaises with and depends upon Batman despite his outlaw status. The squeaky-clean Dent expresses reservations about Gordon's team, which includes some shady figures he investigated in Internal Affairs prior to becoming District Attorney.

About an hour and a half into the film, the Joker is apprehended — a situation that may well have been part of his grand plan. With much delight, he presents Batman and Gotham Police with a "ticking bomb" scenario: Dent and Rachel Dawes, who, with Bruce Wayne, form a love triangle, are trapped in separate warehouses rigged to explode. When the dust settles, Dawes is dead, Dent is gravely injured, and the Joker has escaped. Upon learning of Dawes's death, the grotesquely disfigured Dent becomes the villain Two-Face, abandoning his commitment to legal justice in favor of vengeance dictated by sheer chance (specifically, the flip of a coin). It is important to note that Dent's dangerous predilection toward vengeance is established rather playfully early in the film and reappears in increasingly serious iterations prior to his transformation.

The film's climax and resolution weave four main lines of action. First, the Joker creates mass panic by blowing up a hospital (and freeing Two-Face, who was a patient there). Second, he conducts a social experiment by rigging with bombs two ferries, one full of "ordinary people" (read: middle- and upper-class whites) and the other populated by (ethnically diverse) convicts, and giving each boat a detonator to blow up the other to save its own. Third, Batman uses experimental sonar technology, based on cell phone surveillance, to hunt the Joker, his accomplices, and dozens of hostages from the aforementioned hospital. And fourth, Two-Face attempts to exact revenge on Commissioner Gordon and his family, whose corrupt team facilitated the Joker's scheme (and thus Dawes's death). These lines of action are resolved as follows: the people on the ferries do the right thing and do not blow one another up; Batman finds the Joker in time to prevent him from blowing both up and leaves him hanging — literally — with the SWAT team swarming in to apprehend him; and Batman dashes to the dialogue-heavy Gordon/Two-Face confrontation, which ends in Two-Face's death — but not before the villain has killed numerous people, including two police officers.

The film's final scenes are packed with garrulous philosophizing about good and evil:

> BATMAN: [The Joker] wanted to prove that someone as good as you could fall. And he was right.
> TWO-FACE: You thought we could be decent men in an indecent time. The world is cruel. And the only morality in a cruel world is chance.

As the film ends, Batman convinces Gordon to let him be "whatever Gotham needs him to be"— to let him take the fall for Dent's transgressions so as not to shatter the city's belief in its "White Knight." His rationale: "Sometimes the truth isn't good enough; sometimes people deserve more." As a result, the bat-beacon is publicly destroyed, and Batman — his high-tech infrastructure in tatters and his ally Lucius Fox having resigned — runs into the night, chased by police dogs. He is now, according to Gordon, "more than a hero." Gordon's monologue about Batman's role for Gotham comprises the film's last words: "...We have to chase him. Because he's the hero Gotham deserves, but not the one it needs right now. So we'll hunt him. Because he can take it. Because he's not our hero. He's a silent guardian, a watchful protector. A dark knight."

Critics tended to be not just positive but effusive in their praise of *The Dark Knight*, citing in particular the film's "timeliness" and "relevance." Within a week of the film's release, political readings began to appear in op-ed pages and the blogosphere. Conservative writer Andrew Klavan discharged the opening volley with his *Wall Street Journal* piece, "What Bush and Batman Have in Common." In this article, he argued that the film departed from Hollywood's allegedly left-wing norms and, in particular, recent films about the War on Terror, calling *The Dark Knight* "a paean of praise to the fortitude and moral courage that has been shown by George W. Bush in this time of terror and war." For Klavan, Batman's bending of the rules to catch and interrogate the Joker stands in for the necessary, well-intentioned abrogations of civil liberties (of terrorist suspects as well as ordinary citizens) instituted by the Bush administration. And the caped crusader's self-sacrificing submission to his own vilification at the film's end represents that of Bush (and perhaps Christ as well, Klavan adds):

> When heroes arise who take those difficult duties on themselves, it is tempting for the rest of us to turn our backs on them, to vilify them in order to protect our own appearance of righteousness [...] sometimes men must kill in order to preserve life; that sometimes they must violate their values in order to maintain those values; and that while movie stars may strut in the bright light of our adulation for pretending to be heroes, true heroes often must slink in the shadows, slump-shouldered and despised — then and only then will we be able to pay President Bush his due and make good and true films about the war on terror.[3]

He also notes, perhaps playfully, that "when you trace the outline with your finger," the Bat-insignia resembles a "W."

Klavan's editorial provoked numerous responses, while additional allegorical readings of the film appeared online apparently independent of it. Like Klavan, these authors typically made two interpretive maneuvers: first, they posited particular allegorical relationships between characters and events in the film and real-world people and events related to the War on Terror; and second, they argued how these textual elements shaped the film's political stance. Commentators suggesting the same allegorical relationships sometimes arrived at different conclusions about *The Dark Knight*'s political meaning. Others came to similar conclusions about the film's politics based on different proposed allegorical relationships.

Unsurprisingly, in most cases the political readings of the film were congruent with the writer's worldview, whether explicitly stated or clearly implied. Numerous conservative bloggers and journalists, including Australian pundit Andrew Bolt, affirmed and elaborated upon Klavan's critique.[4] Perhaps revealing conservatives' eagerness to claim a Hollywood superhero for their side, my more–than–forty-item sample of explicitly allegorical interpretations of *The Dark Knight* yielded no pieces from a clearly conservative viewpoint arguing that the film was left-wing or anti–Bush. Worried that Nolan might publicly disown conservatives' allegorical speculation about *The Dark Knight*, one blogger said, "I don't care what he says from here on out. I saw the film. Batman is George W. Bush."[5]

Among writers with liberal/progressive views, though, one finds a wider range of readings: pro– as well as anti–Bush. Predictably, these correspond to, respectively, negative and positive evaluations of the film's message. In an entry on the blog *n+1*, Nikil Saval writes, "*The Dark Knight* does not provoke profound debate about our [American] methods and purposes [in the War on Terror]. It spectacularly affirms them." Drawing on Commissioner Gordon's reference to Dent as "the hero we need" and Batman as "the hero we deserve," Saval writes "nor do we get the comic book movies we need."[6] Spencer Ackerman of *The Washington Independent* likens the film's ethos to Vice President Dick Cheney's oft-quoted statement about the U.S. "working through the dark side; spending time in the shadow," calling *The Dark Knight* a justification for the administration's "architecture of institutionalized abuse."[7]

Others did not read the film as pro–Bush. Two strategies recur in such readings: some commentators point out the ways in which Batman is *not* like Bush, while others argue that he *is* like Bush but that the film's "dark" thematics offer, implicitly or symptomatically, a critique of Bush. According to a blogger known as "Porch Dog," "There is no way that anybody but a child would think that this was a straightforward approval of the Bush administration."[8] Posting on the blog of *Variety*'s Anne Thompson, entertainment journalist David S. Cohen finds the film's critique of Bush in its suggestion that it is Batman's presence that gives rise to a new class of criminal. He argues that "Batman has more in common with his killer-clown foe than with the normal people he means to protect," and asks, "Should we conclude that *The Dark Knight* argues that Bush and bin Laden are two sides of the same coin? If so, the Nolans actually come down somewhere to the left of Michael Moore."[9] Writing for the website of New York's Trinity Church, Nathan Brockman highlights the film's motif of mercy, citing in particular "Batman's reluctance to be callous" (certainly debatable), as well as the grace shown by the ferry passengers. He contrasts these elements with the U.S. response to 9/11, asking, "What if the United States hadn't started two wars after being mercilessly attacked? What if we had unexpectedly shown mercy and humility in our political decision-making?"[10]

The Authorization of Allegory

Now that I have offered an overview of *The Dark Knight* and its reception as political allegory, I turn to a closer examination of the textual features and reading practices that encouraged this phenomenon. Literary scholar Sayre Greenfield offers a model of allegorical interpretation that helps explain the film's cueing of allegory. Conceding that "defining the plane of allegory's existence" is "fraught with difficulty," he writes:

> I find indeterminable the question of whether texts 'are written to' be read allegorically. Nonetheless, whether 'written to' or not, some narratives do encourage readers to read allegorically, given the details of the texts *and* the cultural circumstances of the reader [...] One may still ask, however, what in one text rather than another triggers that strategy.[11]

130 Part Two: Batman and Literary Theory

He defines the reading strategy that leads to intersubjective identification of a text as allegorical as a "base-two system" that must involve *both* metaphoric (comparative, symbolic) and metonymic (associative) connections: "The reader, to read allegorically, must find a series of metaphoric parallels that connect two (or more) associative, metonymic extensions of key ideas." He offers as an example Orwell's *Animal Farm*, in which a system of metonymically linked textual elements (the different animals on the farm) is metaphorically linked to another, corresponding system of metonymically linked elements (Stalin, Trotsky, etc.) of the allegorical pretext (i.e., European totalitarianism). Table 1 charts this model of reading as applied to *The Dark Knight*.

Table 2. Greenfield's Model of Allegorical Reading

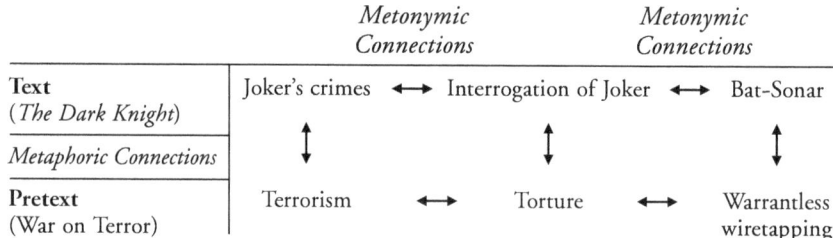

	Metonymic Connections		*Metonymic Connections*	
Text (*The Dark Knight*)	Joker's crimes	←→ Interrogation of Joker	←→	Bat-Sonar
Metaphoric Connections	↕	↕		↕
Pretext (War on Terror)	Terrorism	←→ Torture	←→	Warrantless wiretapping

The Dark Knight contains a critical mass of relatively unambiguous, or at least intersubjectively agreed upon, signifiers that constitute the kind of metonymically linked system of Greenfield's model. Together they cue the War on Terror as an allegorical pretext — but, crucially, only in a skeletal and politically inert fashion. Beyond these baseline cues, viewers can "fill in" metaphorically the rest of this system in different ways, allowing the film to sustain a variety of readings. It is the presence of this *system* of cues that helps explain why *this* film, and not others triggered so many allegorical interpretations. In contrast, *Batman Begins* inspired only a smattering of disparate allegorical readings, such as the one by Kim Newman in *Sight & Sound*. Newman points out that the film's America is one "haunted by a fanatic eastern sect with a charismatic but impossible-to-catch figurehead which is bent on crashing a mode of transport into a skyscraper to trigger an explosion of panic that will destroy society."[12] But the analogy cannot be extended much further, and the strain on the text (e.g., the vagueness of "a mode of transport") shows even here. *Batman Begins* does not have as robust, replete, or systematic a set of cues as *The Dark Knight*, making the latter much more amenable to allegoresis — that is, to triggering the metaphoric and metonymic thinking described above. The film's setting also facilitated these processes. It was shot almost entirely on location in Chicago, and its recognizable urban scenery helped authorize a real-world allegorical pretext for the story. It was frequently noted that the Gotham of *The Dark Knight* appeared far more "real" than the relatively fantastical renderings of the city in all of the previous *Batman* films (including Nolan's), and this effect of realism encouraged commentators to see the film as standing in for, and saying something about, contemporary reality.

Many of *The Dark Knight*'s textual cues relate to the Joker's status as a stand-in for radical Islamic terrorism, specifically Osama bin Laden/Al Qaeda. In fact, he is explicitly called a "terrorist" at least once in the film. At a press conference in which Batman is to reveal his true identity (a demand of the Joker, who promises the daily killing of innocents until the caped crusader is unmasked), Dent asks reporters and the public, "The Batman has offered to turn himself in. But first, consider the situation. Should we give in to this terrorist's demands?" But perhaps the most oft-cited and unambiguous cue for reading the Joker as a terrorist is the scene in which a news program airs a disturbing DIY hostage and execution video featuring the Joker and one of Batman's fans/impersonators in a meat locker. The mise-en-scène of this video (e.g., the hostage being lashed to a chair, along with the hostage's forced recitation of his name and other information) resembles that of a number of hostage/execution videos released by Al Qaeda and other groups in the early through mid–2000s, the most notorious being the beheading of journalist Daniel Pearl.

Immediately prior to viewing this video, Bruce Wayne and Alfred (the butler) have a protracted exchange about the nature of villainy. In one of the film's longest monologues — one that conspicuously brings the rapidly paced film to a near halt — Alfred relates his experience hunting a villain in Burma. He muses, "Some men aren't looking for anything logical, like money. They can't be bought, bullied, reasoned, or negotiated with. They just want to watch the world burn." This passage, which enjoys a privileged position in the film, was featured prominently in several *Dark Knight* trailers. Conservatives and liberals alike have noted the difficulty squaring this statement, and the Joker's ethos, with that of al Qaeda. *National Review Online* columnist Jonah Goldberg evades the problem by noting that terrorists "don't want to see the world burn; they want to see the world in a burqa. But burning the world is preferable to not getting their way."[13] Blogger Matt Huppert argues that the amoral nihilism of the Joker is ill-matched to ideal-driven, "hypermoral" al Qaeda, who "see themselves as holy warriors."[14] *The Dark Knight* is able to evoke for viewers specific icons of Middle Eastern terrorism while simultaneously reducing them to broad, basic themes (e.g., "fear" or "chaos"). In so doing, it creates enough distance between text and pretext to allow for debate as well as plausible deniability.[15]

Commentators repeatedly cited the film's pervasive imagery of verisimilar urban destruction as evocative of 9/11. Following the bombings that kill Dawes and maim Dent, Batman, surrounded by firemen, stands in a pit of steaming wreckage reminiscent of Ground Zero. Later in the film, when the Joker blows up Gotham General Hospital, we see the spectacle of a real building being leveled. In a forty-second take, the Joker walks away from the hospital and toward the camera while small explosions go off behind him. Apparently confused, he tinkers with the detonating device in his hand until a larger explosion occurs. He then smoothly dashes into and hijacks a waiting bus, which drives away as the building collapses. Following an overlapping cut, we are presented with an unobstructed, aerial view of the hospital's destruction and accompanying fireball. Many even cited as evoking 9/11 the film's promotional materials, including its main poster, which features Batman standing before a skyscraper whose upper floors are torn out and engulfed in flames — in the shape of the bat insignia. This poster is emblematic of the film's ambiguous or incoherent — and opportunistic — evocation of 9/11 imagery and related themes: yes, we have a flaming skyscraper, but what does this image really suggest? Surely not that Batman blew it up? Like the film as a whole, the poster succeeds in linking Batman/Gotham to terroristic urban destruction (and thus in establishing the War on Terror as an allegorical pretext) without further clarification or elaboration of more specific metaphoric connections — especially those that would commit the film to particular ideological positions.

A final set of intersubjectively evident cues that triggered allegorical readings of *The Dark Knight* vis-à-vis the post–9/11 U.S. relates to Batman's extreme crimefighting tactics, some of which transgress his supposedly inviolable personal code. First, he performs harsh interrogation techniques upon the Joker in an attempt to extract the locations of Dawes and Dent. Blocking the room's door to prevent Gordon and company from intervening, he punches, throttles, and "walls" the Joker, repeatedly growling, "Where are they?" In an opinion piece for the Christian Broadcasting Network, Jesse Carey writes, "All that was missing was a waterboarding apparatus."[16] Complementing this ethical line-crossing is the use of Bat-sonar, which unmistakably echoes the Bush Administration/National Security Agency's warrantless wiretapping of civilian telecommunications. When Batman reveals the system, which he has independently developed in secret, to Lucius Fox, the two have another didactic exchange:

> BATMAN: Beautiful, isn't it?
> FOX: Beautiful. Unethical. *Dangerous.* You've turned every cell phone in Gotham into a microphone.

BATMAN: And a high-frequency generator-receiver.
FOX: You took my sonar concept and applied it to every phone in the city! With half the city feeding you Sonar, you can image all of Gotham. This is wrong.
BATMAN: I've gotta find this man, Lucius.
FOX: At what cost? [...] This is too much power for one person.
BATMAN: That's why I gave it to you.

Commentators agreed on the allegorical referents of the cues listed above with very few exceptions (e.g. a self–consciously provocative reading that accepted the film as an allegory of the War on Terror but suggested parallels between the Joker and George Bush in certain scenes).[17] However, when it came to pinning down the allegorical referents of other characters and events — and to evaluating the film's stance toward them — there was no such agreement. Some respondents were systematic in their attempts to assign allegorical relationships to numerous major characters and events, while others identified relationships in a more piecemeal fashion. Greenfield's model allows for these gaps and inconsistencies common in allegorical readings, for "a metaphoric extension of a term may occur without precipitating metonymic extensions, and metonymic extensions in one sphere of reference may accrete without metaphoric parallels to connect them to other spheres of reference."[18] Table 2 offers a survey of suggested allegorical relationships in *The Dark Knight*, drawn from the aforementioned sample of the over forty explicitly allegorical readings of the film, along with an additional forty reviews and editorials identifying real-world parallels in the film while not necessarily framing their comments as fleshed-out allegorical interpretations. It shows remarkable diversity in the reading of key textual elements, the most significant of which I will call the "triangle of justice" that includes Batman, Harvey Dent/Two-Face, and Commissioner Gordon/Gotham Police.

Room for Interpretation

While most commentators agree on the allegorical relationships described above, they differ significantly on their political valences. Whereas Klavan and others characterize the harsh interrogation of the Joker as necessary and warranted, those who argue that the film is a critique of Bush policies often point to the fact that these techniques do not work. First, he takes delight in it, cackling maniacally all the way through. Second, he both anticipates and encourages his own torture, which is ultimately what allows him to take a guard hostage, detonate the twin warehouse bombs, and escape to wreak further havoc. Third, the torture does not produce reliable information; consistent with his overall ethic of chaos and subversion, the Joker lies about the locations of Dawes and Dent.

The use of Bat-sonar can be read in similarly contradictory ways. On the one hand, it does lead Batman to the Joker and helps prevent the destruction of the two ferries. On the other, it is revealed during the film's final showdown that it cannot distinguish hostages from villains. Also, Batman destroys it after a single use, and Lucius Fox resigns his position because of his ethical concerns. Those who read the film as a validation of Bush policy can say that it shows how limited incursions into civil liberties are sometimes necessary to maintain freedom; those who read the film as a critique of neo-conservative policy can argue that the limited use of Bat-sonar differentiates it from warrantless wiretapping, which members of the Bush administration have suggested should go unchecked and be instituted permanently.[19]

Once commentators make a case for the War on Terror pretext by assembling the metonymic framework laid out above (i.e., terrorism, urban destruction, torture, and surveillance), their work then turns to sifting through and making sense of the film's thorny thematics concerning justice, heroism, good, and evil to make more specific arguments about further allegorical relationships and the film's politics. Batman's descent into "darkness," most specifically his testing of the moral code (most important, that he will not kill) that in large part defines his identity within the transmedia Batman universe, is central to the thematics of *The Dark Knight*. Because this testing arguably calls into question his very heroism — Manohla Dargis of *The New York Times* went so far as to call *The Dark Knight* "a postheroic superhero movie"–viewers can interpret his journey as either a celebration of the beleaguered Bush and post–9/11 America or a cautionary tale of their transgressions.[20] Indeed, this Batman is undoubtedly a more alienating and inaccessible one than in past installments of the franchise (evidenced, for example, in the distancing, over–the-top gruffness of his voice throughout the film, and the film's almost complete lack of comic asides). Nonetheless, Batman is the film's protagonist by default and is redeemed at the film's end, encouraging viewer allegiance through his self–sacrificing actions (and persecution).[21] It is arguable that commentators' tendency to repeat the film's own talking points led them to overstate the degree to which his "hero" status is threatened in any fundamental way. But because *The Dark Knight* traffics in near-constant, "serious" moral debate, the possibility of different, even opposing, evaluations of Batman's actions (and, by extension, his relationship to real-world political figures) is tightly woven into the fabric of the text.

Complicating matters further is the character arc of Dent/Two-Face, which also accommodates varying interpretations. Viewers can map Bush policies and the "dark journey" of post–9/11 America onto Batman's arc, or onto Harvey Dent's precipitous, and far more grave, moral decline — his becoming a murderous monster upon experiencing loss at the hands of evil. Several bloggers point out that Batman was never anything more than a vigilante, outside the law, whereas Dent, in becoming Two-Face, actually "turns on the values he swore to defend."[22] The mutual admiration, established early in the film, of Dent and Batman for one another's opposing approaches to justice constitutes one dyad in *The Dark Knight*'s "doppelgangland of interlocking pairs."[23] Bruce Wayne/Batman is hopeful for Dent's legitimate, effective meting out of justice, and risks everything at the film's end to sustain the public's faith in "Gotham's true hero." But the film also suggests that the evil threatening Gotham cannot be overcome by Dent's methods alone; for example, he relies on Batman to perform an illegal rendition of a Hong Kong businessman working with the mob. Further, as noted above, the character flaws (including a propensity toward megalomania and fascination with chance) that facilitate Dent's transformation into Two-Face are sown early in the film, signifying a predisposition to lawlessness and potentially casting doubt on his entire enterprise. While evincing the shortcomings of Dent's ethos, *The Dark Knight* also elevates it as Gotham's best hope. Further illustrating the fundamental incoherence of the Batman/Dent duality are Gordon's paired pontifications — oft-quoted in responses to the film, and featured prominently in promotional materials — that Dent is "not the hero Gotham deserved, but the hero we needed," and that Batman is "the hero Gotham deserves, but not the one it needs *right now*." The ambiguities inherent in these characters and events leave the film wide open to different allegorical and political interpretations.

Critics were not always oblivious to the film's inconsistencies and ambivalences. One blogger notes that the film "offers us a number of lengths which *all together* might go to the end, but won't join up without some rather ugly and makeshift knotting."[24] Another maintains that allegory "must be internally consistent to have any true meaning" and sees the film as evidence "that 9/11 has become a pop psychology fad [...] it seems like all roads lead to the twin towers in one way or another."[25] Even while putting forth their own allegorical readings of the film, some commentators questioned the soundness of such endeavors, noting that viewers could find ways to map virtually any political view onto the film.[26] Blogging for theatlantic.com, Matthew Yglesias argues that the film "pulled off the neat hat trick of being both libertarian and fascistic, which is to say it is damn confused ... not bad, but not consistent either."[27]

Some found the film's muddle-headed politics troubling from aesthetic as well as ethical standpoints. For David Cox of *The Guardian*, "the confusion matters. It provides a smokescreen behind which the task of weaving all of those casual allusions into some kind of coherent whole can be persistently ducked."[28] Writing for the World Socialist Website, David Walsh criticizes Christopher Nolan and his co-screenwriter and brother Jonathan Nolan for loading their characters "with doubleness and ambiguity to the point where he or she can hardly stand up under the weight." He further argues that *The Dark Knight* shows "the consequences of not thinking seriously about things, a failure that permits the artist to be picked up by or used by stronger currents in the absence of knowledge and principled opposition."[29] The hard-hitting conclusion of Sival's *n+1* entry illustrates well the tendency (in academic as well as some popular criticism) to read films' inconsistencies, incoherence, gaps, and fissures symptomatically. Arguing that films like *The Dark Knight* help smooth "the task of empire," he writes, "History will record that, while a monumental catastrophe overtook the world financial markets and a new colonialism destroyed the lives of nations, the United States still found time and money to resolve in its films what it could not, for the life of it, perform in the world."[30]

The Dark Knight's Sources and Imperatives

We cannot be certain why, or from where, the allegorical cues or the inconsistencies and ambiguities in *The Dark Knight* arise. But adding to symptomatic and reflectionist approaches to blockbuster ideology a consideration of the potential sources and utility of these textual features can help us understand *The Dark Knight* as both a film and a cultural mega-phenomenon. What follows is, first, an attempt to place the film within the context of its multiple pre–9/11 source materials. Second, I demonstrate that there is reason to believe that the film is a particularly effective and *calculated* implementation of well established tendencies of Hollywood cinema toward polysemy and openness.

A consideration of the film's source materials reveals that the "darkness" of *The Dark Knight* cannot be a simple, unconscious reflection of the presumably "dark" post–9/11 zeitgeist. The vast majority of its major characters and themes can be found, albeit diffusely, in the nearly seventy-year history of Batman comics and other Bat-texts (which are all held, along with Warner Bros., under the Time Warner corporate umbrella). According to Christopher Nolan, he and his brother drew freely from this amalgam of sources, trying "to be influenced by the whole history of the comics, and steep ourselves in it prior to writing."[31] Particularly important sources for the Nolan films, in terms of both storylines and tone, include several pivotal Batman comics and graphic novels published in the mid–to-late 1980s, including Frank Miller's *The Dark Knight Returns* and *Batman: Year One* and Alan Moore's *Batman: The Killing Joke* (this last was particularly important in drawing explicit parallels between the Joker and Batman). These works undertook a "cultural and ideological remodeling" of Batman. Miller's in particular feature strong dystopic and antiheroic currents — scholar Mark Fisher characterizes them as "designer nihilism"— which render Gotham "as an almost apocalyptic scene of urban decay" and highlight the fascistic overtones of Batman's endeavors.[32]

Scholars and comic artists alike typically place these innovative Batman texts in the company of other darker, edgier, and more morally fraught superhero texts of the period, including Moore's *Watchmen* and *V for Vendetta*.[33] These works were widely read as, and acknowledged by the authors to be, loose allegories of Reaganism and Thatcherism. In a 1989 interview, Miller explained his motivations for portraying Batman as a brutal, alcoholic, suicidal man of questionable sanity and Gotham as near-irredeemably corrupt: "I simply put Batman, this unearthly force, into a world that's closer to the one I know. And the world I know is terrifying."[34] Fisher argues that, in Miller's vision, "it is no longer possible to assume the existence of Good."[35] Roberta Pearson and William Uricchio suggest that, although they maintain most of the essential elements of Batman's cosmology, Miller's books nonetheless profoundly altered Batman's relation to the hegemonic order and "widened incipient fissures in the Batman's construction."[36] This conflicted, "dark" Batman may seem ready-made for the post–9/11 age, but he cannot be considered a product of it. Rather, Miller and Moore's works have provided subsequent Bat-authors, including the Nolans, with a rich and appealingly relevant store of icons and situations from which to draw.

As one of the most successful cultural commodities of our time, *The Dark Knight* was able to thrive in both the financial and cultural economies, to use media theorist John Fiske's terms. Fiske has been criticized for offering an overly sanguine outlook on the potential for and utility of viewers' exercising "semiotic power" through "resistant readings." But even if we bracket off this dimension of his argument, we are left with a shrewd and valuable assessment of the economic imperatives of popular media (e.g. blockbuster filmmaking), and how these imperatives might manifest themselves textually. For Fiske, to achieve popularity texts must be able to accommodate great variety in their readings by the myriad groups who consume them. The greater the number of pleasures that can be taken from the text, his argument goes, the greater potential for that text's popularity. Thus, "semiotic excess," polysemy, and openness, all "producerly" or "writerly" textual attributes in the

Barthesian sense, are typically preconditions for popularity. Fiske argues that such imperatives are paradoxical. In order to achieve popularity and maintain their hegemonic position, producers must provide space for viewers to subvert hegemonic or "preferred" readings.[37] Fiske's ideas help explain the strategies of *The Dark Knight*, a blockbuster that not only sought but required near-complete global saturation to be financially successful.[38] But, as I have suggested above, *The Dark Knight* is sufficiently obfuscating such that it would be all but impossible to argue with confidence precisely what its "preferred meanings" vis-à-vis the War on Terror are. And that is precisely the point.

Hollywood has long engineered its texts to appeal to the widest range of audiences, domestic and foreign. In her book *The World According to Hollywood: 1918–1939*, Ruth Vasey documents the institutionalization, under the auspices of the Production Code Administration (PCA) and the Motion Picture Producers and Distributors of America (MPPDA), of "narrative and representational guidelines" aimed to ensure that films would not jeopardize their box-office performance by offending any ethnic, religious, national, or political group among their potential audiences.[39] These guidelines largely regulated denotative rather than connotative meaning in order to allow for plausible deniability–e.g., encouraging vague, non–verisimilar depictions of groups cast in a negative light. Vasey argues that with classical filmmaking, especially following the transition to sound filmmaking, came "the formulation of 'open' texts which were amenable to a variety of different readings [...] ambiguous treatments offering a choice of interpretations helped to compensate for the movies' loss of flexibility" from the silent medium.[40] In an analysis of *Casablanca*, Richard Maltby illustrates that films can be constructed to cater to diverse, unpredictable audiences simultaneously: "incoherence and fissures can [...] be understood as part of the performative work of the movie in communicating with its multiple audiences." In a formulation not so different from Fiske's, he connects this capacity to the imperatives of Hollywood films' "commodity function, to sell the same thing to two or more audiences at the same time."[41]

The terrain has changed much since the classical studio era, and content regulation is no longer institutionalized in the same manner, but the same imperatives of securing wide appeal remain. Thomas Schatz argues that contemporary Hollywood, and particularly blockbuster, filmmaking continues to favor "texts strategically 'open' to multiple readings and multimedia reiteration."[42] Incoherence, gaps, fissures, and enigmas need not necessarily be read as symptomatic of cultural crises or the decline of good storytelling. In reference to *The Dark Knight*, David Bordwell argues that it is "in filmmakers' interests to push a lot of our buttons without worrying whether what comes out is a coherent intellectual position."⁴³ There is a strong and long-established incentive for filmmakers to muddy the pool intentionally.

Christopher Nolan's public statements around the time of *The Dark Knight*'s release support the argument that the film is calculated in its ambiguity regarding real-world events. We must always weigh director's statements about their work — particularly when promoting a film — with caution. Regardless, Nolan's statements clearly demonstrate at the very least an awareness of the film's flirtation with politics as well as the utility of ambiguity and polysemy. A *Los Angeles Times* interviewer proposed to Nolan, "Most of the political message has more to do with the viewer than the filmmaker. It's inferred, not implied." Nolan responded,

> I agree completely. Especially if you do it right [...] If you get that right, people are going to be able to bring a wide variety of interpretations to it depending on who they are. It's allowing the characters to be a conduit to the audience. Allowing an audience to sit there and relate to Batman and his dilemma whether they are Republican or Democrat or whatever.⁴⁴

Nolan was resolutely equivocal and evasive when asked to comment on the film's allegorical dimensions. Discussing whether it was fair to "see shades of Baghdad" in Gotham, he spoke in the broadest terms possible: "Where I suppose I would see a parallel is the threat of chaos, which is something we very much deal with in this film. And in today's world."⁴⁵ He spoke frequently of the interrogation scene, which he called his favorite of the film. In what might lend some credence to those taking an anti–torture message from the film, Nolan said that when Batman "drops the Joker, he has realized the futility of what he's done. You see it in his eyes." But he continues by posing a dilemma, and suggesting that the film does not have a good answer to it: "How do you fight someone who thrives on conflict? It's a very loose end to be left with."⁴⁶ The intellectual terms in which Nolan couches his prevarications dovetail smoothly with both the philosophizing on display in the film itself (e.g. in the privileged monologues and discussions discussed earlier) and the economic incentive toward strategic ambiguity in blockbuster filmmaking.

An aura of cultural relevance is typically a valuable commercial asset for a film — especially those of genres typically branded as escapist fare. *The Dark Knight*'s ponderous thematics, along with its cueing of allegory in a skeletal, porous manner, seek to secure this cultural relevance without overtly committing it to any particular political position. And the strategy worked. Richard Corliss of *Time* praised the film for its "rethinking and transcending of a schlock source," while *USA Today* critic Claudia Puig said, "Despite its comic-book origins and fantasy setting, the story poses timely and compelling ethical dilemmas, demonstrating that popcorn thrillers need not be mindless nor disposable."⁴⁷ Others called it "a superhero movie of unusual psychological complexity" and lauded the film's grappling with "substantive issues and existential questions."⁴⁸ Dargis, who placed the film among her top five of the year, wrote, "Mr. Nolan has found a way to make Batman relevant to his time — meaning, to ours." *The Dark Knight*'s tremendous critical and commercial successes are inseparable from its hard-wired ambiguities associated with its War on Terror pretext.

Conclusions

The Dark Knight was, in a way, the perfect storm. A number of factors — the success of *Batman Begins* as a franchise reboot, an elaborate, well-orchestrated viral marketing campaign, the lure of 70mm IMAX sequences, and most important, actor Heath Ledger's sudden death and the resulting speculation about his performance — fueled intense anticipation for the release. The film itself shrewdly and opportunistically deployed an array of tropes from the *Batman* universe and the superhero and action film genres, combining and tweaking them in a manner that, first, triggered allegorical thinking (of greater or lesser systematicity) among both critics and average moviegoers, and second, left wide latitude for the shape these interpretations could take within the confines of a clear political pretext. That is, the film went beyond garden-variety blockbuster polysemy/openness by overtly intermeshing these qualities with topical political allegory, thus increasing its profit-making potential as well as inviting its reception as a "serious," "intellectual," and "important" film. Debates over these possible interpretations added to the film's buzz, creating a kind of feedback loop in which discussions in various media of the film's cultural relevance boosted its public profile as not just a must-see movie, but a cultural event. It could well be that its carefully ambiguous invocation of the imagined post–9/11 zeitgeist is what earned *The Dark Knight*, for a brief time, such a prominent position within this very discourse, and the public consciousness more broadly.⁴⁹

Table 2. Sample of Suggested Allegorical Relationships in *The Dark Knight*

Batman	George Bush, Dick Cheney, average soldiers, everyday citizens, John McCain, Congress
Harvey Dent	George Bush, Rudy Giuliani, Politicians, U.S. citizens, post–WWII American values, deontology
The Joker	Osama bin Laden/Al-Qaeda/terrorism, George Bush, fear-mongering politicians

The Joker's video	Al-Qaeda execution videos (esp. Daniel Pearl video)
BatSonar	Warrantless wiretapping
Interrogation of Joker	Torture of terrorist suspects
Gotham Police/Gordon	United Nations, conventional law enforcement, Coalition of the Willing, U.S. military, Cold War allies, movie viewers, consequentialism
Lucius Fox	United Nations, Barack Obama, moral guide
Gotham	America, Iraq, World
Alfred	Military recruiter, wizened veteran, moral guide
Bruce Wayne	George Bush
Bat-Imitators	Movie viewers
Police observing interrogation	Movie viewers
"Ordinary people" on ferry	Movie viewers
Convicts on ferry	P.O.W.s
Batman's moral code	Neoconservative democratic realism, virtue ethics

Notes

1. E.g., Geoff Boucher, "Christopher Nolan's 'Knight' Vision," *Los Angeles Times* 6 Jul 2008.

2. A.O. Scott, "Everybody's a Critic of the Critics' Rabid Critics," *The New York Times*, 25 July 2010, AR1.

3. Andrew Klavan, "What Bush and Batman Have in Common," *Wall Street Journal* 25 Jul 2008. http://online.wsj.com/article/SB121694247343482821.html

4. Andrew Bolt, "It's George W. Batman," *The Herald Sun*, 30 Jul 2008. http://blogs.news.com.au/heraldsun/andrewbolt/index.php/heraldsun/comments/column_its_george_w_batman/

5. John Sexton, "More on Bush the Dark Knight," *Verum Serum*, 4 Aug 2008. http:/verumserum.com/?p=2198

6. Nikil Saval, "Review: *The Dark Knight*," *n+1*, 6 Aug 2008. http://www.nplusonemag.com/dark-knight

7. Spencer Ackerman, "Batman's 'Dark Knight' Reflects Cheney Policy," *The Washington Independent*, 21 Jul 2008. http://washingtonindependent.com/509-batmans-dark-knight-reflects-cheney-policy

8. "Batman and Bush," *Porch Dog*, 22 Jul 2008. http://porch-dog.com/?p=418

9. David S. Cohen, "George Bush, The Dark Knight? Be Careful What You Wish For," *Thompson on Hollywood*, 25 Jul 2008. http://weblogs.variety.com/thompsononhollywood/2008/09/george-bush-the-.html

10. Nathan Brockman, "The Dark Knight (of the Soul)," *Trinity Church*, 9 Sep 2008. http://trinitywallstreet.org/welcome/?article&id=1009

11. Sayre N. Greenfield, "Defining Allegory: As Rhetoric, Literary Text, and Reading," *The Ends of Allegory* (Newark: Univ. of DE Press, 1998), 49–55.

12. Kim Newman, "Cape Fear," *Sight & Sound* 15, no. 7 (July 2005). See also Mark Fisher, "Gothic Oedipus: Subjectivity and Capitalism in Christopher Nolan's *Batman Begins*," *Image Text* 2, no. 2 (Winter 2005).

13. Jonah Goldberg, "The Gitmo Five's Burn Notice," *National Review Online*, 13 Mar 2009. http://article.nationalreview.com/?q=M2QzYTFlZTNhZDBlNzBjZGI2ZmExNzI2YTlmN DgyZTg=

14. Matt Huppert, "'The Dark Knight' and the '9/11 Allegory' Fallacy," *Matt's Truthonomics*, 21 Jul 2008. http:/mattstruthonomics.blogspot.com/2008/07/dark-knight-and-911-allegory-fallacy.html

15. For a discussion of the "problem" of difference in allegorical interpretation and composition, see Jon Whitman, "The Allegorical Problem," *Allegory: The Dynamics of an Ancient and Medieval Technique* (Bridgewater, NJ: Replica Books, 1999), 1–13.

16. Jesse Carey, "This Present Darkness," *Christian Broadcasting Network*. http://www.cbn.com/entertainment/screen/carey_DarkKnight.aspx

17. "Andrew Klavan Misses the Point: Why The Dark Knight is Not Allegory for the Bush Administration," *Adamant's Fire*, 29 Jul 2008. http://adamanthenes.blogspot.com/2008/07/andrew-klavan-misses-point-why-dark.html

18. Greenfield, 64–65.

19. E.g., "The Dark Knight, the War on Terror, and Science Fiction's Moral Authority," *Submitted to a Candid World*, 23 Jul 2008. http://www.acandidworld.net/2008/07/23/the-dark-knight-the-war-on-terror-and-science-fictions-moral-authority; Tim Weaver, "Dark Knight Review: How Do You Respond to Terror?" *Not So Subtle*, 20 Jul 2008. http://timm84.wordpress.com/2008/ 07/20/dark-knight-review-how-do-you-respond-to-terror/

20. Manohla Dargis, "Showdown in Gotham Town," *The New York Times*, 18 Jul 2008. http://movies.nytimes.com/2008/07/18/movies/18knig.html

21. I use "allegiance" in the sense established in Murray Smith's *Engaging Characters: Fiction, Emotion, and the Cinema* (NY: Oxford UP, 1995).

22. "Bush Isn't Batman. He's Two-Face," *American History Y?* 25 Jul 2008. http://americanhistoryy.wordpress.com/2008/07/25/bush-isnt-batman-hes-two-face/; "Andrew Klavan Misses the Point."

23. Christopher Orr, "The Movie Review: 'The Dark Knight,'" *The New Republic*, 17 Jul 2008. http://www.tnr.com/politics/story.html?id=757af21c-1026-44f3-918b-ea35b135e350

24. "Allegory Revisited: The Dark Knight," *A Trout in the Milk*, 9 Aug 2008. http://circumstantial.wordpress.com/2008/08/09/allegory-revisited-the-dark-knight/

25. Huppert.

26. E.g. Scott Von Doviak, "Why So Serious? The Dark Knight in the Political World," *The Screengrab*, 31 Jul 2008. http://www.nerve.com/CS/blogs/screengrab/archive/2008/07/31/why-so-serious-the-dark-knight-in-the-political-world.aspx Find others.

27. Matthew Yglesias, "*Dark Knight* Politics," *The Atlantic.com*, 24 Jul 2008. http://matthewyglesias.theatlantic.com/archives/2008/07/dark_knight_politics.php//

28. David Cox, "Why The Dark Knight is So Dim," *Guardian.co.uk*, 28 Jul 2008. http://www.guardian.co.uk/film/2008/jul/28/dark.night/

29. David Walsh, "*The Dark Knight*: Striving to be impressive, but essentially empty," *World Socialist Web Site*, 25 Jul 2008. http://www.wsws.org/articles/2008/jul2008/dark-j25.shtml

30. Saval. A particularly insightful example of such criticism in reference to a different film is Joshua Clover, *The Matrix* (London: BFI Publishing, 2005).

31. Paul Fischer, "Intervew: Christopher Nolan for 'The Dark Knight,'" *Dark Horizons*, 3 Jul 2008. http://darkhorizons.com/interviews/315/christopher-nolan-for-the-dark-knight-. Newman (cited above) traces the comic book origins of many of the characters and themes of the Nolans' take on the Bat-universe.

32. Tony Bennett, "Holy Shifting Signifiers: Forewords" *The Many Lives of the Batman*, eds. Roberta E. Pearson and William Uricchio (NY: Routledge, 1991), vii–ix; Mark Fisher, "Gothic Oedipus: Subjectivity and Capitalism in Christopher Nolan's *Batman Begins*," *Image Text* 2, no. 2 (Winter 2005): 11.

33. Christopher Sharrett, "Batman and the Twilight of the Idols: An Interview with Frank Miller," Pearson and Uricchio, 33–36; Bill Boichel, "Batman: Commodity as Myth," Pearson and Uricchio, 4–7.

34. Sharrett, 38–39.

35. Fisher.

36. William Uricchio and Roberta E. Pearson, "'I'm Not Fooled by That Cheap Disguise,'" Pearson and Uricchio, 209.

37. John Fiske, *Television Culture* (London: Routledge, 2007), 505–513.

38. For a discussion of contemporary global saturation releasing and blockbuster films' seeking "event" status, see Charles Acland's *Screen Traffic: Movies, Multiplexes, and Global Culture* (Durham and London: Duke UP, 2003).

39. Ruth Vasey, *The World According to Hollywood, 1918–1939* (Madison: Univ. of WI Press, 1997), 4–5.

40. Ibid., 226.

41. Richard Maltby, "'A Brief Romantic Interlude': Dick and Jane Go to 3_ Seconds of the Classical Hollywood Cinema," *Post-Theory: Reconstructing Film Studies*, eds. David Bordwell and Noël Carroll (Univ. of WI Press, 1996), 443–444, 452.

42. Thomas Schatz, "The New Hollywood," *Movie Blockbusters*, ed. Julian Stringer (London: Routledge, 2003), 40.

43. David Bordwell, "Superheroes for Sale," *Observations on film art and* Film Art, 16 Aug 2008. http://www.davidbordwell.net/blog/?p=2713

44. Geoff Boucher, "Christopher Nolan on 'Dark Knight' and its box-office billion: 'It's mystifying to me,'" *Hero Complex, The Los Angeles Times*, 27 Oct 2008. http://latimesblogs.com/herocomplex/2008/10/christopher-nol.html

45. Devlin Gordon, "Bat Trick," *Newsweek*, 21 Jul 2008. http://www.newsweek.com/id/145508; see also statements such as "we started to explore the effect one guy could have on an entire population — the ways in which he could upset the balance for people, the ways in which he could take their rules for living, their ethics, their beliefs, their humanity and turn them on themselves. You could say we've seen echoes of that in our own world, which has led me to believe that anarchy and chaos — even the threat of anarchy and chaos — are among the most frightening things society faces, especially in this day and age" (quoted in Walsh).

46. Boucher, "Christopher Nolan revisits and analyzes his favorite scene in 'Dark Knight,' *Hero Complex, The Los Angeles Times*, 28 Oct 2008. http://latimesblogs.com/herocomplex/2008/10/christopher-nol-1.html

47. Richard Corliss, "Batman is Back," *Time*, 9 Jul 2008. http://www.time.com/time/printout/0,8816,18211365,00.html; Claudia Puig, "Ledger's talent lives on as The Joker in 'Dark Knight,'" *USA Today*, 1 Aug 2008. http://www.usatoday.com/life/movies/reviews/2008-07-16-dark-knight-review_N.htm

48. Scott Foundas, "Heath Ledger Peers Into The Abyss in *The Dark Knight*," *The Village Voice*, 16 Jul 2008. http://www.villagevoice.com/2008-07-16/film/heath-ledger-dark-knight/; James Berardinelli, "Batman: The Dark Knight," *ReelViews*. http://www.reelviews.net/php_review_ template.php?identifier=1235

49. Many thanks to Jeff Smith for prompting this insight and for his guidance in the development of this study.

Works Cited

Ackerman, Spencer. "Batman's 'Dark Knight' Reflects Cheney Policy." *The Washington Independent*, 21 Jul 2008. http://washingtonindependent.com/509-batmans-dark-knight-reflects-cheney-policy

Acland, Charles. *Screen Traffic: Movies, Multiplexes, and Global Culture*. Durham: Duke University Press, 2003.

"Batman and Bush," *Porch Dog*, 22 Jul 2008. http://porch-dog.com/?p=418

Bennett, Tony. "Holy Shifting Signifiers: Forewords." *In The Many Lives of the Batman*, eds. Roberta E. Pearson and William Uricchio. NY: Routledge, 1991.

Berardinelli, James. "Batman: The Dark Knight." *ReelViews*. http://www.reelviews.net/php_review_ template.php?identifier=1235

Boichel, Bill. "Batman: Commodity as Myth." *Batman Unmasked: Analyzing a Cultural Icon*. Eds., Pearson and Uricchio. New York: Continuum, 2001.

Bolt, Andrew. "It's George W. Batman." *The Herald Sun*, 30 Jul 2008. http://blogs.news.com. au/heraldsun/andrewbolt/index.php/heraldsun/comments/column_its_george_w_batman/

Bordwell, David. "Superheroes for Sale," *Observations on film art and* Film Art, 16 Aug 2008. http://www.davidbordwell.net/blog/?p=2713

Boucher, Geoff. "Christopher Nolan on 'Dark Knight' and its box-office billion: 'It's mystifying to me.'" *Hero Complex, The Los Angeles Times*, 27 Oct 2008. http://latimesblogs.com/herocomplex/2008/10/christopher-nol.html

_____. "Christopher Nolan revisits and analyzes his favorite scene in 'Dark Knight.'" *Hero Complex, The Los Angeles Times*, 28 Oct 2008. http://latimesblogs.com/hero-complex/2008/10/christopher-nol-1.html

_____. "Christopher Nolan's 'Knight' Vision." *Los Angeles Times*. 6 Jul 2008

Brockman, Nathan. "The Dark Knight (of the Soul)." *Trinity Church*, 9 Sep 2008. http://trinitywallstreet.org/welcome/?article&id=1009

"Bush Isn't Batman. He's Two-Face." *American History Y?* 25 Jul 2008. http://americanhistoryy.wordpress.com/2008/07/25/bush-isnt-batman-hes-two-face/

Carey, Jesse. "This Present Darkness." *Christian Broadcasting Network*. http://www.cbn.com/entertainment/screen/carey_DarkKnight.aspx

Clover, Joshua. *The Matrix*. London: BFI Publishing, 2005.

Cohen, David S. "George Bush, The Dark Knight? Be Careful What You Wish For." *Thompson on Hollywood*, 25 Jul 2008. http://weblogs.variety.com/thompsononhollywood/2008/09/george-bush-the-.html

Corliss, Richard. "Batman is Back." *Time*, 9 Jul 2008. http://www.time.com/time/printout/0,8816,18211365,00.html

Cox, David. "Why The Dark Knight is So Dim." *Guardian.co.uk*, 28 Jul 2008. http://www.guardian.co.uk/film/2008/jul/28/dark.night/
Dargis, Manohla. "Showdown in Gotham Town." *The New York Times*, 18 Jul 2008. http://movies.nytimes.com/2008/07/18/movies/18knig.html
Fischer, Paul. "Intervew: Christopher Nolan for 'The Dark Knight.'" *Dark Horizons*, 3 Jul 2008. http://darkhorizons.com/interviews/315/christopher-nolan-for-the-dark-knight-.
Fisher, Mark."Gothic Oedipus: Subjectivity and Capitalism in Christopher Nolan's *Batman Begins*." *Image Text* 2, no. 2. Winter 2005: 11.
Fiske, John. *Television Culture*. London: Routledge, 2007.
Foundas, Scott. "Heath Ledger Peers Into The Abyss in *The Dark Knight*." *The Village Voice*, 16 Jul 2008. http://www.villagevoice.com/2008-07-16/film/heath-ledger-dark-knight/
Goldberg, Jonah. "The Gitmo Five's Burn Notice." *National Review Online*, 13 Mar 2009. http://article.nationalreview.com/?q=M2QzYTFlZTNhZDBlNzBjZGI2ZmExNzI2YTlmN DgyZTg=
Gordon, Devlin. "Bat Trick." *Newsweek*, 21 Jul 2008. http://www.newsweek.com/id/145508
Greenfield, Sayre N. "Defining Allegory: As Rhetoric, Literary Text, and Reading." *In The Ends of Allegory*. Newark: University of DE Press, 1998.
Huppert, Matt. "'The Dark Knight' and the '9/11 Allegory' Fallacy." *Matt's Truthonomics*, 21 Jul 2008. http:/mattstruthonomics.blogspot.com/2008/07/dark-knight-and-911-allegory-fallacy.html
Klavan, Andrew. "What Bush and Batman Have in Common." *Wall Street Journal* 25 Jul 2008.
Maltby, Richard. "'A Brief Romantic Interlude': Dick and Jane Go to 31/2 Seconds of the Classical Hollywood Cinema." *In Post-Theory: Reconstructing Film Studies*, eds. David Newman, Kim. "Cape Fear," *Sight & Sound* 15, no. 7, July 2005.
Orr, Christopher. "The Movie Review: 'The Dark Knight.'" *The New Republic*, 17 Jul 2008. http://www.tnr.com/politics/story.html?id=757af21c-1026-44f3-918b-ea35b135e350
Puig, Claudia. "Ledger's talent lives on as The Joker in 'Dark Knight.'" *USA Today*, 1 Aug 2008. http://www.usatoday.com/life/movies/reviews/2008-07-16-dark-knight-review_N.htm
Saval, Nikil. "Review: *The Dark Knight*." *n+1*, 6 Aug 2008. http://www.nplusonemag.com/dark-knight
Schatz, Thomas. "The New Hollywood." *Movie Blockbusters*. Ed. Julian Stringer. London: Routledge, 2003.
Scott, A.O. "Everybody's a Critic of the Critics' Rabid Critics." *The New York Times*, 25 July 2010
Sexton, John. "More on Bush the Dark Knight." *Verum Serum*, 4 Aug 2008. http://verumserum.com/?p=2198
Sharrett, Christopher. "Batman and the Twilight of the Idols: An Interview with Frank Miller." *Batman Unmasked: Analyzing a Cultural Icon*. Eds., Pearson and Uricchio. New York: Continuum, 2001.
Smith, Murray. *Engaging Characters: Fiction, Emotion, and the Cinema*. NY: Oxford University Press, 1995.

Uricchio, William and Roberta E. Pearson. "I'm Not Fooled by That Cheap Disguise." *In Batman Unmasked: Analyzing a Cultural Icon*. Eds., Pearson and Uricchio. New York: Continuum, 2001.

Vasey, Ruth. *The World According to Hollywood, 1918–1939*. Madison: University of WI Press, 1997.

Von Doviak, Scott. "Why So Serious? The Dark Knight in the Political World." *The Screengrab*, 31 Jul 2008. http://www.nerve.com/CS/blogs/screengrab/archive/2008/07/31/why-so-serious-the-dark-knight-in-the-political-world.aspx Find others.

Walsh, David. "*The Dark Knight*: Striving to be impressive, but essentially empty," *World Socialist Web Site*, 25 Jul 2008. http://www.wsws.org/articles/2008/jul 2008/dark-j25.shtml

Yglesias, Matthew. "*Dark Knight* Politics." *The Atlantic.com*, 24 Jul 2008. http://matthewyglesias.theatlantic.com/archives/2008/07/dark_knight_politics.php//

Whitman, Jon. "The Allegorical Problem." *In Allegory: The Dynamics of an Ancient and Medieval Technique*. Bridgewater, NJ: Replica Books, 1999.

10

Rolling the Boulder in Gotham

RANDY DUNCAN

In a 1989 tale written by Neil Gaiman, the Riddler asks "When is a man a city? When it's Batman or when it's Gotham. I'd take either answer. Batman is this city." Batman scribes of the past four decades have woven, on both page and screen, a powerful "symbiotic relationship" between the dark knight and his city (Uricchio and Pearson 187). Batman and Gotham City, as they have come to be understood by contemporary audiences, are inseparable concepts.

Jeffery Malpas believes implacement is an ontological condition of experience, and "the nature and identity of individual persons in particular, is to be understood only in relation to place, and in relation to the particular places in which the subject is embedded" (174). Robert Park claims that while "the small community often tolerates eccentricity, the city, on the contrary, rewards it" (126). Park goes on to say that because of the opportunity the great city offers to "the exceptional and abnormal types of man," the city "shows, the good and evil in human nature in excess" (130). Park was not describing Batman's Gotham City, but he could have been.

Evolution of Gotham

Gotham City and Batman were created in an environment of fear in 1939. The country was still coming out of the Depression, war was spreading across Europe and although many of the high profile gangsters were dead or in prison they had left entrenched criminal organizations in their wake. In America's cities, increasing urbanization was creating more slums, gang violence and political corruption. This reality began seeping into the early Batman tales and, after a couple of installments of generic backdrops, the cityscape became increasingly gothic and threatening. Of course, it was not yet Gotham City.

In Batman's first few appearances the city he protected was clearly identified as New York, but "Bob Kane envisioned his version of New York as a maze of concrete canyons where the full moon cast black shadows behind a man with a cloak" (Daniels *DC* 38). Ironically, by the time the name Gotham City was first used (*Batman* # 4, Winter 1940) the dark, foreboding atmosphere of the early stories was being lightened considerably with the introduction of Batman's sidekick, Robin, the Boy Wonder (*Detective Comics* # 38, April, 1940).

The addition of the colorful sidekick brought Batman more in line with the publisher's mindset that they were producing comic books for eleven year-old boys. For most of the 40s, 50s and 60s Gotham, with its huge props and elaborate traps, was a playground for two chums zipping around town in cool vehicles and having exciting adventures. Batman himself went through decades of being by turns generic, silly, or campy.

Beginning in the late 1960s, the staid DC bullpen was reinvigorated by an influx of young talent. With creative teams such as Denny O'Neil and Neal Adams in the early 70s and Steve Englehart and Marshall Rogers in the late 70s the Gotham that had been hinted at in the artwork of those early Batman tales began to emerge. This 1971 description from a Len Wein story is typical of the new tone: "After midnight — among the savage streets of the jungle known as Gotham — where two-legged animals find themselves cornered by the masked hunter of men they call ... The Batman." Yet, even as both Batman and his city were being redefined, the more intense, clench-jawed Batman of the 1970s was spending a good bit of his time outside Gotham. He had adventures in Spain (*Detective Comics* # 404, 1970), India (*Batman* # 232, 1971), a backwater bay south of Gotham (*Batman* # 234, 1971), Vermont (*Batman* # 237, 1971), Las Vegas (*Detective Comics* # 429, 1972), and even took ghetto kids on a camping trip (*Batman* # 250, 1973). In the decades since, Gotham City has become increasingly integral to the Batman mythos. While he might travel the globe or even the cosmos with the Justice League, the Batman presented in the core titles (*Batman* and *Detective Comics*) of recent decades is loath to venture outside the Gotham City limits.

These changes in Batman were only known to a handful of comic book fans until Frank Miller's immensely popular *Batman: The Dark Knight Returns* (1986) not only boosted slumping sales for other Batman titles, but, along with the Tim Burton film that followed a few years later, thrust a new image of Batman into the public consciousness. In the introduction to the trade paperback, Alan Moore describes Miller's Gotham City as "A dark and unfriendly city in decay, populated by rabid and sociopathic street gangs." In the wake of *Dark Knight Returns* and Moore's own dystopian superhero epic, *Watchmen*, Gotham City not only continued to become darker and more dangerous, but was often referred to as "rotten" or "diseased."

In Miller's "Batman: Year One" story arc young police detective James Gordon, on the train to Gotham City to take a job there, muses it is probably best for his wife to travel to the city by airplane because it might "Fool you into thinking it's civilized." Once he has arrived in Gotham, he hopes his wife is not pregnant because "This is no place to raise a family." By the late 1980s the degenerate nature of Gotham City is established firmly enough that the Sam Hamm and Warren Skaaren screenplay for *Batman* (1989) describes the city as "stark angles, creeping shadows, dense, crowded, airless, a random tangle of steel and concrete, as if Hell had erupted through the sidewalk and kept on growing" (Hamm and Skaaren qtd. In Daniels *Batman* 164). In Warren Ellis' *Planetary/Batman: Night on Earth* (2004) crossover story as the Planetary team arrive in Gotham one of the characters describes the city as "...originally designed by English Masons on Opium, exacerbated by absinthe-fiend local architects in the twenties, basically not suitable for human habitation" Reviewer Shave Rivers believes *Batman Begins* (2005) presents "a Gotham City that's oozing darkness and corruption from its every pore" where we "get the sense that the citizens of the city are close to collapsing under the weight of urban decay."

Batman's Gotham City is even more starkly dismal in contrast to Superman's Metropolis. While Metropolis is a city of towering structures and bird's-eye views, "Gotham is a city defined more by its underworld. It's hidden spaces, corners, and traps. The city needs to be read, deciphered, made legible, and the one to do it lives among the bats in his own subterranean hideout" (Bukatman, 203). Batman is such a creature of Gotham that he does not feel comfortable in Superman's gleaming city: "Metropolis." He muses on a reluctant visit, "It is very different from Gotham City and for that alone ... I try to avoid coming here" (Loeb *Beast*). Criminal justice scholars Vollum and Adkinson observe that "In a way, Metropolis and Gotham City represent the dichotomous nature of the great American city"— Metropolis proclaims that cities offer "hope, order, and the American dream" while Gotham reminds us that cities also offer "threatening despair, danger, and anarchy" (99). Metropolis is rooted in a modernist, utopian worldview, reminiscent of the optimism of the 1939 World's Fair World of Tomorrow. Gotham has been portrayed as postmodern and dystopian.

Gotham has become more than simply a dangerous city. Gotham "is a nightmare, a distorted metropolis that corrupts the souls of good men" (Stamp). Kate Spencer has moved to Gotham to become the new District Attorney. In her identity as the superhero Manhunter she perches on one of the city's many gargoyles, in the midst of a gray downpour, and thinks "Usually rain washes a city. The smog, the smells, the accumulated grime all runs down the gutters and away. But Gotham isn't your usual city now, is it? All the rain does here is make the city bathe in a stew of its own filth. What have I gotten myself into?" (Andreyko). It seems everything about Gotham, even the rain, is dark, twisted, even ... hellish.

Gotham Makes Batman

In a dark alley a criminal hears the disembodied voice: "Gotham City is Hell. We are all in Hell." Then Batman makes his dramatic appearance in the alley to declare "And I am the King of Hell!" (Morrison *Gothic*). "Perhaps more than any other person — real or fictional — Batman is integrally linked to his city" (Stamp). There is a strong, mythic connection between the two.

Most city's grew up around a ritual site where animals and humans were sacrificed to the gods and people returned "year after year to dance and to sing on the blood soaked ground" (Erickson 38). Erickson points out that "As the urban center grew it never lost traces of this history. The city is built on the blood of our rituals and their victims. We remember, fundamentally from deep down inside of us, that violence and the city go together" (39).

The Batman himself is spawned from the blood-stained pavement of Crime Alley. Writer Jeph Loeb relates the familiar origin tale in the "Hush" story arc: "That very night, on the street stained with his mother and father's blood, he would make a vow to rid the city of the evil that had taken their lives" (*Legend*)

Mirroring Jesus, who is "the blood sacrifice to end all blood sacrifices," Bruce Wayne is the victim who refuses to be a victim. Erickson describes the ideal Christian response to urban violence: "When we see life threatened, we are to enter into violence as if we were angels sent by God with messages of peace. We are to exchange our lives for that of the threatened other (39). Thus, Bruce Wayne becomes Batman, a savior who will not himself take life and who strives to end the blood sacrifices of violent crime. Perhaps few, if any, Batman writers have consciously applied a Christian ethos to the Batman mythos, but most have portrayed him as avenging angel or a "local saint" dedicated to "To protect. To defend. To guard" Gotham City (Dixon).

Batman as Gotham's Protector

"As the house has its household gods," explains Oswald Spengler, "so has the city its protecting Deity, its local saint" (qtd. in Park 91). Batman is not merely a crime fighter. He is a bulwark against darkness and chaos. In one of many failed attempts to break him Batman is subjected to a nightmare of Gotham in ruins, in flames, with unrestrained violence in the streets. Batman interprets it as "Gotham without The Batman. Chaos. Anarchy. Lack of order." (Talbot).

However, Batman has long been depicted as more than simply a defender. He routinely claims dominion over the city, referring to "my streets" and "my city." In *The Dark Knight Returns*, when Batman defeats the leader of the Mutants, a violent youth gang that has been terrorizing the city, most of the gangsters begin painting a bat symbol on their faces and calling themselves The Sons of Batman. One of the gang members declares to a reporter: "Gotham City belongs to The Batman." (Miller *Dark Knight Returns*). Later in the book, when an electromagnetic pulse plunges Gotham into darkness and chaos, Batman forges the Sons of Batman into an army and tells them "Tonight, we are the law. Tonight, I am the law." The first issue of the new title *Batman: Legends of the Dark Knight* (1989) relates another version of Bruce Wayne's first outing in the Batman costume. After subduing a group of muggers he slams the only one left conscious against the wall and growls "Tell them the streets belong to The Batman" (O'Neil). A 1992 Bryan Talbot story opens with Batman perched on a gargoyle looking out over the city, and his narration tells us "This is my city. At night it belongs to me." (Talbot *Mask, Part One*).

In Gotham, despite its protector, the night is never without its terrors. In reestablishing the Batman character for *Detective Comics* # 0 in 1994, writer Chuck Dixon declares the dark knight's mission is "To stand against the gathering darkness that threatens to wash over Gotham like a poisonous tide." Yet, the very existence of the Batman seems to be a force that pulls that chaotic tide to Gotham's shore.

Batman and Gotham: Who Made Who

Like Batman, the bizarre criminals he fights are "products of Gotham," seemingly "formed from the bowels of the city" (Vollum and Adkinson 100; 104). Perhaps the aspect of Gotham City most responsible for producing madmen is the presence of the Batman.

While Miller presents the Dr. Wolper character in *The Dark Knight Returns* as generally contemptible, perhaps he intends to embed a truth in the psychobabble when he has the doctor explain "Batman's psychotic sublimate/psycho-erotic behavior pattern is like a net: weak-egoed neurotics, like Harvey, are drawn into corresponding intersecting [sic] patterns." Even Batman's friend Commissioner Gordon implies a cause-effect relationship when he refers to Gotham's costumed villains as "**his** people" (Dini, "Ignition"). At the end of *Batman Begins* Gordon worries that Batman's existence could cause escalation. "You're wearing a mask and jumping off rooftops ... take this guy." Holding out a joker playing card he says "A taste for the theatrical, like you." These few sentences foreshadow both the coming flood of weird menaces that will plague Gotham and the fact that Batman share something in common with his foes.

Batman not only contends with the rising tide of supervillains who threaten Gotham, but he wages an internal battle as well. The outwardly confident and uber-competent Batman is inwardly battling his fear. He conquers his childhood fear of bats by becoming what he fears. The fear created that night he saw his parents murdered is turned back on the criminal element of Gotham by becoming a creature that strikes fear into their cowardly hearts. He is plagued by the fear of being like those he fights. In *The Dark Knight Returns* Batman confronts a Harvey Dent whose handsome face has been surgically restored. Batman sees him "as he is"; he perceives the hideously half-scarred visage of Harvey's Two-Face persona. And he sees something else. Looking at Dent, Batman says "I see ... a reflection, Harvey." This is followed by a panel of a close-up of a demonic bat face. Batman sees the demon still within Harvey Dent as reminder of the demon within himself. Perhaps The Batman's greatest fear is of succumbing to that demon, to the madness.

Batman repeatedly confronts and overcomes madness. In the 1989 graphic novel *Arkham Asylum* he stares into his own personal abyss and come back from the edge with his shattered psyche integrated and proves that he is "Stronger than them. Stronger than this place" (Morrison *Arkham*). In the 1992 story "Mask" Bruce Wayne is held captive in a mental institution, pumped full of hallucinogens and made to question the sanity of being the Batman. In the end he emerges unbroken and with his resolve strengthened: "I will not falter again. I am the Batman." (Talbot *Mask, Part Two*).

In the on-going Batman saga fighting crime is still the primary activity, but it is no longer the point of the story. The film *The Dark Knight* (2008) presents the struggle between Batman and the Joker as a battle for the soul of the city. The comic books of the past 25 years have a slightly different subtext. The final words of the Planetary/Batman: Night on Earth story — "Told you. This town is insane."— are not only a comment on the nature of Gotham City, but a clue to the true nature of the war the Batman wages in Gotham. Since that instant when his orderly world was shattered by the senseless murder of his parents Bruce Wayne has struggled to force his world make sense once again. Uricchio and Pearson describe the perpetual struggle between Batman and his arch-nemesis as "the Batman striving to impose order on an unjust universe and the Joker doing his best to enhance the chaos of a meaningless world" (198). During their final confrontation in *The Killing Joke* the Joker rails at Batman: "You had a bad day, and it drove you as crazy as everybody else ... only you won't admit it! You have to keep pretending that life makes sense, that there's some point to all this struggling!" (Moore *Killing*). Of course, one of the most potent elements of the Batman mythos is that he will always continue to struggle. On the final page of *The Dark Knight Returns* an elderly Bruce Wayne is forging reformed gang-bangers into "an army ... to bring sense to a world plagued by worse than thieves and murderers."

Conclusion

Batman was almost immediately iconic at a primitive level, however, it took decades for Batman to become a fully intellectualized icon because he operated in a void. He fought his battles in a city with a name, but with no sense of place, no soul. Until he inhabited a place that had its own identity, Batman was a floating signifier. Batman became more fully defined only as Gotham City became more fully defined. Batman "is a true avatar of Gotham" and "Gotham City itself is an avatar ... of our collective urban paranoia" (Stamp). Gotham City manifests a postmodern dystopia. With its twisted architecture and twisted villains, Gotham is anti-rational. Bruce Wayne becomes the world's greatest detective to make sense of the senselessness of Gotham.

Of course his world will never make sense. Batman stories must have conflict. Jokers, riddlers and scarecrows will continue to bedevil the denizens of Gotham. Batman's very presence makes Gotham less safe; he attracts bizarre nemeses, he attracts violence. The superhero Manhunter has been in Gotham City for less than a month when she realizes what it is like to wage war on crime in Gotham: "What's that myth? Sisyphus? He should be the patron saint of this town" (Andreyko). As the patron saint of the perpetually chaotic Gotham City Batman is fighting a losing, or at least futile battle. We admire Batman not because he wins, but because he will not give up, he will not be broken.

Works Cited

Andreyko, Maac, script. "Strange Bedfellows." *Batman: Streets of Gotham # 1* New York, DC Comics, 2009.
Brooker, Will. *Batman Unmasked: Analyzing a Cultural Icon.* London: Continuum, 2000.
Bukatman, Scott. *Matters of Gravity.* Durham: Duke University Press, 2003.
Burton, Tim, director. *Batman.* Warner Brothers, 1989.
Daniels, Les. *DC Comics: Sixty Years of the World's Favorite Comic Book Heroes.* Boston: Little, Brown, and Company, 1995.
_____. *Batman: The Complete History.* San Francisco: Chronicle Books, 2004.
Dini, Paul. "Ignition." *Batman: Streets of Gotham # 1* New York: DC Comics, 2009.
Dixon, Chuck, script. "Choice of Weapons." *Detective Comics # 0* New York: DC Comics, 1994.
Ellis, Warren, script. "Planetary/Batman: Night on Earth." *Planetary: Crossing Worlds* New York: DC Comics, 2004.
Erickson, Victoria Lee. "On the Town with Georg Simmel: A Socio-Religious Understanding of Urban Interaction." *Cross Currents* 51.1 (2001): 21–45.
Gaiman, Neil, script. "When is a Door? The Secret Origin of the Riddler." *Secret Origins Special # 1* New York: DC Comics, 1989.
Loeb, Jeph, script. "The Legend of the Batman: Who He is and How He Came to Be." *Batman # 608* New York, DC Comics, 2002.
_____, script. "The Beast." *Batman # 610* New York, DC Comics, 2002.
Malpas, Jeffery E. *Place and Experience: A Philosophical Topography.* Cambridge: Cambridge University Press, 1999.
Miller, Frank. *Batman: The Dark Knight Returns.* trade New York: DC Comics, 1986.
_____, script. "Batman Year One: Who I am. How I came to Be." *Batman # 404* New York: DC Comics, 1987.
Moore, Alan. "The Mark of the Batman: An Introduction." *Batman: The Dark Knight Returns* by Frank Miller New York: DC Comics, 1986.
_____, script. *The Killing Joke.* New York: DC Comics, 1988.
Morrison, Grant. *Batman: Arkham Asylum.* New York: DC Comics, 1989.
_____. "Gothic, A Romance, volume one." *Batman: Legends of the Dark Knight # 6.* New York: DC Comics, April 1990.
Nolan, Christopher, director. *Batman Begins.* Warner Brothers, 2005.
_____. *The Dark Knight.* Warner Brothers, 2008.
O'Neil, Dennis. "Shaman." *Batman: Legends of the Dark Knight # 1* New York: DC Comics, 1989.
Park, Robert. "The City: Suggestions for the Investigation of Human Behavior in the Urban Environment." *Classic Essays on the Culture of Cities.* ed. Richard Sennett New York: Appleton-Century-Crofts, 1969.
Rivers, Shane. "Review: Batman Begins." *A1 Movie Reviews* October12, 2009.
Spengler, Oswald. "The Soul of the City." *Classic Essays on the Culture of Cities.* ed. Richard Sennett New York: Appleton-Century-Crofts, 1969.
Stamp, Jimmy. "On Influence: Batman, Gotham City, and an Overzealous Architecture Historian With a Working Knowledge of Explosives." *Life Without Buildings* June 1, 2009 August 12, 2009. http://lifewithoutbuildings.net/2009/06/on-

influence-batman-gotham-city-and-an-overzealous-architecture-historian-with-a-working-knowledge-of-explosives.html

Talbot, Bryan. "Mask, Part One." *Batman: Legends of the Dark Knight # 39*. New York: DC Comics, November 1992.

_____. "Mask, Part Two." *Batman: Legends of the Dark Knight # 40*. New York: DC Comics, November 1992.

Uricchio, William, and Roberta E. Pearson. "I'm Not Fooled by that Cheap Disguise." *The Many Lives of the Batman*. Roberta E. Pearson and William Uricchio, eds London: Routledge, 1991.

Vollum, Scott, and Cary D. Adkinson. "The Portrayal of Crime and Justice in the Comic Book Superhero Mythos." *Journal of Criminal Justice and Popular Culture* 10.2 (2003): 96–108.

Wein, Len, script. *World's Finest Comics # 207* New York: DC Comics, 1971.

11

Figuration of the Superheroic Revolutionary
The Dark Knight of Negation

D.T. KOFOED

In the field of Comics Studies, such as it is, Miller, Jansen, and Varley's *Batman: The Dark Knight Returns* doubtless occupies a foundational spot in the canon, if we grant the very notion of a textual canon any validity. Frank Miller and Lynn Varley's 2001–2 sequel series *Batman: the Dark Knight Strikes Again* has received surprisingly scant critical attention in comparison to its groundbreaking predecessor. Though this trend of silent dismissal and damnation by faint praise is reversing of late, the existing scholarship tends to limit itself to the level of a strictly narrative-textual analysis on the superhero as revolutionary figure within vari-topian realms, depending on the reading (see Murphy's "Gotham (K)Nights"). Not only does this brand of criticism deny the comic its status as graphic narrative, it also devalues its own observations, for the revolutionary icon presented here arises as such through its graphic depiction. The larger popular reaction against *Strikes Again* stems from its very comparison to *Dark Knight Returns*, from the marked increase in Miller's already rampant cultural cynicism and the radical refinement of his visual semantics. As *Returns'* narrative of ideological contestation was based upon and performed through the formalism of an orthogonal page layout and its rupture, emphasizing the television screen as panel — as I've argued elsewhere, Batman's bodily transgression of the rigid panel border positions his iconic figure beyond the influence of that classic ideological apparatus — *Strikes Again* eschews any obviously structured page space. Even figuration is minimal, throwing narrative and graphic emphasis into the negative, liminal spaces of the page, where color signifies in excess and in place of the line art's representational rendering. Characters appear within this negative background space, and in turn are rendered wholly subaltern by Varley's colors, occupying and assuming this space even in the foreground as figuration melds into the scenic frame. The distinction between the media's gaze and the world addressed is effaced in a hybrid landscape within which ideology as traditionally conceived has no place. Combined with Miller's dismissal of petty criminal foils from the plot, Batman's only action in this visual and cultural landscape is that of outright militant revolution against the governmental and social order — the empire of supervillainy. The superheroic icon as liminal subject, and proxy slave, of state tyranny cannot be other than a revolutionary figure, the media image of a politically blank revolutionist.

I cannot long avoid treating the most obvious objection to be raised against my appropriation of terms from Postcolonial studies in the explication of a contemporary mainstream American cultural artifact. Neither Frank Miller's work, nor the general publications of DC Comics, in any way represent a diasporic or marginalized literature. Regardless, a character analysis of the kind thus engaged in must operate from an assumed position within the fictive realm of the text. Cardinal directions, or numbering the world according to its development, are equally performative and ultimately empty shorthand for theories and relations that proceed regardless of one's nomenclature of exclusion. In-between the borders, the liminal space as a conceptual form in contemporary theory, rather than political reality, appears wherever great inequity is evident in a power relationship. The evil empire of Lex Luther's America in *The Dark Knight Strikes Again* is a pure distillation of global inequity while also representing a colonial power in its own right, achieving peace through having "killed just about everyone who disagrees with us!" (16).

In this case of villainous globalization and all its attendant real world contradictions, I am concerned with what Stuart Hall calls the "terrains in between, little interstices, the smaller spaces within which [characters] have to work ... [where] marginality has become a powerful space" (183). The literally representative nature of comics' line art renders — in both senses — the very concept of a subaltern subject with seemingly impossible significance. This figure of the subaltern subject proves uncannily apt, both graphically and narratively, for Miller's work. As Gayatri Spivak famously narrates the process of scholars' first appropriation of the term from centuries of military custom, the "Subaltern Studies" group's impetus to incorporate nationalist insurgencies into historiography ironically allowed "subaltern" to refer to a revolutionary elite, before it assumed the populist connotations now believed to exhaust its reference (78–80). Indeed, as colonial power differentials reduce the subaltern subject to a "shadow," Miller and Varley's emphasis on negative, background space reinforces this signification, for the graphic shadow typically falls behind and is obscured by the foregrounded object in view (Spivak 83). The vestigial elitism of the subaltern is equally informative to my deployment of the term, as it has been generations since any superhero could be genuinely considered a pure figure of populist myth. These catachrestic heroes of the Dark Knight arc begin each series constrained by governmental/media populist/oligarchical forces; while *DKR*'s restrained narrative looked to a mere quartet of anti-heroes, the sequel vigorously effuses obscure references to and appearances from a *melange* of figures either suppressed by the fictive government or ignored by the author—depending on the reader's preference.

While a comparison of Miller's two Dark Knights is useful, it is all too easy to describe the latter work as merely a series of negative absences from the earlier. Miller's line art in *DKSA*, intentionally rough and at times quite ugly, evinces a punk rock aesthetic that seemingly begs disgust from the reader; yet this is nothing new for Miller the draughtsman, marking but the stronger delineation of a personal style refined through the decades since *DKR* in such notable work as the various *Sin City* series. The severing of figuration from setting, through line art devoid of illustrated backgrounds, has developed into the stereotypical hallmark of Miller's compositional rhetoric. Exaggerated proportions in the rendered human body signify reciprocally with the scene— consider the infamous feet that overtly mark the lack of a rendered groundline, which the lack itself redoubles an emphasis upon their own Sasquatch sensibility—such that the design of bodily figuration frequently stands in for setting. This creation of an embodied scene will be explored further with respect to Miller's use of negative spaces. More central to the aesthetic of *DKSA* than character design is a privileged iconic positionality, by which a series of static poses preempt any implication of a narrative motion. The story as such is not dependent upon the progression of bodies through space, the medium's typical simulation of motion across and between panels, but rather rests it narration upon the very presence of bodies in a consequently heightened space. This figural composition, freed from concerns of continuity and relation to the conventions of scene, allows Miller free rein to illustrate a prolonged series of pin-ups—over-articulated poses whose significations draw upon the entire graphic tradition of the superhero genre rather than any specific narrative sequence, a visceral aesthetic quality. The plot relies on the reader's capacity for such instant iconic recognition, as characterization is largely an effect of this graphic iconography, or rather, iconic topography: Captain Marvel's role is simply to be present as the image of himself. While the compositional importance of color is central to this consideration of Miller's characterizations, his employment of Varley as colorist is best discussed with reference to the more general formal mechanics of the page layout.

Despite my prior caveat, a comparison between the opening pages of *DKR* and *DKSA* immediately emphasizes the differing structural and artistic conventions at work, yet the role of these initial spreads is identical in detailing the formal concerns of their respective works as a whole — Miller is literally up-front regarding his narrative system. *DKR* establishes in two pages the rigid grid of the multiframe (to borrow my critical terminology from Groensteen) which composes larger panels by simple addition of these constituent units, along with the uniquely differentiated frame of the television screen, an interpellative apparatus of the narrative. *DKSA* extends its schematic introduction over three pages, establishing a fluid layout which remains wholly variable both in panel dimensions and panel count, unified through the negative space depiction of the hero, a dissected icon of absence. On opening to the textual cacophony of that first page, one might not recognize Batman in the almost completely black background, until a turn of the page reveals the move obvious background figurations of his profile and fist (15–7). The static grid has here devolved into a mutable articulation of panels within a splash page aesthetic, presenting an ambiguous multiple simultaneity of happenings without recourse to a central event. The lack of distinct frames presents an equal rhetorical tone to each panel instance, irredeemably blurring the boundary between the in-person reality and its media exposure — the television has disappeared, dissolved into the fabric of a reality from which it is inseparable.

Jimmy Olsen personifies the hazard of this narrative system, as he cannot be definitively accredited with either the role of screaming bystander or media commentator; only his directed address towards the reader is certain. Yet this seeming interpellative move on behalf of the narrative is undercut by the character's varying eye line and the lack of any structural support for the panel frame that would reinforce a reading of electronic transmission. These panels occupy a middle position that is never fully either end of the media's transmission system, a liminal space of uncertainty, without meaning. The ideology of political consumerism in Miller's fiction is in flux: structurally ambiguous paneling juxtaposes news, commercials, and commentary with the piecemeal outline of his hero as hyperframe border of containment. Throughout, the focus of the multiframe lies behind these panels, suffusing and privileging the negative space of the composition as its site of signification, the voice and figuration of, to borrow a phrase from Scott McCloud, "blood in the gutter" (see Chapter 3). Surely Miller's Dark Knight, occupant of this heightened subordination, would approve of the moniker. Despite the accidental militancy evoked by this phrase, it is sufficient to note the primacy of the background space among the formal aspects of the text, which figuration will be more fully grasped following some discussion of Varley's contribution to the *mise-en-page*.

The coloring in *DKSA* is the two-ton hot-pink-striped-Photoshop-filtered elephant hovering in the back of any discussion on the comic. Outside the received constraints of the heroes' costumes, the governing aesthetic regarding human figures is clearly non-representational. Rather than merely decorate the existing line art, Varley's colors are compositional in the strict sense, drafting the layout with renderings that often replace traditional illustration. Color signifies, and it carries the narrative. Most obvious is its affective quality, by which depictions of great violence are given to visible pixelation; at other instances, color striations centralize similar effects around figures of agency, exemplified by Superman's cathartic destruction of a planet-destroying asteroid (66). Indeed, Superman frequently embodies these effects of the coloring's emotional indication. The bookends of his character arc — defeat at Batman's hands and the final assumption of his power over humans — present Varley's most heavily pixelated images, which oppositionally double, and challenge, the representation of the line art (80–9, 221). As he streaks towards Batman's cave, Miller illustrates Superman's cape as an aerodynamic streamlined shape falling straight along his back, which Varley emphasizes with a sweeping conglomeration of color blocks reminiscent of flame which flow around and beyond the depicted form — the narrative rage of Superman's character is given graphic figuration despite his staid, traditional illustration (80). This convention, once established in the narrative, is extended for the delineation of fundamental character in the villain Brainiac: its eyes are composed of similar pixelated blocks with their effective association of violence, which the character gleefully fulfills (140–2, 150–64, 223–4, 234).

Miller and Varley are not content with the use of color as mere accent on effect. Elsewhere and often, the coloration is no longer subordinate to the containment of line borders it physically exceeds, a literal boundary-blurring visible throughout the majority of pages — witness Laura's climactic defeat of Brainiac (234–7). Batman, who surprisingly appears on the page less often than the rest of Miller's heroic menagerie, is unique in that his coloration remains muted and flat throughout an otherwise kaleidoscopic work; the simple over-representation of the black in his cape and cowl compresses his figure into an overtly two-dimensional space, operating behind the illusory third dimension of the action. Beyond accentuating scenic affect, the coloration is itself figural, composing bodies and space. Wonder Woman's wielding of Zeus' lighting bolt is a minor, distinct exemplar of Miller's compositional reliance on color as the extension of line (152–3). Traditionally illustrated backgrounds are almost wholly absent in favor of color fields, evident as complex structured spaces in their own right, while Braniac is at times wholly absent from Miller's original penciling — a creature of pure color. Most evident in the frequent splash pages, where the line art occupies a dramatically smaller portion of the page space — the abstract city behind Catgirl's escape with the Atom (31), the spiral destruction of the Flash's rescue (58–60), Superman and Wonder Woman's flying sex scene (118–122), Batman's public unveiling (168–9), and the devastation of Metropolis (190–1) are easily recognizable instances — the construction of scene by color extends throughout the text as an equal part and partner to the artistic design.

Emphasis is repeatedly pressed upon the background, the negative space of the page, and its panels. As the often garish color draws attention from the overtly dramatized poses of the foreground figures, Varley's work assumes its primary function as site of the reader's affective response, the barometer of the comic's emotional register. In addition to this signposting by the color, the turning of the reader's gaze, Varley frequently seeks to wholly dissolve the line art figures into their surrounding panels. In rendering characters as indistinguishable from her intricately composed negative spaces, the very division between figure and scene is revealed as an arbitrary and inconsequential categorization — the subaltern hero is the background space personified, whose agency is constituted as limited. Though numerous examples of this prevalent technique are available, I will highlight a few of the most literal, where the illustrated figure is colored over with the background, saving to mention in another context the depiction of characters as and in the background space. The opening action paints Catgirl into the wall behind her, temporarily ignoring the animal print usually depicted as part of her costume (28); in his nocturnal wanderings, the Question exactly matches the lighting and shadow of his rooftop surroundings (46); while surveying the ruins of Metropolis, Wonder Woman is depicted with both the color and texture of the ashes of desolation (176–81). To appropriate an archaism, Varley has limned Miller's figures to be liminal.

This composition of negative space that positively signifies to the characterization, through the colors, offers a challenge to theoreticians of the comics medium, which I have no pretension of answering with these few initial observations. A provocative corollary can nonetheless be teased from the beginning of Homi K. Bhabha's extended argument on the inherent and constitutive liminal marginalia of the modern nation, "DissemiNation," through his recounted anecdote from Bakhtin: "the recurrent metaphor of landscape as the inscape of national identity emphasizes the quality of light [and] the power of the eye" (143). The corollary for light in the graphic identity of *DKSA* is Varley's coloring, both in the literal sense of the physical properties by which the eye perceives color and the artistic replication and depiction of colors, as well as in the figurative associations that the coloring creates in this particular body of work. The proposed visual composition of national identity is mirrored in the distinctions of color which construct the icon and the varied permutations of its fictive world. Both landscapes are highly saturated.

As seen from the first pages of *DKSA*, the negative space is not empty, but the domain of the superheroic icon. Batman occupies — is — the literal and figurative background of the first book, appearing in person only for the final three pages, a distantly articulated echo of the first three, both iterations culminating with his exaggerated fist. Bhabha here reminds us, through Heidegger, that "the boundary becomes the place from which *something begins its presencing*" (5). Having already deconstructed the icon of the hero in *DKR*, Miller's Batman is initially an empty silhouette, a framing device for introducing an ambiguous media effect: note that the panels throughout the initial sequence are entirely bordered by the backdrop of Batman, whose voice graphically resides outside the public discourse. This is the liminal space to which the heroes have been pushed, their relation to the cynical politics of a democratic totalitarianism. The scene immediately cuts to Ray Palmer in the literally liminal realm of a petri dish, on a scale detectable only by microscopes, comparable to Hal Jordan's existence in some quark realm (18–24, 173–6). Superman's introduction to the narrative echoes that of Batman, a framing silhouette that doesn't delay the gratification of his full figuration in the pages immediately following (34–8). Yet the simplistic regime of the evil empire in *DKSA* does not allow for the ideological contestation of heroic titans that formed the core of *DKR*, such that the almost immediate public return of the heroes becomes little more than a note in the larger mediascape, the purported revolution limited to a select cadre of heroes already positioned outside society and politics. Miller's America in *DKSA* is a world-colonizing totality, overseen by supervillains, which has physically enslaved some heroes, co-opted others into collaboration, and dismissed all public discourse as inconsequential noise. As per the accepted connotation of the resulting heroic liminal space as that in-between state, a "process of symbolic interaction" which is ultimately constructive by definition, this second Dark Knight might reasonably evoke some anticipation for a third act, socially constitutive resurrection of the icon (Bhabha 4). Upon the heroes' reemergence, however, the citizenry has no framework within which to conceive the position of the superhero, considering a pop music act in costume as equivalent to the Last Son of Krypton and demanding "better service than this" when Metropolis is razed to ashes (150). Narration and figuration diverge: graphically liminal icons of revolution subsist in a fiction whose own logic rejects them. The subaltern hero presented here is thus further removed from cultural and political relevance than that resulting from the modernist Deconstruction of the icon in Miller's previous work.

The Dark Knight Returns famously ends with a truce between the defeated Superman and the resurgent Batman, a temporary reprieve and resumption of the status quo, a truce inevitably broken at the onset of *Strikes Again*. The unresolved dialectic between Statist and Militant forces encapsulated by Batman and Superman's climactic battle in *DKR* would seem to finally be brought to synthesis here in the character of Laura, the daughter of Superman who willingly completes Batman's war against "a world plagued by worse than thieves and murderers" at her father's behest (*DKR* 199). While this dialectic was previously enabled through the identification of the heroes as ideological proxies, Miller's dramatically different approach to the worlding of *DKSA* renders any such ideological framework irrelevant. The dialectic cannot resolve in the sequel, for it no longer exists. With editorial free rein of DC continuity, Miller has rejected the reality-inflected political dimensions of *DKR* to create instead a classic superhero/supervillain conflict. While not denying Miller his frequent satirical jests within *DKSA*, these heroes are not in retreat from political defeat and the loss of public opinion, but have simply lost their fight against the supervillains, who now control the world, having finally achieved their master plan. The co-opted heroes remaining in the world of *DKSA* naively wait for, as Wonder Woman asserts, "just one slender chance. That's all we've ever needed. In all our adventures. Over all the years" (114).

Despite appearances — the unprecedented visual style, the nods to contemporary politics and internet culture — the plot has stepped back from the high modernist aesthetic of iconic deconstruction into a nostalgic mode, where the heroes are just that, and the villains are irredeemably evil. And to be clear that the final global revolution is not the triumph of an alternate ideology or radical politics, the plot concludes with the ultimate "Deus Ex Crisis," where Hal Jordan as Uber-Parallax, the Green God Lantern introduced only in the final issue, single-handedly alters the planet, rendering the combined efforts and suffering of every other character superfluous (225–30). The last of the heroes to return, living farther past the border demarcating the beyond than his more corporeal associates, Green Lantern at least fits easily into Bhabha's basic model of a subject's return from liminality that informs and assumes "part of a revisionary time ... to reinscribe our human, historic commonality [and] *touch the future on its hither side*," enacting the fate of a millenarian alternate subjectivity that is already quite superhuman in its theorization (7). Such revisionist subjectivity implicitly rejects Hegelian notions of progress and the dialectic, as well as the Marxist ideology which generated the initial

Superman/Batman opposition. Rather than taking the modernized icon of *DKR* into a second staging of deconstruction, Miller's *DKSA* dilutes the narrative of the heroic icon in a fantasy of imperialist globalization. The constitutive formalism of the comics medium as a merging of image and text reaches its paradoxical height in rendering the superhero as a revolutionary icon beyond social borders of control while narrating a political vacuum for the revolution's mediated staging.

Iconic deconstruction as it has been theorized — exposure of the fantastic icon to a realistic world and the resulting dissolution of the icon's definitional traits with the withdrawal of fantasy's buttress system — cannot function when its requisite screen of reality is re-fantasized, yet it would be a mistake to periodize *DKSA* as a postmodern text merely for not replicating the recognized modernist qualities of its predecessor. If anything, the presence of Miller and Varley as creators in the high modernist tradition is most evident in this particular work, offering an expression of personal style so thorough it borders on the overbearing and alienating. Behind this popular figure of the triumphant creative consciousness lies a fundamentally traditional plot, returning the deconstructed hero to an unapologetic fantasy world, to battle fantastic supervillains for the fate of the planet in a hypermodernist phantasmagoria. It is the villain that dominates this continuity, against and through which the fantasy of the superhero regains its solidarity as a media image, a partial re-articulation of prior unity. Miller has been publicly skeptical of the deconstructive notion universally attributed to his earlier work, *The Dark Knight Returns*, yet acknowledges in a promotional interview that by exploring "the boundaries of what a superhero comic book could do [we] broke those boundaries," and with his subsequent work, he is simply trying to fix the toy he broke, an effort which by its very nature can only ever be partially successful (Brownstein).

Naturally one can't ignore the comics' second climax, the surprise return and death of Dick Grayson the Robin/Joker, and its bloody two-page spread of incredibly small panels (238–9), yet I'll treat its place in my analysis analogous to its place in the narrative — an afterthought, an autonomous concluding tail like the coda at the end of a musical score or the surprise escape of a lizard in your grasp. The effect of suddenly turning the page to confront these densely packed rows and columns is shocking given the text's firmly established pacing and dominant visual semantics of openness and variability. Individually, the panels are consistent with prior articulations of inset panels as marking simultaneous action within a larger semantic context. The reciprocal reinforcement of repetition, the claustrophobia of the orthogonal grid and its shrinking panels, visually dissecting the action with obsession to detail effectively feeds into the immediacy and drama of the minutely graphic violence. The style is unique within *DKSA* while nostalgically harkening back to the style of *DKR*. This sudden introduction of a previously non-existent character — in the penultimate moment — is a final assertion of Miller's inclination towards over-compensatory fantasy. The reader leaves the comic on a note of the unreal, the fantastic, the coincidental illogic of nostalgic plotting, which precludes any willing suspension of disbelief. It can only be followed by an abrupt end.

Works Cited

Bhabha, Homi K. *The Location of Culture*. 1994. New York: Routledge, 2005.
Brownstein, Charles. "Returning to the Dark Knight: Frank Miller Interview." *Comic Book Resources*, 21 April 2000. http://www.comicbookresources.com/?page=article&id=192.
Groensteen, Thierry. *The System of Comics*. 1999. Trans. Bart Beaty and Nick Nguyen. Jackson: University Press Mississippi, 2007.
Hall, Stuart. "The Local and the Global: Globalization and Ethnicity." 1991. *Dangerous Liaisons: Gender, Nation, and Postcolonial Perspectives*. Ed. Anne McClintock, Aamir Mufti, and Ella Shohat. Minneapolis: University Minnesota Press, 1997. 173–87.
Kofoed, DT. "Breaking the Frame: Political Acts of Body in the Televised Dark Knight." *ImageTexT: Interdisciplinary Comics Studies* 5.1 (2010). Dept of English, University of Florida. http://www.english.ufl.edu/imagetext/archives/v5_1/Kofoed/.
McCloud, Scott. *Understanding Comics: the Invisible Art*. 1993. New York: HarperCollins, 1994.
Miller, Frank (w/p/i), and Lynn Varley (c). *Batman: The Dark Knight Strikes Again*. 2001–2. Ed. Bob Schreck. New York: DC Comics, 2002.
Miller, Frank (w/p), Klaus Janson (i), and Lynn Varley (c). *Batman: The Dark Knight Returns*. 1986. Ed. Archie Goodwin and Bob Kahan. New York: DC Comics, 1996.
Murphy, Graham J. "Gotham (K)Nights: Utopianism, American Mythology, and Frank Miller's Bat(-topia)." *ImageTexT: Interdisciplinary Comics Studies* 4.2 (2008). Dept of English, University of Florida. http://www.english.ufl.edu/imagetext/archives/v4_2/murphy/.
Spivak, Gayatri Chakravorty. "Can the Subaltern Speak?" *Marxism and the Interpretation of Culture*. Ed. Cary Nelson and Lawrence Grossberg. Urbana: University Illinois Press, 1988. 66–111.

Part Three

Batman and Beyond

12

"One May Smile, and Smile, and Be a Villain"
Grim Humor and the Warrior Ethos

MELANIE WILSON

Batman fits into a long tradition of stoic, morally ambivalent warriors who are masters of ironic humor. Of course, there are obvious connections between him and the characters of Alan Moore's *Watchmen*, but he also has a much older counterpart: the Icelandic *Njal's Saga*'s Skarphedin. Unlike most emotionally stoic warriors, Skarhpedin does not merely joke; he grins. This sort of behavior is still a mode of expression for modern warriors, particularly morally ambiguous heroes such as *Watchmen*'s Comedian and Rorschach and *The Dark Knight Return*'s Batman. Although most people assume that humor is always a positive phenomenon, this is not always the case. For Skarphedin, the Comedian, Rorschach, and Batman, humor serves as a repressive tool that expresses displeasure with society.

A brief examination of two theories of laughter and humor will prove helpful in examining these warriors in their diverse situations. The first theory is that people laugh when something is unexpected. Most frequently, the surprise that triggers laughter is a good surprise, relatively unaccompanied by danger or pain. This theory, in its broadest sense, applies to many types of incongruity, including verbal irony and wordplay, juxtapositions of seemingly incompatible ideas, and juxtapositions of people or objects that appear to be opposites. According to this theory, things are only funny if one understands the expected norms of a situation. This explains why young children often do not understand jokes; they do not know the accepted societal patterns of behavior well enough to realize when and how these patterns have been disrupted. The incongruity theory also explains why many jokes are not universally funny; cultural norms are different. This provides a problem in determining whether or not the understatements of the Icelanders would have been considered humorous by their contemporaries; however, based on the ways other characters respond to them, it is difficult to interpret them any other way.

Another common theory of laughter is that laughter results from a feeling of superiority over the person or object that is the cause of the laughter. Plato, whom most critics identify as the first person to offer a theory of laughter, popularized this theory; because of laughter's negative nature, he strongly advised people to avoid laughter. Laughter that originates in feelings of superiority is problematic on a variety of levels. Sometimes laughter of superiority is tinged with affection, as when people laugh at children or animals for doing things that appear to be illogical, but more frequently, it is compassionless laughter. This is most often evident when people laugh at people who exhibit characteristics of otherness such as disease, disorder, or racial difference. Though it may be negative in nature, however, this type of laughter can be useful as a defense mechanism. This is particularly true in the warrior ethos, where warriors must detach themselves from their opponents' humanity to triumph in battle. This detachment, while a necessary part of the heroic mode, can become so extreme that the hero becomes an anti-hero.

Of course, all of these theories of laughter have loopholes. Most of these loopholes arise from the fact that much scholarship is, as neuroembryologist Robert Provine notes, "mired in its prescientific phase where logic and anecdote, not empirical data, reign" (11). Many theorists seem eager to establish laughter and humor as legitimate fields of scholarly inquiry. In attempting to establish its importance, they frequently neglect the negative incarnations of laughter in favor of presenting the therapeutic value of positive laughter. However, this supposition that laughter is always positive is clearly biased, ignoring such disturbing instances of laughter as that of the psychopath or the laughter of ridicule. As Provine summarizes, "Laughter is a harlequin that shows two faces — one smiling and friendly, the other dark and ominous" (2). John Morreall offers a theory of laughter which he may have more convincingly offered as a theory of humor: "Laughter Results from a Pleasant Psychological Shift" (39). Of course, one must keep in mind that pleasantness is a subjective experience; that is, while one person may find it pleasant to spend a relaxing weekend at the beach, another person may find it pleasant to disembowel puppies. Theorists are also hampered by their assumption that laughter is always a response to humor. In fact, according to numerous studies that Robert Provine conducted, most laughter is primarily a social phenomenon that has very little to do with humor. It is far more productive to approach the laughter of a person — or a character — with a variety of theories about humor and laughter stimuli.

Smiles are equally problematic. In today's world, broad smiles indicate that a person is open, friendly, and warm. As recently as the early twentieth century, however, such smiles were a breach in propriety. In an exhaustive study of portraiture and popular advertisements, Fred E. H. Schroeder notes that tooth-baring smiles are almost entirely absent from portraits or advertisements before the 1930's. Angus Trumble, author of the exhaustive *A Brief History of the Smile*, offers a similar observation: "In short, as far as I could see, most teeth and open mouths in art belonged to dirty old men, misers, drunks, whores, gypsies, people undergoing experiences of religious ecstasy, dwarves, lunatics, monsters, ghosts, the possessed, the damned, and — all together now — tax collectors" (xxxi). Schroeder concludes, "The smiling subjects are variously not in control of their expressions; they are innocents like children and peasants; madmen, seniles, drunks, outcasts, people lost in passions of lust, greed power, chicanery, cruelty; and at the fundament, they are barely human" (110). Both Schroeder and Trumble feature passages from etiquette books that discourage smiling. These books cite the impropriety of showing the teeth, which have animalistic connotations. Further, Trumble observes that the Old English *grin* "applied equally to men and animals" (82). Smiles, then, were expressions of bestial emotions, and the lingering connotations can still cause a smile to be unnerving. Trumble concludes:

> [W]e should remember that, more than ever before, [...] teeth still have widespread associations with vampire myths, bizarre crime, the savage biting of hand-to-hand combat (even sport), unstoppable monsters of science fiction, and dozens of other manifestations of the horror esthetic. In fact, the dark irony with which many contemporary artists attack the meanings of the modern smile may reflect the unlikely persistence of that very ancient impulse to measure it against fluctuating standards of decorum, permissible boundaries of lewdness, and various conventions of concealment and display[.] (155)

Trumble's observations are immensely helpful in making sense of the meanings of smiles and other expressions that involve bared teeth in *Njal's Saga* and graphic novels.

Literary laughter and smiles play a particularly interesting yet subtle role in both *Njal's Saga* and graphic novels revolving around heroes, especially those heroes without supernatural ability. Graphic novels draw on many motifs and themes common in ancient texts that relate the exploits of warriors, especially when the tone of the ancient text is not epic in nature. The laughter in ancient texts is seldom a simple response to a conventionally pleasurable stimulus. Because ancient heroes are products of a warrior-centered society, their laughter is borne of anguish and a need for distance. As such, their humor is frequently grim and sometimes chilling. Further, because these warriors seldom verbally express their emotions, it is nearly impossible to determine the object of their grim amusement. Because of their taciturn nature, studying the humor of these impassive heroes necessitates an examination of not only laughter and jokes but also smiles.

Jacques Le Goff identifies two main types of laughter in Christian culture: positive laughter and negative laughter (161). The prevalent form in *Njal's Saga* is negative laughter, and Le Goff further identifies two forms of it: "derision or mockery, and *subsannatio*, the sniggering characteristic of malevolence" (161). Both are obvious throughout *Njal's Saga*. One obvious form of mockery is the understatement. These understatements provide examples of verbal incongruity by describing large, frequently horrific events as small, inconsequential events. Sometimes, these understatements are callous and dismissive. Thjostalf murders Hallgerd's husband to please her; when she asks why his axe is bloody, he responds, "I've done something [...] which will permit you to marry a second time" (23). Later, after Hrapp kills Gudrun, Gudrun also asks why Hrapp's axe is bloody. Hrapp replies, "I have been taking care of Asvard's backache" (143). Both Hrapp and Thjostalf are nefarious characters bragging about their deeds; however, sometimes characters also use understatement for less offensive purposes. For example, when Gunnar's attackers lay siege to his house, Gunnar stabs Thorgrim in the waist with his halberd from inside the building. When Gizur asks if Gunnar is at home, Thorgrim replies, "Find that out for yourselves, but I've found out one thing — that his halberd's at home" (126). Thorgrim's quip serves to deflect attention from the gravity of his situation by employing understatement. In all of these cases, the understatement serves to separate the person from the situation being mocked. The reason Hrapp and Thjostolf's humor is offensive is that they attempt to use humor to soften the brutality of their actions. Although violence is a constant fact of life in *Njal's Saga*, none of the noble characters treat it as a laughing matter. Violent death is, on the contrary, one of the most serious things in the culture, and it requires either monetary recompense or, more frequently, blood vengeance to settle the debt. The ways in which different characters use understatements to describe violence, therefore, is always revealing.

Another important form of humor in *Njal's Saga* is the exchange of insults. This is another clear example of laughter that expresses superiority. The most obvious example is that of Sigmund Lambason, whom the other characters value as a poet. Sigmund joins with Hallgerd to devise some particularly damaging slander that incites Njal's sons to violence. Hallgerd begins by suggesting, "Let's call [Njal] 'Old Beardless,' and his sons 'Dungbeardlings'" (74). She then requests that Sigmund create a poem about her insults, and Sigmund obliges. The humor that both Sigmund and Hallgerd apply here is a textbook example of Le Goff's *subsannatio*. However, while Sigmund and Hallgerd think that this slander is funny, neither Gunnar nor the author of the saga agrees with them. Gunnar distances himself from this sort of mocking humor in an earlier exchange in which he tells Sigmund, "You're not at all like me: you are given to mockery and sarcasm, while I am not. You get along well with Hallgerd, because you have more in common with her" (73). The author of the saga points to this slanderous behavior as the catalyst for the violence which destroys Sigmund. Although Hallgerd and her friends appear to have been amused by Sigmund's offensive verses, the ultimate consequences of this slander are violent and fatal to Sigmund, and the author's sympathies clearly do not lie with him. Through the use of repeated hunting imagery, the author portrays Sigmund as prey that rises to Hallgerd's bait. This imagery suggests that Sigmund is directly responsible for his own death.

The understatement and the insult are two cornerstones of humor in *Njal's Saga*. Skarphedin, however, is an enigmatic figure who smiles in response to events that would cause most other men in the saga to employ violence. His smile is aggressive in itself, a warning that he is contemplating action. Of course, one obvious problem with observing Skarphedin as a character is that *Njal's Saga* is, ostensibly, a history. Viewing Skarphedin as a character rather than an historical figure seems illogical. However, the author of *Njal's Saga* appears to have taken some poetic license with the story. Although a man named Njal did die when a group of people besieged his house and set fire to it, the various conversations and personalities which the author constructs for the saga are fictional. Therefore, it is plausible to examine Skarphedin as a deliberately constructed character. Specifically, the author invents Skarphedin as the sort of grim hero that now populates the pages of comic books.

Skarphedin's heroic qualities are obvious. He is so powerful and fearsome that even after he is dead, people are hesitant to approach his corpse. According to the saga author, when the people discover Skarphedin's body, "Everybody said that it was easier to be in the presence of the dead Skarphedin than they had expected, for no one was afraid of him" (230). Their hesitance is nto surprising; the things Skarphedin has done in battle throughout the text are awe-inspiring, and the author of the saga tinges them with drama. The most obvious demonstration of his skill comes during his famous battle on the ice:

> A broad slab of ice, smooth as glass, had formed on the other side of the river, and Thrain and his men were standing in the middle of it. Skarphedin took off into the air and leaped across the river from one ice ledge to the other and made a steady landing and shot on in a glide. The ice slab was very smooth,

and Skarphedin went along as fast as a bird in flight. Thrain was about to put on his helmet, but Skarphedin came at him first and swung his axe at him and hit him on his head and split it down to the jaw, so that the molars fell out on the ice. This happened in such rapid sequence that no one could land a blow on Skarphedin; he went gliding away at a furious speed [159–60].

This sequence does indeed carry a sense of magic and drama, but it is the same sort of magic and drama that accompanies many of Batman's dramatic entrances in contemporary literature. That is, it is not supernatural; it is a result of Skarphedin's athletic prowess and showmanship.

It is also important to consider what prompts both this attack and every other attack which Skarphedin participates in. A central problem of *Njal's Saga* is justice. Although the characters continually return to the Althing to seek compensation for their various murdered kinsmen, none of these lawsuits ends satisfactorily. As translator Robert Cook notes, "In *Njal's Saga* there are many feuds and many killings, and a number of cases are brought to the Althing for trial, but not one legal case is ever concluded. [...] [E]ven though arbitration and vengeance were socially acceptable elements of feud, one would hope that the court trials would have a higher score than zero in a saga so obsessed with law" (xxv). The characters in *Njal's Saga*, particularly Njal himself, face a growing disillusionment with their legal system's ability to administer justice. The deficiencies of their legal system are procedural; it is a legal system in which lawyers win or lose cases depending on how well they follow procedure and not on the actual merits of the case. Further, there is no way to enforce the pronouncements of the Althing. Skarphedin gives up on the legal system long before Njal does, taking justice into his own hands. This sort of vigilante justice resembles the behavior of today's superheroes except that Skarphedin does not adopt a mission to pursue world- or even city-wide justice. Although Skarphedin's brand of justice is not as wide-reaching as Batman's or most other comic book heroes, he does seek retribution for things that the legal system will not take care of for him.

It is nearly always in the context of Skarphedin's quest for justice that he grins. He directs his first grin at Njal; when Njal shows Skarphedin the money that he has received as compensation for Njal's servant Svart, Skarphedin says, "It may turn out to be useful," and grins (61). Skarphedin's smile is clearly not a pleasant smile. The money in question is the money for the first death in the feud, so the pattern that dominates the saga has not yet been established; there is no precedent yet for people to overturn the ruling of the Althing which the monetary settlement represents and opt for blood vengeance instead. Skarphedin's mocking grin clearly anticipates this pattern, however, and returns when his anticipation is justified. He grins again after

Atli kills Kol, who is the person responsible for killing Svart. The grin follows another of Skarphedin's wisecracks: "Slaves are much more active than they used to be: then they just got into brawls, and that seemed harmless enough, but now they're out to kill each other" (63). Taken without the grin, this statement might be read as a simple expression of nostalgia. However, his grin renders this statement mocking.

As the saga progresses, Skarphedin's humor begins to fragment. Njal returns from a hearing in which he receives settlement for the murder of Thord, Skarphedin's foster-father. Skarphedin first attempts humor: "They thought they needed a lot of help," he observes in response to the news that three people ambushed Thord (72). Within the same quotation, he abandons this defense mechanism in favor of expressing genuine frustration: "But how far must this go before we can raise our hands?" (72). Unlike Njal, Skarphedin realizes the limitations of the legal system to truly carry out justice. Skarphedin's frustration is not entirely valid here; after all, Njal has received compensation for the murder, so the guilty parties have been punished. However, Skarphedin's anger rings true despite the technicalities. The monetary fine does not remove the guilt of the ambushers; futher, Skarphedin knows that Hallgerd will incite her family to continue assaulting and insulting Njal's family. In his society, the only effective form of punishment is blood vengeance.

Skarphedin's grin becomes ever-present as the proceedings of the Althing intended to prosecute him for the murder of Hoskuld, Njal's foster-son, commence. Skarphedin insults one person after another with increasing intensity as his lawyer attempts to gain support for him. These insults are virulent and erupt from Skarphedin with very little provocation. Each potential ally asks who Skarphedin is, following this question with a vaguely insulting description of him. Perhaps the worst of Skarphedin's tirades is directed against Thorkel, who asks, "Who is that big and frightening man who goes fifth in line, pale-looking and sharp-featured, with a wicked and luckless look about him?" (204). This question, while certainly insulting, is no match for Skarphedin's answer:

> My name is Skarphedin and there's no need for you pick out insulting words for me, an innocent man. It's never happened that I threatened my own father or fought him, as you did with your father. Also, you haven't come to the Althing often or taken part in lawsuits, and you're probably handier at dairy work amidst your little household at Oxara. You really ought to pick from your teeth the pieces from the mare's arse you ate before riding to the Thing — your shepherd watched you and was shocked that you could do such a filthy thing [204].

This tirade comes even after Asgrim tactfully suggests before they enter Thorkel's tent, "I must ask you, Skarphedin, not to take part in the conversation" (203). Skarphedin, naturally, grins at this suggestion. Needless to say, the counsel with Thorkel does not end well. When Asgrim admits defeat, Skarphedin responds, "Off to our booth, bored with begging" (205). This comment explains his behavior throughout the Althing. Given his already-established distrust of law, he must realize that whatever happens at the Althing will not resolve the problem of his guilt in Hoskuld's murder. In this sequence, his grins and jeers indicate that he recognizes the irony of "begging" people to support him during this irrelevant court case. As Low Soon Ai suggests, "[I]n his attitude to the chieftains from whom the Njalssons try to solicit support, and to the proceedings at the Al?ing, it is clear that he rejects the societal, legal machinery by which his crime is reckoned and quantified" (106). Le Goff additionally suggests that Skarphedin's expression is "the grin of the unfortunate, the man against whom fate regularly turns. [...] Skarphedinn laughs either through incomprehension of the misfortune awaiting him, or as a form of defence—defiance towards this bad luck" (163). Skarphedin's mocking laughter here embraces his own fate and the corrupt legal system which will bring it to pass.

Skarphedin's grin makes a final appearance when Flosi burns Njal's house. Although Skarphedin fights heroically, it is clear that he realizes that they are doomed. Throughout the ordeal, Skarphedin uses mocking humor. He jokes with the men who try to build the fire that will consume Njal's family, "Building a fire, boys? Are you going to cook something?" (219). Later, when Njal gets into bed and prepares for death, Skarphedin comments, "Our father has gone to bed early, which is to be expected—he's an old man" (222). These jests again establish Skarphedin as a strong, emotionally invulnerable character who maintains his invulnerability by using humor to place distance between himself and the events occurring around him. It is this heroic attitude that inspires Skarphedin's final grin. During the battle, Kari calls Skarphedin the bravest of them all, to which Skarphedin responds by "stretch[ing] his lips into a grin" (219). This grin simultaneously affirms and denies what Kari says, expressing Skarphedin's ambivalence about the society that produced him.

The condition of Skarphedin's body is revealing: "[H]e had been standing up against the gable wall, and his legs were burned off almost up to the knees, but the rest of him was unburned. He had bitten into his upper lip. His eyes were open and not swollen. He had driven his axe into the gable wall so hard that half the blade was buried, and it had not lost its temper" (230). Two prominent images emerge from this description: the axe and the teeth. The axe that "had not lost its temper" reflects the ideal, controlled version of Skarphedin from early in the text. Although Skarphedin tests the axe, it does not break or even bend. Skarphedin uses humor to maintain his heroic façade.

However, Skarphedin must suppress or repress much of his actual emotion; the grins and humor that erupt from him function as release valves for this pressure. As these grins become more prevalent, however, they become increasingly subversive. Skarphedin becomes insolent as he loses control of his emotions. The teeth that emerge from behind Skarphedin's lips assert the animalistic violence that is at the heart of his nature.

The Skarphedin that emerges from *Njal's Saga* is a deeply conflicted man. In many ways, he is the ideal Icelandic warrior, as evidenced by the author's introductory description of him:

> Skarphedin [...] was a big and strong man and a good fighter. He swam like a seal and was swift of foot, quick to make up his mind and sure of himself; he spoke to the point and was quick to do so, though mostly he was even-tempered. His hair was reddish-brown and curled and he had fine eyes; his face was pale and sharp-featured, with a bent nose, a broad row of upper teeth and an ugly mouth, and yet he was very like a warrior [44].

At the beginning of the saga, Skarphedin possesses athletic prowess, emotional control, and rhetorical effectiveness. All of these qualities make him an ideal member of Icelandic society. However, Skarphedin is unable to accept the Icelandic legal system as a valid means of enforcing justice. As the saga progresses, his even temper erodes as his grins multiply. These grins express his disdain for those who believe the legal system can prevail over bloodlust. Still, he cannot quite bring himself to directly oppose the ideals that his father espouses. His mocking smile is not only for the establishment but for himself and his emotional vulnerability, as well.

Skarphedin's dilemma is the same one that some of the most critically-acclaimed Reagan-era comic book heroes face. Many of them echo Skarphedin's distaste for the legal system and his desire for justice along with his coping mechanisms, specifically a bizarre or disturbing sense of humor. The ultimate end of these expressions is the same; all of these heroic figures defy the horror of the dissolving establishment with their ironic humor. Two of these characters are Alan Moore's Comedian and Rorschach, both of whom would be more accurately defined as anti-heroes. The landscape of Moore's *Watchmen* is notoriously dark and grim; no hero in the classic sense of the word emerges at all. Rather, each character develops in ambiguous ways that contain elements of good and evil. Rorschach and the Comedian are the two characters who emerge from the series with the most pessimistic views of humanity, yet they are the two who most frequently engage in humor.

The Comedian is, as one might expect in a postmodern text, hardly a comedian. His brand of humor is completely derisive, and the crux of his worldview is that life is just a bad joke. In many ways, the Comedian and his horrifying sense of humor are at the center of the text. The first panel of the graphic novel is the Comedian's badge, a classic yellow smiley face, in a pool of blood. The final panel is a clear homage to the opening panel — an editor's assistant's smiley face shirt with a splotch of ketchup that is identical to the splotch of blood on the Comedian's badge in the first panel. These bookend smiley faces that enclose the horrific events of the graphic novel reinforce the Comedian's motto that life is a horrible joke.

As the Comedian famously tells John in a Vietnamese bar, "Once you figure out what a joke everything is, being the Comedian's the only thing that makes sense. [...] I never said it was a good joke! I'm just playin' along with the gag..." (2.13). He later says something similar to Nite Owl as the two of them try to stop a riot: "I keep things in proportion an' try ta see the funny side" (2.19). The idea of the Comedian as a balanced person is almost laughable. Numerous panels show the Comedian observing or participating in horrific acts, all the while wearing an unnerving grin. One example comes from John's memories of him in Vietnam; he sprays fire while grinning diabolically. The concluding panel on the page features this chilling smile in close-up (4.19). What is most disturbing about the Comedian's attitude is that the other characters see him as a realist. Rorschach suggests that the Comedian's loneliness stems from the fact that he sees the flaws of society so clearly; the clarity of his perception leads him, Rorschach suggests, "to become a reflection, a parody of it" (2.27). Critic Taneli Kukkonen supports Rorschach's diagnosis, identifying the Comedian as a Kierkegaardian ironist: "conducting himself in a certain manner while inwardly not believing in the ideals he superficially espous[e]s" (200). Understood this way, the Comedian becomes an incredibly perceptive character. His laughter enables him to live in the horror-filled world of the twentieth century; it also blinds him to the sad beauty of flawed humanity which emerges at the end of the text. More practically, his humor is not an impenetrable shield. When the Comedian finds out about Ozymandias's plan to stage an alien invasion in order to avert nuclear war, his sense of humor fails him: "I mean, I thought I knew how it was, how the world was. But then I found out about this gag, this joke. [...] I mean, what's funny? What's so goddamned funny? I don't get it. Somebody explain ... somebody explain it to me" (2.22–3). Without his humor to protect him from the horror, the Comedian is utterly defenseless.

However often the other characters identify the Comedian as the character who understands the most about modern society, most readers do not view him as the protagonist. More frequently, they point to Rorschach. Rorschach's sense of humor also places him in an interesting position in the heroic tradition. His humor is exceptionally dark, and most of the characters who encounter it do not know how to respond to it. One of his earliest jokes regards the Comedian's badge. Dan Dreiberg, finding that Rorschach has broken into his house and is eating a can of his beans, assumes that the stain on the badge is bean juice. "That's right. Human bean juice. Ha ha" (1.11), Rorschach responds. He concludes the second chapter by telling a joke: "Man goes to doctor. Says he's depressed. Says life seems harsh and cruel. Says he feels all alone in a threatening world where what lies ahead is vague and uncertain. Doctor says 'Treatment is simple. Great clown Pagliacci is in town tonight. Go and see him. That should pick you up.' Man bursts into tears. Says 'But, Doctor ... I am Pagliacci'" (2.27). Alan Moore and Dave Gibbon spread this joke across five panels, which alternately depict the horrors of the Comedian's life and the brutality of the Comedian's death. The juxtaposition of this dark joke with the even darker art is incredibly effective, presenting the tragedy of the Comedian's life and death succinctly and powerfully. "Good joke. Everybody laugh," Rorschach appends to this sequence (2.28). It is particularly interesting that Rorschach implicitly compares the Comedian to the clown Pagliacci. Clowns, according to humor theorists, elicit laughter because the audience feels detached from them. The ridicule which the audience engages in as a clown undergoes various traumatic experiences can only result from the audience distancing itself from the humanity of the clown. The Comedian is simultaneously audience and clown, purposely trying to make people laugh at the horrors of the world, all the while ridiculing its tragic flaws by attempting, if Rorschach is right, to parody it. More interesting is that Rorschach deems this joke a good joke. In fact, Rorschach is more of a Pagliacci figure than the Comedian is.

Rorschach's humor most frequently bubbles to the surface when he confronts underworld thugs. This humor is often bullying and aggressive. When he tries to get information about the Comedian's murder from Moloch, a retired super-villain, Rorschach pushes the powerless, cancer-ridden old man into the refrigerator, observing, "You're sweating. Looks unpleasant. Should cool down" (5.5). Moloch does not ultimately yield any useful information during Rorschach's interrogation, however. As the disappointed Rorschach leaves, he wryly remarks, "Sorry about mess. Can't make omelette without breaking few eggs" (5.6). This remark refers to both Rorschach's method of questioning and the literal eggshells which Rorschach has left on the floor. Both of these jokes rely on verbal irony for their effects. He uses this same sort of punning during his later encounters with a diminutive criminal, Mr. Figure, whom Rorschach is responsible for imprisoning. When Figure approaches Rorschach's cell, Rorschach greets him, "Big figure. Small world" (8.6). Of course, Figure does not find this particularly humorous, although he feigns laughter. After Figure spends some time threatening him, Rorschach tersely remarks, "Tall order" (5.7). He uses these kinds of puns again when Figure returns during a prison riot to kill Rorschach. One hefty henchman notes that Rorschach is not making any wisecracks about Figure's height, concluding, "Maybe he figured out that once we slice these bars we're gonna make **him** a little shorter" (8.14). Rorschach replies, "Fat chance" (8.14). The henchman bursts into a fit of rage which enables Rorschach to defeat him by tying him to the prison bars in front of the lock. The other men have to kill him to unlock the door. When they do get in, Rorschach breaks the toilet so that water gushes onto the floor. This water electrocutes the henchman who enters carrying a welding torch. Rorschach comments, "Never disposed of sewage with toilet before. Obvious, really" (8.17). Figure, realizing that all of his henchmen are now dead, flees the scene. Rorschach pursues him, running into his would-be rescuers, Dan and Laurie. "Have to visit men's room," Rorschach excuses himself, presumably to follow and dispose of Figure (8.20). As Dan and Laurie discuss the awkwardness of the encounter, they hear a toilet flush. When Rorschach finally emerges from the restroom, he says, "There. Did what had to be done. Can leave now" (8.20). Laurie sarcastically responds, "Really? I mean, are you sure? We don't want to get too reckless and go diving head-first into things!" (8.20). Rorschach trumps her sarcasm, although he is the only one who really gets the joke: "Hurm. Good advice. Sure there are many who'd agree with you" (8.20), including, presumably, Figure. The water flooding from beneath the bathroom door suggests that Rorschach has murdered by drowning him in the toilet. The *Watchmen* film is less ambiguous, clearly showing Figure's presence in the restroom and his growing terror between swoops of the swinging restroom door. The humor of this entire sequence is founded on Rorschach's fondness for puns.

Based on this brief examination of the Comedian and Rorschach, it is easy to identify several connections with the tradition of the grim hero which Skarphedin embodies. Like Skarphedin, both Rorschach and the Comedian take pleasure in deeds of violence, executing them with formidable prowess. All of these characters use expressions that society traditionally considers positive to express darker sentiments. The characters use humor to express their skepticism of the law. The Comedian's defense mechanism of mocking the world for its blindness is not unlike Skarphedin's defense mechanism. Rorschach's witticisms also have the same effect as Skarphedin's grin. Rorschach differs in that his humor is reserved for the criminals rather than the law itself, although he is not adverse to attacking them if they cross him.

Like Rorschach, Frank Miller's version of Batman in *Batman: The Dark Knight Returns* views the legal system as an ineffective institution which enables criminals to thrive. Although Bruce Wayne, whom critic Chuck Tate describes as "the alter-ego of the Batman" (139), expresses a desire to believe in the law's transformative possibilities, it is clear that Batman does not. This Batman, filled with fury about society's ills, takes a grim pleasure in doling out punishment. The extent to which he enjoys inflicting pain on the criminals that he attacks is a matter of some critical controversy. Terrence R. Wandtke suggests that Batman "act[s] pragmatically and not cruelly" (94). He then cites a scene in which Batman catches and disables a criminal, purposely choosing a defense which would enable him to disarm and injure the criminal over three of them that would have disarmed the criminal without injuring him. This action is pragmatic in that the criminal will presumably stop committing crimes. Chuck Tate, on the other hand, argues that Batman is entirely motivated by the pleasure he takes in hurting criminals; as Tate points out, although Batman does help people, he does not appear to be primarily interested in doing so. Rather than accept praise or thanks from the people he helps, Tate notes, "he has been known to chastise victims for not taking precautions to avoid becoming targets" (140). Batman's grim pleasure is a direct reflection of warrior ideals in *Njal's Saga*, specifically Skarphedin's. That Batman enjoys his work is obvious in the showmanship which he employs. Batman makes numerous dramatic entrances in the heroic tradition of Skarphedin's ice-skating decapitation. One of these entrances is Batman's elaborately staged rescue of the heir to the Ridley fortune (61–65).

Given that most critics and readers identify Batman as the darkest and most mysterious of the major superheroes, it is interesting that character after character comments on the ubiquity of Batman's laughter. In fact, a clipping by Jimmy Olson from *The Daily Planet* that prefaces the comic explains that underworld figures never talk about Batman: "They talk about a Man of Steel. An Amazon Princess. But they never talk about the mean one. The one who couldn't fly or bend steel in his bare hands. The one who scared the crap out of everybody and laughed at all of the rest of us for being the envious cowards we were" (9). When Batman catches Harvey Dent and stops his plan to blow up one of Gotham's Twin Towers, Dent urges Batman, "Take a look ... have your laugh" (55). Superman also accuses him of laughter: "When the noise started from the parents' groups and the subcommittee called us in for questioning — you were the one who laughed ... that scary laugh of yours..." 'Sure we're criminals,' you said. 'We've always been criminals. We have to be criminals'" (135). After the Coldbringer detonates despite Superman's best intentions, Superman feels excruciating agony at the horrors that humankind perpetuates. "They can do this ... and you laugh..." he says in disbelief (173). If Batman does, in fact, laugh, the reader never sees it. Rather, Batman continues to behave with his grimly detached stoicisim. Perhaps the reason that all of these characters from reporter to criminal to superhero perceive Batman's laughter is that they sense his detachment and the judgment which accompanies it. They know that Batman finds them unworthy and that he, to some degree, is mocking them.

In his book about film archetypes, James F. Iaccino identifies Batman's repressed laughter as the cement that binds him to his shadow, the Joker: "This super villain [the Joker] is the very antithesis of the Batman figure who gives into his 'dark humor shadow' completely, allowing it to twist his personality into everything foul and wicked" (106). In this context, Iaccino refers to the 1989 film *Batman*. The shadow relationship between Batman and the Joker, however, is evident throughout *Batman* literature. Certainly, the Joker functions as Batman's shadow in *The Dark Knight Returns*, where the two are ensnared in a symbiotic relationship. News of Batman's re-emergence wakes the Joker from his coma, causing the Joker to shift from a neutral face to a broad, tooth-baring grin in the space of five consecutive panels (41). This grin becomes a focal point in the fifth panel, becoming so large that it takes two panels to show it in its entirety. The Joker's grin is antithetical to Batman's increasingly aggressive grimaces, yet both expressions evoke fear. The exposed teeth of both Batman and the Joker are the sorts of animalistic expressions of savagery which both Trumble and Schroeder identify as inherent to smiles in art. This animalistic behavior is evident to critics, too; Chuck Tate focuses on Batman's "familiar menacing grin," suggesting that it denotes "a pleasure [in causing pain] revealed each time he grins as he delivers a ferocious blow to a criminal's body" (142, 144). Terrence Wandtke notes that Batman's animalistic behavior emphasizes his role as as a perpetual outsider to society: "In one of his first depicted confrontations with thugs, he growls, becoming more clearly the 'other' thing which strikes fear" (94). The Joker's bizarre laughter expresses the same rejection of social norms that Batman's growls do; both are manifestations of otherness.

Key to understanding the dynamic of the relationship between Batman and the Joker is the idea of duality, a motif which pervades most *Batman* texts. Batman and the Joker share the same concerns, yet they take opposite stances on these concerns. One such concern is the chaos which the Joker personifies and which is completely foreign to Batman's mode of thinking. This is true in numerous Batman stories. In Miller's *The Dark Knight Returns*, Batman continues to hear the Joker laugh maniacally even after the Joker dies. Staring at the wildly grinning body of the Joker as it burns, Batman pleads, "Stop ... Stop laughing..." (156). The Joker's disembodied laugh is the epitome of the chaos which Batman fights. It is not only in *The Dark Knight Returns* that the Joker is chaotic. In the Afterword to the Deluxe Edition of *The Killing Joke*, Brian Bollard states "I [...] would never have chosen to reveal a Joker origin. I think of this as just one of a number of possible origin stories manifesting itself in the Joker's fevered brain." This provocative analysis of the Joker's character is consistent with the sheer madness which he embodies, a madness captured perfectly in the 2008 film *Batman: The Dark Knight*, in which the Joker offers several origin stories for himself. Alfred succinctly summarizes the Joker's character, explicitly telling Bruce Wayne, "Some men just want to watch the world burn."

The shadow relationship between Batman and the Joker is the subject of Alan Moore's *Batman: The Killing Joke*. This book, noted by many Batman fans as the definitive Joker comic, outlines a confrontation between Batman and the Joker while also revealing a Joker origin story. One major motif in this comic is the bond between Batman and the Joker. Batman wants to avoid what he sees as an inevitable destiny: "I've been thinking lately. About you and me. About what's going to happen to us, in the end. We're going to kill each other, aren't we? Perhaps you'll kill me. Perhaps I'll kill you. Perhaps sooner. Perhaps later. I just wanted to know that I'd made a genuine attempt to talk things over and avert that outcome. Just once" (4). At the end of the comic, Batman tries again to have this conversation, yet he fails. The reason he fails is that there is no way the polar opposites which Batman and the Joker represent can be reconciled. Still, the crux of their relationship is that they are often unnervingly similar.

The conversation between the Joker and Batman at the end of *The Killing Joke* is helpful in revealing the similarities and differences that bind them. Although disturbed smiles pepper the pages of this comic, most of them belonging to the Joker and some of them belonging to his victim, Batman only smiles once: on the final page as he responds to the Joker's joke. This joke is particularly helpful in understanding the point of the comic. Batman offers to rehabilitate the Joker, ending the need for one of them to kill the other. The Joker considers for the space of a panel before responding that he cannot accept Batman's offer, and then he tells a joke to illustrate his reason:

> See, there were these two guys in a lunatic asylum ... and one night, one night they decide they don't like living in an asylum any more. They decide they're going to escape! So, like, they get up onto the roof and there, just across this narrow gap, they see the rooftops of the town, stretching away in the moonlight ... stretching away to freedom. Now, the first guy, he jumps right across with no problem. But his friend, his friend daredn't make the leap. Y'see ... y'see, he's afraid of falling. So then, the first guy has an idea ... he says 'Hey! I have a flashlight with me! I'll shine it across the gap between the buildings.

You can walk along the beam and join me!' B-but the second guy just shakes his head. He suh-says ... he says 'Wh-what do you think I am? CRAZY? You'd turn it off when I was half way across!'" [47].

This situation parallels the one between Batman and the Joker; both of them reject the insanity of society and have chosen to deny its inherent madness. Still, neither one is the epitome of sanity. The idea of Batman helping the Joker live a normal life is, realistically, ridiculous. Batman and the Joker unite in laughter at the end of this comic, emphasizing their similarities, yet the ambiguous ending simultaneously reinforces their differences. Their laughter is grim, and it ends suddenly with the arrival of the police and the disappearance of Batman and the Joker from the final two panels.

Understanding the Joker's humor as an analogue of Batman's unexpressed dark humor is enlightening. The Joker's humor echoes that of Rorschach and the Comedian. It is characterized by a combination of detached puns and the lunatic laughter of psychological release. After he shoots Jim Gordon's daughter, Barbara, he commences with a litany of library jokes: "Please don't worry. It's a psychological complaint, common amongst ex-librarians. You see, she thinks she's a coffee table edition," he quips as she falls onto the glass coffee table (14). He further remarks, "I can't say much for the volume's condition. I mean, there's a hole in the jacket and the spine appears to be damaged. [...] Frankly, she won't be walking off the shelves in that state of repair. In fact, the idea of her walking anywhere seems increasingly remote. But then, that's always a problem with softbacks" (14). At the end of the comic, the Joker also offers a diatribe that could have come directly from the mouth of the Comedian; this diatribe contains an example of the Joker's hysterical laughter: "Do you know what triggered the last World War? An argument over how many telegraph poles Germany owed its war debt creditors! Telegraph poles! Ha ha ha ha HA! It's all a joke! Everything anybody ever valued or struggled for ... it's all a monstrous, demented gag! So why can't you see the funny side? Why aren't you laughing?" (39). Further, laughter is how the Joker responds to his own chemical transformation into the Joker — in a panel that encompasses half a page, he stands grinning before a background of exaggerated "HA"s (32). In both of these cases, his laughter is hysterical. As humor theorist John Morreall explains, "By reacting with laughter the hysterical person is rejecting the reality of the shocking situation. He is unable to face the horror, and so his nervous system takes over with a behavior that expresses not horror but amusement. [...] [T]his laughter and rejection of reality 'works,' for it gives the person some distance, at least temporarily, from the horror" (57). Robert Provine suggests additionally that hysterical laughter can result from "the intimate neurological relation between laughter [...] and crying" (187). The Joker, then, responds to horror with denial and the shadow of tears. Batman has an equally strong response to the random horror of modern life, yet his response is a mirror image of the Joker's. That is, he responds with anger and savage aggression directed at restoring order rather than laughter and insane violence directed at creating chaos. The Joker, as Batman's nemesis, represents the potential depravity of pleasure which Batman takes in harming people. Of course, Batman remains a hero because his motives are to stop crime, and, even if it is not his primary goal, he generally helps innocent people; the Joker, on the other hand, only serves his own chaotic ends. Batman's destructive behavior as a vigilante seems to serve the greater good; however, if everyone took justice into their own hands, the chaos that the Joker personifies and perpetuates would ensue.

The grim heroic deeds of Rorschach, the Comedian, and Batman follow the heroic tradition which Skarphedin embodies in *Njal's Saga*. These warriors are all characterized by a dark humor that enables them to distance themselves from the horrors that surround them. This shield of humor enables them to carry out their heroic deeds and compensate for the impotence of the legal system. However, their humor is hardly the unambiguously positive phenomenon described by many humor theorists. Still, each hero ironically emerges from the text as the voice of reason and sanity, largely because he finds the ungoverned chaos of the world laughably absurd. The humor of the warrior ethos simultaneously separates a warrior from society and enables him or her to fight its evils. Therefore, while all laughter is not necessarily the uncomplicatedly positive experience which many humor theorists identify it as, it is an integral and useful part of the warrior ethos.

Works Cited

Ai, Low Soon. "The Mirthless Content of Skarphedin's Grin." *Medium Aevum* 65.1 (1996): 101–108.
Batman: The Dark Knight. Dir. Christopher Nolan. Perf. Christian Bale and Heath Ledger. Warner Brothers: 2008.
Bollard, Brian. "Afterword." *Batman: The Killing Joke: The Deluxe Edition.* New York: DC, 2008. 60–61.
Cook, Robert. "Introduction." *Njal's Saga.* Trans. Robert cook. New York: Penguin, 2001. vii–xxxiii.
Iaccino, James F. *Jungian Reflections within the Cinema: A Psychological Analysis of Sci-Fi and Fantasy Archetypes.* Westport, Connecticut: Praeger, 1998.
Kukkonen, Taneli. "What's So Goddamned Funny? The Comedian and Rorschach on Life's Way." *Watchmen and Philosophy.* Hoboken: Wiley, 2009.
Le Goff, Jacques. "Laughter in *Brennu-Njals Saga*." *From Sagas to Society: Comparative Approaches to Early Iceland.* 1992. 161–165.

Miller, Frank. *Batman: The Dark Knight Returns.* New York: DC, 2002.
Moore, Alan, and Brian Bollard. *Batman: The Killing Joke: The Deluxe Edition.* New York: DC, 2008.
Moore, Alan, and Dave Gibbons. *Watchmen.* New York: DC, 2005.
Morreall, John. *Taking Laughter Seriously.* Albany: State University of New York, 1983.
Njal's Saga. Trans. Robert Cook. New York: Penguin, 2001.
The Tain. Trans. Robert Kinsella. Chatham, Kent: Oxford University Press, 1988.
Provine, Robert R. *Laughter: A Scientific Investigation.* New York: Penguin, 2000.
Shakespeare, William. *Romeo and Juliet. The Riverside Shakespeare.* Ed. G. Blakemeore Evans et al. 2nd ed. Boston: Houghton Mifflin, 1997. 1101–1145.
Schroeder, Fred E.H. "*Say Cheese!* The Revolution in the Aesthetics of Smiles." *Journal of Popular Culture.* 32.2 (1998): 103–145.
Tate, Chuck. "An Appetite for Desctruction: Aggression and the Batman." *The Psychology of Superheroes: An Unauthorized Exploration.* Dallas: Benbella, 2008. 135–145.
Trumble, Angus. *A Brief History of the Smile.* New York: Basic, 2004.
Wandtke, Terrence R. "Frank Miller Strikes Again and Batman Becomes a Postmodern Anti-Hero: The Tragi(Comic) Reformulation of the Dark Knight." *The Amazing Transforming Superhero!* Ed. Terrence R. Wandtke. Jefferson, North Carolina: McFarland, 2007. 87–111.

13

"And Doesn't All the World Love a Clown?"
Finding the Joker and the Representation of His Evil

MICHAEL SMITH

He takes off his hat, sweeps that large purple fedora — a pimp hat, really, with its ridiculous two-foot wide brim and giant, improbably orange feather — off his head, and really, that is all it takes. One unshadowed look at that face, and we *get* it. We see that white, white skin, the red, red lips, the mop of green hair above the too-long horse face wracked with twisted glee, and the wide yellow of the eyes mapped with angry red veins, and we just *know*. We know, not knowing or stopping to think *how* we know, this stone-chill certainty buried, perhaps, in childhood associations (for weren't we all afraid of clowns?): Here is evil and insanity distilled, its essence personified. Here is a badness and a madness that walks on two stilt-long legs, wearing a well-tailored purple pinstriped zoot suit, an orange tuxedo shirt and an incongruous black jacquard silk long string tie, in the preferred style of riverboat gamblers and gentlemen callers everywhere...

We *know*.

Here is maniac. Madman. Psychopath and psychotic. Lunatic and loon. Here is a crazy — a nutcase, a headcase, a real freaking fruitcake. A total psycho, a pure sicko, an absolute sociopath. Here is bugged and buggy. Gone billy. Bonkers.

Here, then, is *batty*.

(If you call him any of these things, incidentally, if you look him in the eye and say them to his face — and he'll only take a bow and thank you politely for the compliment, saying "Charmed, I'm sure," or "You flatter me," or "Guilty as charged....")

If we move past this immediate visceral reaction, though, this wonderful revulsion and that first spark of dark energy and the delightful anticipation of terror the "Harlequin of Hate" brings whenever he *first* steps out, takes off his hat, and reveals himself to be the prime criminal mover in this or that Batman tale (Oh, goody! This one's a *Joker* story!), where does the Joker take us? At the end of a Joker story, what are we left with?

There is a Peggy Lee song that asks the question: "Is That All There Is?" In the second stanza, the character recounts being taken to the circus when she's twelve years old. All of the things common to a circus were present — clowns, elephants, dancing bears, acrobats of all sorts. Yet, despite the "marvelous spectacle," the child felt that something wasn't right; that something was missing. Confused, she asks herself if that is all there is to a circus (Lee).

Like a circus, the Joker's schemes are loud, grand, goofy affairs, suffused with danger and deadly possibility. But as with a circus, they are pure spectacle, theatre without apparent object or inherent meaning, and so they can also get — well, a little boring. In the end, don't we sometimes find ourselves experiencing something like the incongruous disappointment, the improbable ennui expressed by Peggy Lee? How quickly we cease to be impressed by dancing bears and trapeze acrobats and motocross bikes racing around inside giant spheres made of mesh. How soon before all the randomness eventually strikes us as kind of empty?

So, yes, the Joker is perhaps the most distinctive villain in comic book history. His look is, in its own way, at least as iconic as Batman's. If we could place him on a scale and measure the factor of his immediate recognizability among non-comic book fans, he'd be right up there, sitting comfortably next to his nemesis and Superman.

But while the Joker is the most fully realized villain *visually*, he is also the *least* realized as a character, and it may be that *that* is also why we find ourselves experiencing a little of Peggy Lee's ennui whenever we come out the other side of another Joker story. Yes, certainly, we know him when we see him. (We *know*....) But what we don't know is much of anything — anything at all — about him. When it comes to the Joker's origin, we have only tidbits of who he was and how he came to be, and conflicting tidbits at that. What is more, the various forms of the Joker's origin have always proven grossly inadequate as any kind of an explanation for who the Joker *is* — for his monstrosity, for his silliness. *Why* does he do it? "He is just insane, crazy, psychotic, loony, mad, nutty, sick, et cetera" can never be a satisfying answer to this question, though it is the one we have most often been given.

It is not like there hasn't been time. This is someone who has been around for fifty-seven years. That is a long, long, *long* time to maintain a consistent, recurring presence in comics and still remain *under*-explained, *under*-examined. By now, we might suppose that anything having anything at all to do with the Joker's behavior and motivations — indeed, every last bit of minutiae involving him — would have been told, revised, revisited, re-aligned, re-positioned, re-worked, and re-told ("ret-conned" in comic parlance) a thousand times. You would think that, by now, some writer or other must have written a story examining precisely *why*, exactly, it is that the Joker favors jacquard silk long string ties.

It is important to consider that the man even had his own monthly comic *series* in the early 1980s. Yes, it lasted only nine issues, but nine issues still seems like plenty of time to at least begin to scratch the surface of the title character's psychology. In retrospect, though, the hapless writers assigned to *The Joker* series appear, more than anything, to have been at a complete loss — unsure, exactly, how to get their arms around him or how to handle the Joker in his own book. The solution they came up with was actually to put the Joker in the background, make him the foil, a supporting character, and center each issue around a guest hero (such as the Creeper, a second-stringer who, interestingly, resembles the Joker somewhat in appearance and in attitude, and appeared in the third issue) or, in a couple of cases, another villain who was at least approachable from their perspective (the frankly sane and straightforward Lex Luthor of the seventh issue).

The Joker's first appearance, in *Batman* #1 in 1940, certainly offers few clues about why the Joker does what he does and none about where he might have come from or how he got that way. Like the serpent in the garden, he just appears one day to cause trouble in Gotham, his chilling voice interrupting a radio broadcast to brazenly announce his intentions to steal a diamond and kill a wealthy and prominent citizen of Gotham at a precise date and hour. He returns us to our regularly scheduled programming with "The Joker has spoken!" Of course, the wealthy citizen is quickly given police protection, but he collapses and dies anyway at the appointed hour, his facial muscles pulling into a ghastly grin: "the sign of death from the Joker!" The diamond that is still sitting in the safe is then found to be a fake. Clever Joker, it seems, snuck into the man's mansion the night *before*, injected him in his sleep with a 24-hour time delay solution, and then made off with the diamond. "If the police expect to play against the Joker," the Joker tells us, "they had best be prepared to be dealt from the bottom of the deck."

The Joker doesn't laugh, not once, in *Batman* #1, and indeed, there's nothing the least bit funny about him. That "bottom-of-the-deck" line is the closest he comes to a joke. He is, in fact, deadly serious, and he goes on to repeat the pattern of radio announcement, then murder and theft, and manages to outwit and escape a now-on-the-case Batman in the process. He seems in-control, even calm and rational about the whole process — except for the fact that greed, alone, does not appear to be his motivation. The murders are not truly necessary, and it is certainly not necessary for him to make them so *creatively* grisly. At the same time, there's nothing the least bit loose or fun about him during his showdowns with the Batman. No jokes, no puns, nothing. He says, quite simply: "I'm going to kill you," and he punches Batman in the head. He pulls a gun and says, flatly, "Prepare to die." Later, he throws his emptied gun at Batman and offers a variation on this theme: "I'll kill you." (Interestingly, it is Batman and Robin who insist on making jokes and puns in this issue, Robin saying, "Looks like I'm the ace in the hole, Joker," and Batman noting, "You've played your last hand!") But he is defeated and sent to jail.

One might ask, at this point: Is that all there is? *Batman* #1 was sixty-eight pages and featured four stories. In the last story, the Joker makes a return appearance. But his murderous schemes are eventually foiled again. The Joker even appears to die after Batman slugs him, and he falls off a ship and plummets into the ocean — to his death, presumably. It turns out, however, that the Joker is most assuredly *not* dead; indeed, he is only going about the business of breaking new ground in comics. In the introduction to *The Greatest Joker Stories Ever Told*, Mark Gold tells us that this death was very likely the first instance of what was to become a well-honored tradition — that of the "unkilled villain." The Joker is back just a few issues later.

It's important to note two things, here. The Joker's first "unkilling" — his first resurrection — is also the occasion of his first mad, out-of-control laughter. He gets picked up by a passing ship, and the innocent sailors drop him ashore ("Queer sort of duck, ain't he?" one of them remarks). The Joker makes his way to his secret lair and lets loose: "Ha! Ha! Ha! I'm alive! Ha! Ha! Ha!" Besides his first unhinging, what's also important about the Joker's return is that it also establishes a particular pattern, for he seems possessed of a very peculiar and specific *kind* of immortality. Or perhaps it is that he is just more susceptible to a certain kind of death and resurrection. In any case, this business of the Joker falling as if from a great height, plummeting into a body of liquid and disappearing only to come back later is the single most consistent and oft-repeated method of his death-disappearance-resurrection. He gets punched and falls, or he trips and falls, or he slips and falls, or he's electrocuted and falls, or he's trapped in something that falls, or something shifts suddenly beneath him and he falls, but always — nearly *always* — he falls, and he falls, and he falls: from ships, catwalks, ledges, buildings, suspended steel girders, trapezes, telephone poles, antennas, fire escapes, planes, helicopters, blimps, bi-planes—just about anything high in the air. Usually, he laughs as he falls. And eventually he hits liquid—usually water, usually the ocean, but sometimes a river, occasionally a vat of chemicals or oil. He hits, and the laughter stops abruptly. He never comes up. More often than not, we are given an entire panel where we are shown the slow spreading of the ripples left on the surface, and it is this image we are left to ponder as we contemplate, once again, his disappearance. No matter the exact nature of the body of water—whether ocean, or oil—these ripples resemble those on a lake after a stone has been tossed in.

He *falls*, yes, but we do not ever get to see the Joker recovering, gathering his energies like Satan and cursing God, as Milton might have it, or even Batman at the bottom of this lake. Though, if we stop a moment to consult Dante Alighieri's *Inferno*, we find that the seventh circle of hell is reserved for murderers, and that it is a lake where "those who do injury to others violently, boil" (133). Murder, of course, is the Joker's stock in trade. Through all his mad schemes and his multitude of random crimes—the thefts and the ransoms and even the time he ran for mayor of Gotham City (and won)—there is one thing that doesn't change: his fondness and capacity for homicide. That is the one crime that the Joker is most guilty of, so perhaps it is no accident that when he falls, he plummets into liquid. Dante's Seventh Circle of Hell is also reserved for sodomites, but that will be discussed later.

The Joker would fall, and come back, and fall, and come back, for approximately eleven more years before the first gestures toward an origin story were attempted. In 1951's "The Man Behind the Red Hood" (*Detective Comics* #168), Batman is hired to teach a class in criminology at State University. "Professor Batman" assigns his eager students the task of solving a mystery that has stumped him for over a decade: a string of gang robberies led by a man in a tuxedo and red hood and cape. The hood completely covered the man's face—not even eyeholes were visible. After one last narrow escape from Batman, the Red Hood disappeared, his identity a secret. Once the students re-open the case and start sniffing around, however, the Red Hood comes out of retirement and starts robbing again. Eventually, he is captured, his hood (actually, it turns out to be more of a red helmet, rather than a hood, with "two-way red mirrored lenses" to see through) is removed to reveal the Joker, who then proceeds to lay out the complete story of his origin in no less than *three* panels. Once upon a time, he tells us, he was a lab worker whose "skin coloring was normal, just like yours!" and he decided to "steal $1,000,000 and retire." So, he "became the Red Hood," and he did eventually reach his goal by "stealing from the Monarch playing card company," the "hood's oxygen tube" enabling him to escape by "swimming under the surface of the pool of chemical wastes." But when he got home and took off his hood/helmet, he found that "the chemical vapor" had turned "my hair green, my lips rouge, my skin chalk-white! I look like an evil clown! What a joke on me!" (63). Realizing his new face could "terrify people," the Joker named himself after "the card with the face of a clown" (it *was* a playing card company's chemical waste, after all) and started "a new career path"—graduating from simple robbery to robbery-homicide, presumably.

And that, really, is all there is. And that's how the Joker's origin would more or less remain for the next thirty-seven or so years. He continued to turn up about once a month in one or another of the Batman's half-dozen or so titles, although with the coming of the Comics Code Authority in the mid-fifties, he left the scene for a while (perhaps he was believed to be a bit *too* intense for the kiddies), although he did eventually reappear, albeit with a slightly toned down act (Gold 7). The 1960s and the *Batman* TV show brought an increasingly campy, goofy, ineffectually slapstick Joker to the comics, his laugh no longer chilling and instead just plain silly. It wasn't until 1973 that the Joker regained any of his murderous edge, gruesomely (and pointlessly) killing off former members of his gang in Denny O'Neil's "The Joker's Five-Way Revenge" (Batman 251), the story most often credited with restoring the luster of pure homicidal madness to the Joker. It should be noted, however, that not even that story, or any of the ones which were influenced by it and followed directly in its wake, which by and large feature a kill-crazy Joker in the midst of one pointless, randomly impossible scheme after another (attempting to copyright the smiling faces of poisoned fish is perhaps the best example), can do much to satisfy a reader looking for any kind of an explanation beyond: "The guy is just insane, crazy, psychotic, loony, mad, nutty, sick, et cetera."

If that, indeed, is all there is, then it follows that the Joker could not be responsible for his own actions. He doesn't know what he is doing. He doesn't know right from wrong. He doesn't *know* he is insane, crazy, psychotic. Or does he?

If we look more closely, it would seem, actually, that he *does* know it. For as often as we have seen the Joker fall as if from a great height into water, there is another kind of Joker scene that's repeated again and again throughout his history. It is the exchange that goes like this:

ROBIN (tied to an enormous roman candle): "You're insane, Joker. You're out of your mind."

JOKER: "Gloriously so! Isn't it wonderful?"

Or like this:

COMMISSIONER GORDON (held at gun point): "You're crazy, man! A lunatic!"
JOKER: "Of course! But I taste oh-so-delicious!"

Or even:

BATMAN (in chains, about to be lowered, perhaps, into a shark tank): "You are hopelessly, hopelessly mad, Joker. You know that, don't you?"
JOKER (shrugging, pulling the lever that drops Batman in the tank): "*Tsk, tsk,* Batman. Your last words, and you can't think to tell me something I *don't* know."

Moreover, if we select, at random, a half-dozen Joker stories, from any period or from all periods, we are sure to encounter a host of moments like this, with dialogue coming from the Joker that is almost precisely like this:

BATMAN (clenching his fists): "What's the matter, Joker? Afraid to meet me in a fair fight?"
JOKER (running away): "You're kidding, right? I may be insane, but I'm *not* crazy."

Indeed, as far back as "The Crazy Crime Clown" in January 1953, we have evidence that the Joker knows *exactly* what he's doing. In this story, he steals utterly worthless items and *fakes* insanity in order to get himself committed to an asylum where he'll have access to a patient who knows the secret location of $1,000,000. To this end, he even hires a lawyer and a psychologist who will arrange a phony diagnosis: "Hebophrenic Schizophrenia"—an insanity "marked by extremely foolish behavior" (103).

So what, exactly, is it that is going on in that head of his? In Frank Miller's *The Dark Knight Returns* (1986), we are given our first real access to the Joker's brain, and these bits of internal monologue would seem to indicate that the Joker, at least, understands what it is he's trying to accomplish, even if we don't. Early on, the Joker emerges from a ten-year-catatonic state at very nearly the same moment Batman emerges from retirement. An indulgent, namby-pamby psychologist obsessed with the media spotlight seizes on this and turns the Joker into a product of the culture of victimization, arguing that the Joker has long suffered from "Batman Psychosis" and gets him a booking on the "David Endochrine [read: Letterman] Show." The Joker steps out on stage, looks at the audience, and thinks: "So many faces—so different from one another ... so few *smiles*..." (21) When asked by host Endochrine how many people he's killed—some estimates place the number well over 600—the Joker replies: "I don't keep count." (There is a deadly seriousness, and a flatness, to his delivery that is reminiscent of his very first appearance in *Batman* #1—"I'm going to kill you" and "Prepare to die"). He gestures with his cigarette at the studio audience and says, quite evenly: "I'm going to kill everyone in this room," (22) which he then proceeds to do, kissing another guest — a certain sex therapist by the name of "Dr. Ruth Weisenheimer" — full on the mouth (his lipstick is poisoned) and dosing everyone else (Endochrine included) with his lethal laughing gas (he is apparently immune to the effect of his own chemicals) and bringing the death smile to their faces.

From there, the Joker moves to the country fair, where he hands out his poisoned cotton candy to hundreds of children. It is here, again, that we move inside his brain: "They could put me in a helicopter and fly me up into the air and line the bodies head to toe on the ground in delightful geometric patterns like an endless June Taylor dancers routine — and it would never be enough. No, I don't keep count. But *you* do. And I love you for it" (36).

The Joker's referencing of June Taylor reinforces the notion and importance of spectacle, of *show*, while the "you" in the Joker's reverie, of course, is Batman (or God, if the Joker is the Devil), who arrives on the scene and has determined, finally, that he must kill the Joker. It has taken the Batman precisely this long to acknowledge consciously what some part of him has known and resisted all along: the Joker is in control of his actions. The Joker *is* responsible. We learn this through a bit of Batman's own internal monologue: "From the beginning, I knew ... that there's nothing wrong with you ... that I can't fix ... with my hands..." (38) Their no-holds-barred fight terminates in the "Tunnel of Love," with the Joker stabbing Batman repeatedly in the stomach with a knife held just below the level of his abdomen, and Batman clutching the Joker's head in his massive hands.

It is here we must pause, briefly, to consider the implication of this image, and the nature of their long relationship. The matter of the Joker's sexual orientation is a cloudy one. There have been hints, here and there, throughout his long history that he might —*possibly*— be homosexual. There are many moments, for example, like the one when he bursts into a city office, seeking the copyright for those smiling fish. A bureaucrat exclaims "Good Lord!" and the Joker whirls around, says "Where?" and then, realizing his mistake, proceeds to drape himself all over the man's desk, cooing: "Oh, hahhahahhahaaa, I *see*! It was just an expression — of *endearment*, eh, Mr. Francis? Come on, you can tell *me*! You've always secretly *admired* me, haven't you?" (Englehart 233). There, too, is the way the Joker refers to Batman as "Darling" throughout the *Dark Knight Returns*— a small thing, perhaps, but then, the Joker has historically been shown to have taken particular delight in addressing burly male superheroes in their long underwear as "honey," "sweetie," "snookums," "cutie-pie." Finally, there is simply the manner in which he is drawn: the long-legged dandy-ness, the extravagantly tailored and colored clothing, the foppish posture and posturing — all of this in-keeping, in some way, with a ludicrously stereotypical representation of homosexuality.

A bit of apocrypha surrounding *The Dark Knight Returns* is that a scene clarifying the initial reason for Batman's retirement was eliminated before publication by the editors at DC. Why? Supposedly, the Joker captured and then raped and murdered Jason Todd, the second Robin. This doesn't register as an act that has much of anything to do with sexual orientation, however (here or, for that matter, in real life). Instead, it strikes one as more an expression of power and hate. If such a scene did exist (or was even contemplated), it doesn't really reinforce the notion that the Joker must be a homosexual, or that homosexuality (or repressed homosexuality) has much of anything to do with why he does why he does. Instead, it would suggest that the Joker does what he does out of a conscious decision to maximize suffering and to do the most evil thing he can think of — whatever that may be at the time. And it is the cruelest joke, perhaps, the Joker could ever play on Batman, whose own relationship with Robin the Boy Wonder has often been characterized (by comedians and scholars alike) as somewhat less than entirely wholesome.

Still, it is hard to look at the "Tunnel of Love" sequence in *The Dark Knight Returns*, and *not* see some sort of homoerotic dynamic at work here: the two of them are locked in a fierce embrace in a dark, wet cave, and they are building, together, toward a mutual moment of simultaneous death — the Joker thrusting with his knife, Batman exerting pressure and lifting him by the neck. But at the moment of climax, Batman refuses to kill the Joker, and instead, he opts for paralysis, dropping him to the cave's floor. Here, the Joker mocks him: "I'm really ... very disappointed in you, my sweet.... The moment was perfect ... and you ... didn't have the nerve.... Paralysis ... really..." And the Joker laughs, and he keeps laughing, and with "a devil's strength ... he twists, and twists, and what's left of his spine ... goes..." He dies, and "whatever's in him *rustles* as it leaves."(46)

It is difficult to resist noting, here, that since Batman just cannot bring himself to "go all the way," the Joker, in effect, has to complete the act himself. Also, if we once more consult Dante, we find that besides murders and sodomites, *suicides* go to the lake in the Seventh Circle of Hell, as well.

We are given additional access to the Joker's interior life in Alan Moore's *The Killing Joke* (1988), and here is stronger evidence yet that he does what he does for a well-calculated reason. In this one-shot issue, the Joker's "Man in the Red Hood" origin story is finally revisited and re-cast. Curiously, there has been some resistance to Moore's story among hardcore comic fans and critics alike, most of it based on arguments that Moore went too far in humanizing the Mirthful Madman and that what he winds up giving us is a "kinder, gentler Joker." This is a strange argument, since in the story, the Joker: 1) shoots Commissioner Gordon's daughter through her spine, permanently paralyzing her; 2) takes his time stripping her naked; 3) snaps leering photographs of her in the throes of her nude and bleeding agony; 4) sends those photos to Batman; 5) abducts Commissioner Gordon and strips *him* naked, and 6) tries to drive Gordon insane in an Amusement Park Funhouse.

In *The Killing Joke*, we learn that the Joker was once upon a time a lab assistant who quit his job to pursue a career as a stand-up comedian. He is not successful or even, it appears, the least bit funny. Struggling to support his very pregnant wife, Jeanne, he tells her she's married to a loser and then collapses into her arms, crying: "Jeez ... I have to go, I have to go and stand up there and nobody laughs ... and you think, you think I ... Oh God. Oh God I'm *sorry...*"(5). He is evidently not a criminal, but hoping for some quick money nevertheless, he falls in with a group of crooks, and becomes their patsy in the robbery of the playing card company (it is next door to the chemical plant he used to work in). The crooks have a distinctive gimmick for their crimes, one they've apparently repeated: they recruit a new patsy for each robbery and dress him in a flashy red hood/helmet and tuxedo to draw the police's focus and media attention away from themselves.

The same day the crime is to be carried out, the comedian's wife and unborn child are killed by — of all things — an electrical short from a bargain-basement baby formula warmer she is testing. Utterly destroyed, he tries to back out, but the crooks force him to carry out the robbery in the chemical plant anyway, which is foiled by the police and Batman. Dressed in this red hood/helmet — he can barely see, and he sees double, through those "red, two-way mirrored lenses" — and absolutely frantic to escape, he jumps off a catwalk and into the polluted river and once again, or actually for the first time, he falls from a great height into liquid. Scrabbling to the river bank, he takes off his helmet, and in a reflective puddle, sees that the chemicals have turned his skin white, his lips red, and his hair green. He starts laughing, and the Joker is born (29–32).

The most important element of this ret-con is the Joker's former status as "a loser." He's a screw-up, but a regular, boring, every day kind of screw-up. There's no meanness in him, but there's also nothing the least bit special about him. He's a schlub, really, and he has the everyday schlub's dream of "One day, I'll be rich and famous, I'm not sure how, yet, but...." Later in Moore's story, the Joker tells the Batman that it is only "one bad day" that makes him different from the multitude of humanity — one bad day that separated him, in effect, from the rest of the schlubs: "Something like that happened to me once...," he says. "I ... I'm not exactly sure what it was. Sometimes

I remember it one way, sometimes another..." (39) Given a bad *enough* day, then, we might extrapolate from this that *anyone* can be as "insane, crazy, psychotic, loony, mad, nutty, sick, et cetera" as he is.

In *The Killing Joke*, this is the equation the Joker is solving for. It's why he shoots Gordon's daughter and kidnaps Gordon: this is Gordon's "one bad day." It's why the Joker kills or torments *anyone*, in fact. He's giving them — or their friends and family — their "one bad day." That one bad day justifies and — more than that — it *excuses* the Joker's murderous insanity. In the Joker's mind, even the sanest man has to be just *that* close to losing it. It is his reason for doing what he does, his why.

Except, Commissioner Gordon *doesn't* lose it. The Joker's equation falls apart. Not everybody loses it. Not even *most* people. Not even the Joker's victims or, actually, their families. Because people die in horrible freak accidents all the time. People slip and fall in the shower. People get in their cars, turn their heads to back out of their driveway, and somehow the neck achieves precisely the proper angle to cut off the flow of blood to the brain, and they die. Kids batting in Little League get hit in the chest with a pitched ball and die halfway to first base. And, of course, people are murdered and tortured *every* day, by the thousands. Sometimes there's an explanation given for these, and sometimes that explanation is political or religious. But the more one stares at those explanations, the more inadequate they truly seem, until eventually, these deaths may seem all the more random and haphazard.

Stop to consider that the Joker emerged full-bloom in the 1940s, a time when *millions* were being subjected to unspeakable deprivation and degradation, when *millions* died horribly — all victims of a highly organized, bureaucratic, industrial system of death (a great deal of it accomplished, as with the Joker, through the use of gas). None of it made any sense, really. "One bad day," maybe a failed painter with black, oily hair and a silly mustache — formerly a schlub of the first order — went nuts, or maybe he didn't, but somehow an unspeakable, inexplicable evil came into the world.

To the people who lived and who died in the camps he had built, it surely must have seemed to have had nothing at all to do with anything resembling fairness or sense. Kurt Vonnegut, Jr., for one, wrote about this particular kind of insight, wrote with it and about it repeatedly, although nowhere as succinctly as in a 1945 letter to his parents, in which he first describes how, during his time as a prisoner of war in Dresden, the Allied bombing "killed 250,000 people in twenty-four hours and destroyed all of Dresden — perhaps the world's most beautiful city. But not me." [11]. Still, when it was over, the survivors and their loved ones moved on. Not easily, but somehow. Life, they say, goes on, even after one bad day.

Schlubs, it would seem, are a remarkably resilient lot. They recover quickly from trauma. That is because they do not spend too much time trying to make evil make sense. That is the only way they are able to continue. Claude Lanzmann, producer and director of the acclaimed Holocaust documentary *Shoah* (1985), is the most prominent — and loudest — person to hold to this point-of-view: that those who attempt to make sense of evil, to examine it and quantify it, to understand it, and review its history and somehow explain it, must inevitably end up justifying it, excusing it. And evil *cannot* be excused — otherwise, it is not evil; it is human, and so, we might forgive it. But the Holocaust *cannot* be forgiven. If it is forgiven, it can be forgotten. And thus, it could happen again. For Lanzmann, evil *cannot* make sense (Rosenbaum 251–266). To explain it is to dismiss it. That is why evil must remain Other. It must be forever outside, supernatural, and inexplicable.

We can extend Lanzmann's reasoning, however, for there is an even larger, existential terror we schlubs avoid by keeping evil inexplicable. For if we ever recognize Adolf Hitler, say, as an actual human being, then we are forced to recognize that one simple, tiny silly human being could matter *so* much — and how *easily* so very much could happen. If evil is ever seen in this light, in the fullness (or smallness) of what it really is — as the stupid, easy result of an incredibly complicated chain of individual *human* decisions and random interactions and events — how could we *ever* once step out of the house?

In the graphic novel *Arkham Asylum* (1988), a psychologist tells Batman that the Joker's "a special case. Some of us feel he may be *beyond* treatment. In fact, we're not even sure he can be properly defined as *insane*." She likens the Joker's syndrome to Tourette's and goes on to offer the somewhat contradictory, impenetrable — but tantalizing — proposition that "we may actually be looking at some kind of super-sanity here ... a brilliant new modification of human perception, more suited to urban life at the end of the twentieth century.... Unlike you or I, the Joker seems to have no control over the sensory information he's receiving from the world" (Morrison 27). At first glance, this would seem to be a bit of psychological doggerel or double-speak, something similar to the "My patient suffers from Batman psychosis" victimization of the Joker by his fame-obsessed psychologist in *The Dark Knight Returns*: he's not in control, he's not responsible, et cetera. But this psychologist may have stumbled on to something that's useful for our purposes. For the term "super-sanity" does not imply a *lack* of awareness or self-control. In fact, "super-sanity" would seem to suggest *exactly* the opposite — an abundance, even an *over*-abundance, of consciousness and perspective. Perhaps, it is too *much* perspective.

If we then *combine* this idea with the notion that evil *must* have no explanation (for if evil moves away from its status as Other and "starts to make sense," the schlubs would not be able to leave the house), we get the following way of looking at the Joker: He must forever insist that evil is *not* every day, *not* human, *not* banal, *not* something that "just happens to people" (as it happened to his wife), but that evil is instead something that is supernatural, inexplicable, unexplained, outsized, extraordinary, beyond belief—yes, even funny or silly. Think of trying to explain in concrete, reasonable terms just *why* it is that something makes one laugh. It can't be done. "Funny" just *is*. Laughter, itself, is almost a supernatural act.

The Joker establishes, again and again, that evil belongs to the Other, to those in the Seventh Circle of Hell, to the "insane, crazy, psychotic, loony, mad, nutty, sick, et cetera." That, really, is "super-sanity": the Joker's conscious recognition that someone must *play* that role, and since he recognizes that someone *must* play it, *he* will be the one to play it.

If Satan—who came from nowhere and whose origin and motivation defy explanation—has gone from the world, or if he never existed in the first place, someone must take on the Devil's responsibilities. Someone must insist on good or, at least, on evil, for there is the greater, grasping terror of the mundane. There is, quite simply, *hope* in the idea of good and evil.

Perhaps this is why the Joker kills randomly, utterly senselessly, without purpose or motivation or meaning. He embraces randomness; he embraces chaos, but it is a deliberate randomness, a deliberate senselessness, one designed to produce an effect. That is why his schemes make no sense—they make no sense on purpose. That is why he nods affirmatively, even proudly, and says, "Yes, hilariously so!" (or something similar) whenever anyone calls him insane ("Yes, well, I had *better* be insane, no? Thank God!"). That is why he occasionally makes a show of faux-homosexuality: homosexuality is Other, it is cast as alien, monstrous. The Joker has to be crazy so we can stay sane. This, actually, is why he isn't even all that funny. Or even, ultimately, satisfying. He is like a performance artist, inhabiting his own work. And like most performance artists, the Joker is trying too hard.

This identification of the Joker's insanity as "too much sanity" is, admittedly, pretty circular, even a little cute, as is the whole notion of "deliberate randomness." For seeing too much and having too much perspective, one might suggest, would make one insane, and being deliberately random isn't really being random at all—except, of course, it sort of *is*.

This is very circular, so let's consider circles. *The Killing Joke* begins and ends by repeating an image whose recurrence I've indicated previously: those ripples on water, spreading out from the center. Here, they occur on the surface of a puddle and are caused by a drop of rain. Elsewhere, we have seen these ripples whenever the Joker falls from a great height. Interestingly, the spread of ripples on any liquid surface is expressed mathematically through the number PI (⅔). PI also "sits in the pupil of the eye.... PI can be found in waves and ripples and spectra of all kinds, and therefore PI occurs in colors and music." Given the Joker's propensity for homicide, it is even more interesting that "PI occurs naturally in tables of death, in what is known as a Gaussian distribution of deaths in a population; that is, when a person dies, the event 'impacts' PI" (Preston).

PI is a "transcendent number." It has no end and stretches to infinity. There is something supernatural and inexplicable about PI. Like the Joker, it departs from rational explanations, avoids attempts to locate it; it is virtually indescribable and can't be found. Yet, it clearly exists. The evidence for it is everywhere. It, like the Joker and his evil, cannot be ignored. It can be demonstrated and witnessed, but not comprehended. It is a circus without end or beginning. And that's all there is.

Works Cited

Englehart, Steve. "The Laughing Fish." *The Greatest Joker Stories Ever Told*. Ed. Mike Gold. New York: DC Comics, 1988. 226–242.
Gold, Mike. "The Joker's Dozen" (Introduction). *The Greatest Joker Stories Ever Told*. New York: DC Comics, 1988. 6–10.
Lee, Peggy. "Is That All There Is?" By Jerry Leiber and Mike Stoller. Rec. 1969. *Peggy Lee — All-Time Greatest Hits*. Curb Records, 1990.
Miller, Frank. *The Dark Knight Returns*. New York: DC Comics, 1986.
Moore, Alan and Brian Bolland. *Batman: The Killing Joke*. New York: DC Comics, 1988.
Morrison, Grant and Dave McKean. *Arkham Asylum*. New York: DC Comics, 1989.
Preston, Richard. "The Mountains of PI." *The New Yorker* 2 March 2 1992. September 4, 2005 http://www.newyorker.com/archive/content/?050411fr_archive01
Rosenbaum, Ron. *Explaining Hitler*. New York. HarperPerennial, 1999.
Vonnegut, Kurt. *Armageddon in Retrospect*. New York. G.P. Putnam & Sons, 2007.

14

Call It (Friendo)
Flipism and Folklore in *No Country for Old Men* and *The Dark Knight*

MATTHEW FOTIS

> Whenever you're called on to make up your mind, and you're hampered by not having any, the best way to solve the dilemma, you'll find, is simply by spinning a penny. No — not so that chance shall decide the affair while you're passively standing there moping; but the moment the penny is up in the air, you suddenly know what you're hoping — Piet Hein, *A Psychological Tip* (Hein 1969)

Heads or tails — that's all it takes. Some call it in the air and let it hit the ground. Others call it before the toss, catch the coin in one hand and slap it on the back of the other. Whatever the method, flipping a coin has a long tradition in Western culture. From Caesar's "head" settling disputes, Donald Duck's adventures with Flipism[1], the modern day use of a coin toss in sports, to the naming of Portland, OR, flipping a coin has been an influential part of Western and Anglo-American folklore for centuries. A seemingly simple game of chance has been a popular gambling and children's game, a mode of divination, a way to settle disputes, and used to argue for the power of reason and prove the prudence of a legal system based on a jury of one's peers.

Like many aspects of folklore, coin tossing has made its way into film. Two of the most critically acclaimed films of 2007 and 2008 prominently feature coin tosses. Anton Chigurh (Javier Bardem), the cold blooded villain of the Coen Brothers Academy Award winning *No Country for Old Men*, and Harvey Dent (Aaron Eckhart), the white knight district attorney in Christopher Nolan's *The Dark Knight*, both use coin tosses throughout their respective films. The use of Flipism by Chigurh and Dent seemingly suggests a world ordered by fate, destiny and the cosmos. It is my contention, however, that

Flipism is used by the filmmakers to argue for the supremacy of free will in a chaotic world. Rather than leaving things to chance as tossing a coin seemingly suggests, both characters are fully aware of the choices they are making throughout, and the use of coin tosses is a calculated psychological tool implemented by two highly intelligent characters — not as a means to make decisions.

In order to fully understand how Flipism works in each film I will be first charting a brief history of coin tossing to help establish a background and folk tradition. This will frame the discussion as well as provide insight into how Chigurh and Dent implement and manipulate Flipism. I will then examine the ways in which Chigurh and Dent use Flipism, with specific examples of their particular brands of Flipism in action. Finally, I will show why Flipism is a psychological tool and not an agent of fate.

Coin Toss — A Brief History

Heads and Tails is a coin tossing game in contemporary America that derives from the British game Cross and Pile. As is so often the case with Western traditions, Cross and Pile actually originated in Ancient Greece. In the Greek game, according to William Wood Seymour, "a shell was smeared on one side with pitch, while the other was left in its original whiteness; when tossed in the air, the cry was night or day" (466). We can see in the whiteness and darkness of the seashell the beginning of one of the folk beliefs often associated with coin tosses, that of light and dark or good and evil. This idea is personified in the films by Dent and Chigurh. The new Gotham District Attorney, Dent is repeatedly referred to as the city's "White Knight," while Chigurh is seen as evil incarnate, as film critic David DuBos notes, "the black-appareled Chigurh walks and stalks ... dispensing Death wherever he goes ... with a simple flip of a coin" ("No Exit").

The belief in the righteousness of heads in part stems from the positive associations with the heads side of the coin. Coin flipping as a decision making tool dates to Roman times. While coins had been around for centuries, it wasn't until Julius Caesar came to power that using a coin flip to make a decision emerged. Caesar's head was on one side of every coin, so "heads" determined the winner. It was thought that "heads" meant that Caesar agreed with the decision. It was also believed that the coin flip revealed the gods decision. In more modern times, this idea has merged into the belief that a coin toss, particularly the heads side of the coin, shows God's will. The Roman method of coin flipping was taken very seriously and was used to resolve disputes, property litigation, marriage issues, and even employed in criminal court. Caesar's head on coins not only showed the right answer in any dispute, but it also is the root of the popular saying "Heads you win, tails you lose" (Batchelor and de Lys 52–54).

The idea of light versus dark, good versus evil, et cetera is further solidified with the British. While still used as a means to settle disputes, although not carrying the same legal stature as in Roman times, coin tossing in Britain is more associated as a gambling game, named Cross and Pile because historically English coins were stamped on one side with a cross. By pitting the cross, signifying what Christians would argue is the ultimate symbol of light, versus the bottom part of the die, which can be seen to symbolize Hell, the game intentionally or not heightened the belief of good versus evil. The cross has considerable significance in the Christian world, and "in popular lore it is regarded as a charm, the most potent protection against evil in existence" (Larousse 129). Furthermore, according to David Pickering, "because of its sacred associations, the cross is widely reputed to repel evil spirits of all kinds, from vampires to the devil" (65). With the heavenly symbol of the cross on one side, and the corporeal pile side, we again see the contrast between the gods and man.

When the cross was replaced on British coins by the crown around 1600, the game took on further significance. The notion of the divine right of kings posited that a monarch derives his right to rule directly from the will of God (Figgis 1). With the British crown seen as having a divine connection, the calling of heads or tails again signifies more than a simple game of chance. Much like with Caesar, the heads side of the coin became associated with righteousness. By coming up heads, it is implied that the king (or Caesar) agrees with the decision, and by proxy so too does God. Due in part to the positive connotations of the heads side of the coin, there is even a belief among many that heads is more likely to be the result of a coin toss, even though a fairly weighted coin will yield a fifty-fifty result. Many people are familiar with the saying "see a penny, pick it up, and all day long you'll have good luck." However many people also won't pick up a coin unless it is heads up, "Face up, pick it up. Face down, leave it down." Picking up a tails side up coin is thought to bring bad luck.

The idea of coin flipping revealing God's will has carried into American folklore. The heads side of the coin in American currency is embossed with the words "In God We Trust." As Proverbs 16:20 states, "He who gives attention to the word will find good/And blessed is he who trusts in the Lord" (*New American Standard Bible*). As Christianity so often preaches, faith in God will be rewarded, likewise going against His will can be punished, so picking the heads side of the coin can be seen as putting one's trust in God. On the flip side, the tails side of the coin has long been associated with darkness, evil, and humanism; it is, after all, the side of the coin you can't see. In American currency, it does not feature any religious overtones; rather it features the phrase "E Pluribus Unum"—out of many, one. This highly secular phrase can be interpreted as completely incompatible to Christianity in which there is one clear leader. E Pluribus Unum suggests a society that is strongest when it is following the will of the people, rather than the will of God. It argues for the power of reason over the philosophy of faith. With the Enlightenment and its challenges to God's will, the tails side of the coin began to take on an even more secular — i.e. negative — connotation, and heightens the notion of God's will (heads) versus free will (tails).

In contemporary America, coin tossing has come to represent a flippant, fair or arbitrary way to make a decision, a sort of watered down version of the Roman system. As noted above, there is still a seeming preference for the heads side of the coin and a strong belief that a coin flip reveals God's will, fate and destiny. But coin flips are rarely still used for large decisions, instead it has become a way to settle trivial arguments and disputes. Do I want chocolate or vanilla ice cream? Which team will get the ball first in the Super Bowl?

Coin flipping has a long and winding tradition, and as a result, there are several important beliefs about coin flipping that pervade American life. There is the idea that a coin flip is revealing God's will or is simply fate. Some believe in the righteousness of the heads side of the coin, seeing it as heavenly and the tails side as secular and, consequently, evil or dark. Some see a coin flip as the most fair and arbitrary way to settle a small dispute. The debate concerning if flipping a coin is totally random or a predetermined outcome is not important. What is important is that these folk beliefs are exploited by Chigurh and Dent in their respective films.

Anton and Harvey Flip a Coin

Before exploring the actual coin tosses in the films, first let us quickly look at Dent and Chigurh. The idea of good versus evil in a coin toss can be seen in the good versus evil portrayed by Dent and Chigurh. One is literally seen as death or the devil, while the other is "Gotham's White Knight," who has a crisis of faith near the end of the film where he questions just which side of the coin he represents. Not only do they symbolize certain sides of the coin in their respective films, but juxtaposed they also represent an interesting dichotomy. Dent can be seen to represent the heroic and righteous heads side of the coin, while Chigurh represents the dark, tails side.

Dent is the stereotypical hero. Director Christopher Nolan cast Eckhart for the role because he embodies "that kind of chiseled, American hero quality" (Jolin). Further playing up the light versus dark motif, Eckhart even had his hair lightened for the role. While Dent stands for the hero, one way of viewing the film is to consider that Dent is essentially moving from the heads side of the coin to the tails side due to The Joker's injection of chaos into Gotham. In the end though, because of Batman's actions, Dent ultimately represents the heads side — the slain leader who sacrificed everything for the common good. Interestingly, Eckhart modeled the character on Robert F. Kennedy, who was "idealistic, held a grudge and took on the mob" (Keck). RFK, like Dent, had both light and dark qualities that made him good at his job.

While Dent represents the stereotypical hero, Chigurh is the prototypical villain. He is a ruthless murderer who displays little emotion. While Eckhart is a Waspish "chiseled American hero," Chigurh is ethnic. He isn't given an exact ethnicity, but one can assume based on the Southwest location that Chigurh is Mexican-American. This feeds on long held negative connotations about non-white peoples, as well as representing the idea that evil is dark. Richard Dyer's *White* argues that whiteness has become synonymous with goodness. As Dyer argues that it is said, even in liberal textbooks, "that there are inevitable associations of white with light and therefore safety, and black with dark and therefore danger." These associations, argues Dyer, originate with the "Jewish and Christian use of white and black to symbolize good and evil, as carried still in such expressions as 'a black mark,' 'white magic,' 'to blacken the character'" (qtd. in Hooks 38). We have seen the connotations in coin flipping as well, where heads can be seen to equal white (Dent) and tails equal dark (Chigurh). Howard Thurman echoes these sentiments, arguing that race has purposely been mythologized so that white equals good, while "black is ugly, black is evil, black is demonic" (qtd. in Hooks 189).

Tellingly, all of the people that Chigurh hunts and kills are white, furthering negative stereotypes and fears about Mexican immigration. As Leo Braudy notes, Chigurh's evil "has no conscience or human nature that can be appealed to, and it is foreign" (10). He is foreign not only in ethnicity, but also as a part of the white world. He seemingly drops from the sky into the film, and at the end, vanishes again. All of this fuels his villainy. Adding to his foreign nature is the manner in which he kills his victims. For much of the film, he uses a cattle gun, shooting his victims in the forehead. This deprives them of their humanity, turning them into livestock. Jay Ellis argues that it also "deprives them of their living sight while imprinting in them a symbolic third eye — a visual representation of the enlightenment on matters of chance and destiny" (229). Chigurh then represents the secular side of the coin, while Dent is ultimately eulogized as a hero, looking over the city from above.

It is important to note that both films also use the heads side of the coin as the positive side of the coin. For example, when Chigurh flips a coin to determine if he will kill a gas station owner, the man calls "heads" and is allowed to live. Likewise Dent uses heads as the life giving side of the coin, telling one potential victim, "Heads you get to keep your head. Tails not so lucky." The assumption is that heads equals life, while tails equals death; a motif that runs through both *No Country for Old Men* and *The Dark Knight*.

Now that we have a general idea of the history and folklore of coin tossing, let's look at the coin tosses in the films, beginning with Anton Chigurh in *No Country for Old Men*. The film is set in west Texas in 1980, and "tells the story of a sheriff struggling along in the bloody wake of a psychopathic murderer [Chigurh]" (Cooper 37). Llewelyn Moss (Josh Brolin), a local resident out hunting, stumbles upon a busted drug deal ... and a bag with two million dollars. Moss takes the money and kicks off a series of cat and mouse games. Chigurh begins chasing Moss to recover the money, while Sheriff Ed Tom Bell (Tommy Lee Jones) tries to track down either Moss or Chigurh. There are several bloody encounters, including a shoot out between Moss and Chigurh in a border town that leaves both of them wounded. Chigurh then tracks down Moss, kills him and takes the money. Bell nearly catches Chigurh at the scene of the final showdown, but Chigurh is able to avoid detection. Chigurh, true to his word, then tracks down Moss's wife and kills her. As he leaves the scene, he is involved in a nasty car accident, and despite a severely broken arm, he is able to leave the scene before the police arrive. The movie ends with Chigurh still on the loose.

In many ways, the film follows a folktale narrative style. Linda Degh argues in "Folk Narrative" that folktales can be categorized by three basic qualities; first, a framed, narrated structure (Bell); second, formulaic speech patterns; and third, formulaic narrative arcs and character types (60–61). *No Country for Old Men* satisfies all of these requirements, and interestingly, can be viewed as a type of folktale in its own right. The plot is a Pandora's Box type cautionary tale. As Cooper states, "Moss, an ordinary 'everyman,' stumbles upon a temptation (the cash), and upon succumbing to the temptation is pursued by a Vice character, Chigurh, who is also an archetypal 'Devil,' and a Virtue character, Bell, who tries and fails to get Moss to do the right thing by turning the money into the police" (48). Bell even offers a moral at the end of the film, borrowing from Rip Van Winkle, when he comments that Moss and company "woke up and they don't know how they got where they're at."

Not only is the plot similar to a fairytale, but so too are the characters, as their archetypes suggest. Much like the two sides of a coin, Bell and Chigurh represent two sides of the film's moral code. As Cooper argues, "nihilism (represented by Chigurh) and morality (represented by Bell) defend their cases against each other ... [the film ends] with the nihilist exiting the stage while the moralist remains, diffident and undefended" (39). Not only does Chigurh represent the Christian idea of the Devil, but he also can be associated with the border folklore idea of the devil as a shape shifter. Chigurh is so terrifying to Bell and others because he does not kill for malice. This is incongruous with the Christian Devil, and is actually more in line with "an arbitrary wreaker-of-havoc like Native American tricksters" (Cooper 49). Additionally, his survival of three near death experiences and his ability to seemingly vanish, such as at the end of the film, is more comparable to the trickster type than the Devil. The trickster or shape-shifter can change their external shape at will, while retaining a consistent identity. Thus, the evil witch can appear as a young woman or beautiful princess, but their essential identity is the same (Garry and El-Shamy 126).

Chigurh's character in many ways is comparable to a character type in folklore because he is seemingly two-dimensional. As Vladimir Propp points out in *Theory and History of Folklore*, characters in folklore differ from characters in literature primarily because, in folklore, characters are "types," not individuals (27). Cooper believes that Chigurh is not only "a typed character, but he is also depicted with supernatural overtones. At one point ... Sheriff Bell assures himself and another deputy that Chigurh is, in the final analysis, not a ghost. The other man replies, 'I guess if he was a ghost you wouldn't have to worry about him'" (43). Chigurh also engages each of his victims in a dialogue, much like the stereotypical fairytale villain. Like the big bad wolf huffing and puffing, Chigurh forces a conversation with his victims before ultimately deciding their fate.

Chigurh and Bell both ultimately posses jobs in which they decide other men's fates; Bell as a sheriff and Chigurh as a hit man. Bell follows the standard of the law, while Chigurh follows his own code, represented in the film by a coin toss. There are two examples in the film where Chigurh uses a coin toss to seemingly decide the fate of his victim, once early in the movie with a "random" gas station attendant and then again at the end of the film with Carla Jean. I will also be looking at one other incident in the film where Chigurh does not offer his victim the chance to "call it."

In the first coin flipping scene, an unnamed gas station owner encounters

Chigurh and makes a few remarks about Chigurh (specifically that he is from out of town, i.e. foreign) that alerts Chigurh to a possible complication. The conversation quickly moves from small talk to something more. In an instant, Chigurh has begun to evaluate the situation, and the old man is quite aware of what has just walked into his gas station. At the height of the intensity, Chigurh asks, "What's the most that you have ever lost on a coin toss?" Before the man can grasp what is happening and answer, Chigurh flips a coin, covers it with his hand, and states, "Call it." While there is a definite sense of malice and almost joy in Chigurh's voice, it is also completely controlled, which is simply terrifying to the man.

After a moment of silence, Chigurh again extols the man to call it, telling him, "You need to call it. I can't call it for you. It wouldn't be fair." The man replies that he hasn't "put nothin' up." Chigurh replies that, indeed, he has been "putting it up" his whole life. During the conversation, we learn that the man married into owning the gas station, and therefore, according to Chigurh, hasn't earned what he has become. Chigurh seems to imply that the man's actions have brought this moment into being. Terrified, the man asks what he stands to win, and Chigurh simply replies "Everything ... Now call it." The man calls heads, which is the "correct" call. Chigurh does not kill him and actually gives the quarter to the man to keep as his "lucky quarter."

The second episode that I would like to analyze does not actually involve a coin toss, and that is precisely why it is important. This encounter is between Chigurh and fellow hit man Carson Wells (Woody Harrelson). Wells has been hired by Moss to kill Chigurh, yet it is Chigurh who tracks down Wells. Unlike the encounter at the gas station, there is a personal history between the two men. Wells is brash, arrogant, predatory, and manipulative, so he does not elicit the same type of sympathy as the gas station owner. Unlike Chigurh, who never gives a clear reason for his line of work, Wells is clearly a less than moral character that is more than willing to exploit and kill people to make a buck. To make him even more unseemly, he seems to relish his line of work. This arrogance, however, proves to be his undoing.

Wells has grossly underestimated Chigurh, referring to him as a "garden variety homicidal maniac." Chigurh seems to be somewhat perturbed by the fact that Wells does not recognize that he is not up against a run of the mill hit man. When Chigurh and Wells come face to face (Chigurh with a shotgun in hand), this time there is no offer of a coin flip. For Wells, there is no opportunity for a reprieve, or as I argue, there is no illusion of a reprieve. Chigurh seemingly wants Wells to admit that he is going to die and accept his fate. He asks Wells "if the rule that you have followed brought you to this point ... then what use is the rule?" At the beginning of the question Chigurh is smiling, but by the end his patented stare is splashed across his face. Wells tries to offer Chigurh money to spare his life, but again, Wells misunderstands the man he is up against. Finally Wells utters the trademark line, "You don't have to do this." Chigurh simply replies, "They all say that," and then kills Wells.

Chigurh seems completely unfazed by having just killed a man. He simply kicks his feet up so that his shoes won't become soaked with blood and answers the ringing phone. As "fate" would have it, the phone call is from Llewelyn Moss. Chigurh tells Moss to turn in the money. If Moss does so, Chigurh vows to spare Moss's wife Carla Jean (though not Moss), noting that it is "the best he can do." Moss, out of fear, vows to keep running, which leads to the third encounter I will analyze between Chigurh and Carla Jean.

Chigurh finds Carla Jean at her mother's house. By this point, he has already recovered the money and killed Llewelyn. As the two sit opposite one another, Chigurh is clearly not relishing the encounter the way he did with Wells and does not have the same electricity that was present with the gas station owner. Instead, he seems resigned, resigned to the fact that he must kill Carla Jean because Llewelyn refused to turn over the money. When Chigurh informs Carla Jean that her husband had the chance to save her, she pleads ignorance and innocence. Like many of his victims she tells Chigurh, "You don't have to do this." Chigurh pauses for a moment and unlike earlier encounters where he was using the silence to build fear, this time he appears to be hesitant. It is in this moment that he decides to offer Carla Jean a chance.

Unlike the gas station attendant, Carla Jean refuses to play the game. Chigurh urges her to "call it." Yet she refuses, telling him "The coin don't have no say in it. It's just you." Chigurh seems to weigh this response, before telling her that he "got here the same way as the coin did." She still refuses to play the game, and a moment later, we see him leaving her house checking the soles of his shoes to make sure that he is not tracking any of her blood.

Was Carla Jean able to see something that Chigurh's other victims could not? Did she uncover the ruse of his game or waste her last chance at life? The coin flip does not represent God's will or fate, as some have argued; rather, it is a calculated move by a killer that steadfastly adheres to logic. Chigurh follows a strong sense of cause and effect. He is after all a byproduct of society (including the Vietnam War); he did not just fall from the sky. He firmly believes that his actions are simply a part of a long chain of connected events. It is his victims that have caused their own demise. They have put themselves into the crosshairs; Chigurh is simply the end result (or effect) of their choices and actions.

In the scene with gas station attendant, Chigurh is happy to pay and be on his way. It is not until the man begins asking questions that Chigurh acts. Chigurh made a conscious choice to let the man go; the coin flip had nothing to do with his fate. The coin flip quite simply put the fear of God into the man. Chigurh needed to ensure that the man would not follow up on his earlier questions about Chigurh and his plans. One should remember that, at this point, Chigurh has recently killed a police officer and several others and is hunting a man carrying two million dollars of illegal Mexican drug money, so it is reasonable to assume that Chigurh wants to cover his bases. Rather than kill the man, which would have aroused more suspicion and given away his location, Chigurh decides to leave the man be, knowing that after the encounter he won't be talking to anyone about Anton Chigurh out of pure fear. What better way to arouse fear than to present yourself as someone willing to *kill* based on pure chance? As Chigurh states at the end after giving the coin to the man, "don't put it in your pocket ... where it will be mixed in with the others and become just a coin." Chigurh then pauses, cracks a half smile, and says, "Which it is." What seems like a menacing exit line is actually a rather telling line about Chigurh's coin tossing philosophy. He was never going to kill the man based on a coin flip.

Another reason that Chigurh does not kill the man is because, as absurd as it seems, Chigurh does not needlessly kill. Apart from the logical reasons not to kill the man — it would create a scene, the police would come, etc — it also isn't necessary. While Chigurh does kill several other "innocent" people throughout the film, he does not do so purely for the thrill of the kill. The hotel clerk for example, is killed because Chigurh knows that Moss is at the hotel. Chigurh assumes that he will kill Moss, which means that the police will be coming. Therefore, in his mind, he needs to eliminate any witnesses that can put him at the scene of the crime. Furthermore, he isn't creating an entirely new crime scene as he would if he killed the gas station owner, rather he is only adding to the one he plans to create anyway. Chigurh is the ultimate hit man, at the pinnacle of his profession. He knows when he killing someone is necessary and when it is not. While he has no qualms with killing someone that is simply in the wrong place at the wrong time, he does not kill for pure pleasure. The legend of Chigurh, fed by the idea that he kills based on a coin flip, actually makes it easier for Chigurh not to kill. He doesn't have to prove anything to anyone, so he is able to let innocent people like the gas station owner live. His next encounter, with a less accomplished and seasoned hit man/bounty hunter, further demonstrates Chigurh's ability to asses a situation and shows the value he places on life.

The encounter with Wells shows that Chigurh is in complete control of his choices and is not an agent of God or the Devil or anyone. He is the result of reason. Wells chose to try to kill Chigurh for a quick buck. The likely outcome of the situation was that either he would kill Chigurh or vice versa. By grossly underestimating Chigurh, Wells has flipped his own coin so to speak. The rules of the agreement Wells made dictate that someone must die, in this case Wells. Likewise with Carla Jean, Chigurh already offered to let her go free. Carla Jean's husband stole the money, so one could argue that she had no role in the affair. But she did nothing to try to stop him, and in Chigurh's world, she also chose to marry Llewelyn, knowing his faults—although perhaps not knowing one of those faults would be to forfeit a chance to save her life. In that way, she is an accomplice, yet Chigurh is willing to forgive her and spare her life. If Moss returns the money and turns himself in, she lives; if he does not, she dies. Simple cause and effect. Since Moss did not turn in the money, in Chigurh's world, she must therefore die. She recognizes this cause and effect reasoning and therefore does not submit to his coin flipping charade. Chigurh is simply trying, as unfathomable as it may seem, to give Carla Jean the illusion that she has some agency over her life, since, much like the gas station owner, it was not her direct action that led Chigurh to this point. She sees through this and declines to call it, knowing that heads or tails, she is dead.

While Chigurh might be one of the most iconic villains of all time, *The Dark Knight's* Harvey Dent is "the hero Gotham needs." Set a single year after *Batman Begins*, the film follows Batman's (Christian Bale) quest to rid Gotham of the mob. Aiding in his quest are Lt. James Gordon (Gary Oldman) and the new district attorney, Harvey Dent. The three men form a revolving heroic triumvirate, countered by the psychopathic criminal The Joker (Heath Ledger). Dent manages to lock up nearly all of the city's criminals, but his achievements are spoiled by The Joker, who sets up a series of either/or ethical challenges that wreak havoc on the city and the film's heroes. The Joker's ultimate test forces Batman to choose between saving Dent or their mutual love interest Rachel Dawes (Maggie Gyllenhaal). Batman chooses to save Dent, although Dent's face gets mutilated in a fantastic explosion. Dent then goes on a spree of revenge, turning into the villain from the comic series Two Face[2] before he is ultimately killed by Batman. Knowing that the city needs the symbol of Dent to live on, Batman takes the blame for Dent's spree, leaving Dent as the city's white knight, and Batman as the dark knight. As Lt. Gordon sums up their relationship, "One the hero Gotham needs, the other the hero Gotham deserves."

Much like Chigurh and Bell, Dent and Batman can be viewed as two sides of the same coin. For that matter, there are a series of coin pairs in the film: Batman and The Joker; Dent and The Joker; Gordon and Batman, Dent and Two Face among others. In each pair there is clearly a "good guy" and a "bad guy." Batman is also a coin; both a symbol of hope to many and a member of the criminal underground to others. Bruce Wayne, as a playboy billionaire and a masked vigilante furthers the two sides of the coin motif. The film itself can also be seen as a battle being waged with light and dark, fire and shadows. The Joker wants to create a dark world by using fire, while Batman presents a symbol of hope by wearing a mask and operating under the cloak of darkness to bring about peace and order. Dent is so appealing to both Gotham and Batman because he is bringing light to the city in broad daylight. With all of the light and dark connotations, it should come as no surprise that the film has implemented coin tossing.

There are nine scenes in the film that feature a coin toss. First, I will examine Dent's very first coin flip scene in court, second his coin flip with a captured criminal, and finally his coin flipping montage after his accident when he is essentially Two Face. I shall only focus on a few here to demonstrate that Dent, much like Chigurh, is not leaving anything up to chance. For the first three quarters of the film, Dent cannot leave it to chance because he is using a double-headed Peace Quarter (notice that it is not double-tails since Dent is a hero). As the film begins, Dent has just been elected Gotham's new D.A.. He exudes a heroic quality and vows to clean up the city. He is literally the face of hope that Batman cannot be, the heads to Batman's tails. As Bruce Wayne notes, "Gotham needs a hero with a face."

The first instance of a coin flip comes at the trial of mobster Sal Maroni. Dent is slightly late to the trial and when he arrives, Assistant District Attorney, and Bruce's childhood friend and ex-girlfriend, Rachel Dawes starts to tear into Dent. Exuding charm, he offers to let her chair the case based on a coin flip, "Heads I take it, tails it's yours." Again, notice that heads is the positive choice. Rachel indignantly replies, "Flip a coin?... And leave something this big to chance?" Dent flips the coin, and of course it comes up heads, to which he replies, "I make my own luck." At this point in the film, the audience is not yet aware that Dent is using a double-sided coin. Yet, that is partially irrelevant. Much like Chigurh, Dent has already made his decision and is using the coin flip to achieve another goal. In this instance, he is trying to prove his prowess, both as a lawyer and a potential lover. He seemingly is leaving an important case to chance, yet once the trial begins he displays an amazing talent and preparedness, disarming a potential assassin and getting a confession.

The second time we see a coin flip, Dent is interrogating a criminal in the back of an ambulance after an assassination attempt on the mayor. The criminal thinks that he has an emotional Dent right where he wants him and plays coy. That is when Dent takes out his coin. He points his gun at the criminal's head and says, "Heads you keep your head, tails not so lucky." The criminal doesn't quite believe Dent, who flips the coin and, of course, it comes up heads. The criminal laughs, but Dent stops him by flipping the coin again. This causes the man to scream in terror and plead with Dent that he doesn't have any useful information about The Joker. Batman interjects, asking Dent why he is leaving the situation to chance, to which Dent, again replies that he isn't. He flips the coin to Batman, who along with the audience sees that Dent is using a double sided coin. Again, we see that Dent is not using the coin toss to make a decision, but is using it as a psychological tool to manipulate the other person.

The final set of coin flips that I will analyze take place after Dent has had half of his face burned off. The explosion also left Dent's coin burned on one side, so for the first time in the film, he has a coin with two sides. After a hospital visit from The Joker, in which The Joker convinces Dent/Two Face that there are no rules, only chaos, Dent sets out to get revenge for the murder of his fiancée Rachel. On his quest for revenge, Dent/Two Face uses his new coin on The Joker, two police officers who betrayed him, Batman, himself, and Gordon's young son. Interestingly, the first person that Dent/Two Face shoots based on a coin flip, the dirty cop Wirtz, is actually not a coin flip. He spins the coin on a bar top, and when the burned side comes up (of course, the clean heads side still represents life) Dent/Two Face shoots Wirtz. It is a slight distinction, but the audience never actually sees Dent/Two Face kill Wirtz. The coin comes to rest on the dark side and then Dent/Two Face fires his gun. While it is implied that Wirtz has been killed, it is not certain.

Similarly, when Dent/Two Face shoots Sal Maroni's driver based on a coin flip, we do not actually see the violence. Just moments before Maroni had "survived" his own coin flip, but his driver "wasn't so lucky." All that the audience sees is Dent/Two Face putting on his seat belt and then firing his gun, causing the car to spin out of control and crash. Again, it can be assumed that the driver and Maroni are dead, but it is not certain, after all Dent/Two Face walked away from the accident. Furthermore, in the aftermath of Dent/Two Face's spree, it is noted that several people were left unconscious in the wake of violence. It isn't absurd to assume that Maroni and his driver fall into this category.

The end of the film features a series of interesting and revealing coin flips. Dent/Two Face has brought Lt. Gordon's family to the site of Rachel's murder. He wants to make Gordon watch a loved one die, much like he had to listen to Rachel die. After determining that Gordon's son (who, of course, is the only member of the family with bright blonde hair) is the person whom

Gordon loves the most, Dent/Two Face sets out on his coin flips. Batman, who arrives fresh from defeating The Joker, is the first to have his fate flipped. The coin comes up on the dark side, and so Dent/Two Face shoots him. It's important to note that he shoots Batman in the stomach. This suggests that he doesn't want to kill Batman, because throughout the course of the film, Dent and Batman have seen how important they are to each other and to the future of Gotham. The next coin flip is for Dent/Two Face himself. The coin comes up heads, so he lives. The final flip is for Gordon's son, but while the coin is in the air Batman knocks Dent/Two Face away, sending him plummeting to his death. As Dent lies dead, the coin comes to rest on heads. Knowing that Gotham's new-found hope would be destroyed, and the cases he made against the mob would be dismissed should Dent/Two-Face's crimes become known, Batman and Gordon decide to trick Gotham into thinking that Batman, in a vengeful fury, has committed all of Dent/Two-Face's murders. The symbol of Dent lives on, not as the dark side of his personality, but as the light side. Much like the two sides of the coin, Dent lives on as the pristine heads side, the white knight.

The film shows two different uses for coin flipping. As Dent, coin flipping is not a decision making tool, rather it is a device to achieve a different end — a psychological advantage. As Two Face, coin flipping becomes a decision making tool, leaving several dead. In this way, the film both reinforces and subverts folk beliefs. Initially, Dent uses the folk belief to his advantage, but as Two Face he uses the folk belief to make choices, in a way, absolving himself from the consequences.

Yet, even when Dent is at his most villainous, the coin flipping has slight distinctions. As noted above, when he shoots Wirtz he spins the coin, which suggests that Dent/Two Face has already made up his mind as to what he is going to do. Likewise, when the coin comes up black for Batman, Dent/Two Face shoots him in the abdomen, again suggesting that killing Batman is not his goal. Instead, he is trying to show Gordon that if the coin comes up black, he will pull the trigger. Whether or not he will actually kill the boy is not relevant at that moment (and a decision I do not think Dent/Two Face has made yet or wants to make. By not killing Batman, it can be argued that he is subconsciously avoiding making the decision, knowing that Batman will intervene). He wants to put Gordon through the agony of having to talk to someone in a seemingly hopeless situation and "lie" to them that everything is going to be okay. Shooting Batman achieves this state, killing him is not necessary. It is also noteworthy that Dent/Two Face is also angry at Gordon for not standing up to corruption in the police force, which led to Rachel's death. Even as a villain, Dent/Two Face is worried about government corruption.

Call It

While the Romans used a coin toss as a serious and legally binding way to solve problems, and coin flipping has long been associated with demonstrating God's will, coin flipping in *No Country for Old Men* and *The Dark Knight* actually works to show man's superiority over his own fate. Rather than leaving things to chance as tossing a coin seemingly suggests, both characters are fully aware of the choices they are making throughout, and rather than follow folk beliefs, they actually manipulate those beliefs. As Robert Georges and Michael Owen Jones note in *Folkloristics*, "folklore is first and foremost a behavioral phenomenon" (231). Georges and Owens argue that folklore is not simply a traditional artifact, but it can be an active phenomenon. In researching how children play games, they state "ignoring how a child alters the rules of play or employs strategies to turn chance into something to be controlled and exploited overlooks an important fact of human behavior ... Individuals ... personalize folklore, utilize it for psychological or spiritual ends, and even exploit it as a means of self-aggrandizement" (264).

So, why did the filmmakers change the traditional folk belief? With nearly every single instance of coin flipping in the films, the outcome of the coin toss is not a determining factor in what happens next. Rather it is a psychological tool employed by Chigurh and Dent to gain an edge over their adversary. They are using the folk beliefs that are associated with coin flipping to their advantage. The people on the other side of the coin flips are assuming that Chigurh and Dent are going to act based on a random act of chance. They also believe that the outcome of the coin toss is in some way a valid verdict, a binding decision that is a direct descendant of the Roman belief. Yet neither character, both of whom are, in their own way, obsessive and carefully crafted, would leave major decisions to chance. They each have a plan, and flipping a coin is a part of the plan — a means to achieve an end, not the end in itself.

Therefore, the randomness of a coin toss works to make Chigurh an even more terrifying figure. It helps transform him into an evil, killing machine. Deciding to kill someone based on a coin flip feeds his legend and builds him into something that he is not. Chigurh does not kill based on a coin toss; he kills based on action, choices, and consequences. The coin tossing works to make him a figure that you don't want to cross; it doesn't determine your fate however — it shows that you determine your own fate. The "randomness" of a coin toss in Dent's case gives him a psychological advantage over the criminals in his city and adds to his own charm and effectiveness. With a double-sided coin he dictates the outcome of his coin tosses, while making others believe that he is leaving things to chance. In one way, he is also using the folk belief that coin tosses show God's will ... and He happens to be on Harvey Dent's side.

Coin flipping, then, is not a random act that shows us God's will. It is a calculated method employed by two incredibly intelligent and strong-willed characters to gain an advantage. By manipulating the traditional folk beliefs associated with coin flipping, they give themselves an edge over their adversary. By using a coin flip to seemingly make decisions, Chigurh and Dent help tip the odds from a flip of the coin to their side.

Notes

1. Disney animator Carl Barks coined the term Flipism in his 1953 Donald Duck comic "Flip Decision." The term has come to represent the philosophy of making decisions by flipping a coin. As Professor Batty tells Donald in the comic, "Life is but a gamble! Let Flipism chart your ramble!" (Barks).

2. Nolan insists that Dent is dead at the end of the movie, leaving the villain Two Face dead as well. In that sense, the film is much more about Dent and his heroic symbolism than solely his transformation into a villain.

Works Cited

Barks, Carl. *Flip Decision, Walt Disney Comics & Stories* 149, Vol. 13, No. 5 (1953).
Barrier, Michael. *Carl Barks and the Art of the Comic Book. New York:* M. Lilien Publishers, 1981.
Batchelor, Julie Forsyth, and Claudia de Lys. *Superstitious? Here's Why!* New York: Scholastic, 1954.
Braudy, Leo. "Whose Country?" *Film Quarterly.* Summer 2008, Vol. 61, No 4, pgs 10–11.
Cooper, Lydia. "He's a Psychopathic Killer, but So What?": Folklore and Morality in Cormac McCarthy's *No Country for Old Men.*" *Papers on Language and Literature,* Winter 2009, 37–59.
Dark Knight, The. Dir. Christopher Nolan. Warner Bros, 2008.
Degh, Linda. "Folk Narrative." *Folklore and Folklife.* Ed. Richard M. Dorson. Chicago: University of Chicago Press, 1972. 53–84.
DuBos, David. "No Exit: Film review of *No Country for Old Men.*" *New Orleans Magazine.* February 7, 2008.
Ellis, Jay. *No Place for Home.* New York: Routledge, 2006.
Figgis, John Neville. *The Divine Right of Kings.* New York: Harper & Row, 1965.
Garry, Jane, and Hasan El-Shamy, eds. *Archetypes and Motifs in Folklore and Literature.* Armonk, NY: M.E. Sharpe, 2005.
Georges, Robert A., and Michael Owen Jones. *Folkloristics: An Introduction.* Bloomington, IN: Indiana University Press, 1995.

Gomme, Alice B. *The Traditional Games of England, Scotland, and Ireland.* New York: Dover Publications, 1964.
Hazlitt, William Carew. *Faiths & Folklore: A Dictionary of national beliefs, superstitions and popular customs.* London: Reeves & Turner, 1905.
Hein, Piet. *Grooks.* New York: Doubleday, 1969.
hooks, bell. *Killing Rage: Ending Racism.* New York: Holt Publishers, 1995.
Jolin, Dan. "Fear Has a Face." *Empire* 223: 87–88. http://www.empireonline.com/magazine/covers/image.asp?id=24227&gallery=1365&cation=%23223%20%28January%202008%29
Keck, William. "Aaron Eckhart puts on his best acting face." *USA Today.* 28 July 2008. http://www.usatoday.com/life/people/2008-07-28-eckhart_N.htm.
Landesman, Cosmo. "The Dark Knight— the Sunday Times review." *The Sunday Times.* 27 July 2008. http://entertainment.timesonline.co.uk/tol/arts_and_entertainment/film/ film_reviews/article4386375.ece.
Locke, John. *The Works of John Locke in Nine Volumes.* London: Rivington, 1824 12th ed.. Vol. 2.
New American Standard Bible. Anaheim, California: Foundation Publications, 1995.
Newell, William Wells. *Games and Songs of American Children.* New York: Dover Publications, 1963.
No Country for Old Men. Dir. Ethan and Joel Coen. Vantage Paramount, 2007.
Opie, Iona, and Peter Opie. *Children's Games in Street and Playground.* Oxford: Oxford University Press, 1969.
The Papers of Thomas Jefferson. Edited by Julian P. Boyd et al. Princeton: Princeton UniversityPress. "The Founders' Constitution." Volume 5, Amendment VII, Document 13. http://press-pubs.uchicago.edu/founders/documents/amendVIIs13.html.
Propp, Vladimir. *Theory and History of Folklore.* Trans. Ariadna Y. Martin and Richard P. Martin. Ed. Anatoly Liberman. Minneapolis: University of Minnesota Press, 1984.
Seymour, William Wood. *The Cross in Tradition, History and Art.* London: G.P. Putnam's Sons: 1898.
Strutt, Joseph. *Sports and Pastimes of the People of England.* London: Methuen, 1903.
Wärneryd, Karl. "Religion, Ritual, and Randomization." Public Choice Society Annual Meeting, San Antonio, Texas, March, 2008.
Woodson, Linda. "You are the Battleground:' Materiality, Moral Responsibility, and Determinism in *No Country for Old Men.*" *The Cormac McCarthy Journal* 5.1 (2005): 5–26.

About the Contributors

Christopher Bundrick is an assistant professor of English at the University of South Carolina–Lancaster. He has published extensively in American literature, particularly in the American gothic tradition in addition to his work in composition and popular culture studies.

Stephanie Carmichael is a graduate student writing on comics and video games, while serving as comics editor for GirlEntertainmentNetwork.

Andrea Comiskey is the 2009 Jarchow Fellow and a teaching assistant at the University of Wisconsin–Madison. She is a member of the Society for Cinema and Media Studies whose research in silent film has been widely recognized.

Randy Duncan is an award-winning professor of communication at Henderson State University. He has published extensively on the Comic Arts and is a cofounder of the Comics Arts Conference.

Kevin K. Durand teaches AP calculus and science and is chair of the Mathematics Department at the LISA Academy Collegiate Prep School in Little Rock, Arkansas. In addition to his work with philosophy and popular culture in *Buffy Meets the Academy* and *The Universe of Oz,* he has published essays exploring mathematics in the works of Plato, Aristotle, Descartes, Kant, and Whitehead.

Matthew Fotis is an award-winning playwright who is a Playwrights' Center Core Grant recipient and a two-time Illinois Arts Council grant recipient. He is completing a doctorate at the University of Missouri–Columbia.

Mitch Frye is a doctoral candidate at Louisiana State University. In addition to his interest in the *Batman* universe, he has contributed to *Dracula: The Sourcebook* and presented essays in popular culture addressing topics from theodicy to superheroes.

D. T. Kofoed is a graduate student at Michigan State University. He has presented and published widely in comic theory, particularly with regard to examining the modern/post-modern divide in the American superhero genre.

Mary K. Leigh is a doctoral academy fellow at the University of Arkansas exploring the dynamic relationship between philosophy and literature in Victorian England.

In addition to her interests in Eliot and Thackeray, she was co-editor of *The Universe of Oz*, and she has presented numerous essays on various topics related to philosophy, literature, and popular culture.

Sudipto Sanyal is a graduate student at Bowling Green State University whose interests range from Sherlock Holmes and Sir Arthur Conan Doyle to contemporary American literature and vocal music.

Michael Smith is an assistant professor of Rhetoric, Writing, and Technical Communication at James Madison University with widely varied interests in popular culture, particularly television and film studies.

Jenée Wilde is a graduate doctoral teaching fellow at the University of Oregon as well as the director of the Queering Academic Studies Research Interest Group at the Center for the Study of Women in Society.

Melanie Wilson is completing her doctoral work at Texas Tech University. She published an essay in *Buffy Meets the Academy* and is exploring 19th-century British literature, with a particular interest in Gothic fiction.

Index

Adorno, Theodor 3, 4, 5, 6, 7, 8, 10, 14
Aeschylus 5, 26
Ai, Low Soon 185
Alfred Pennyworth 11, 17, 21, 22, 35, 38, 44, 45, 48, 55, 59, 60, 62, 64, 69, 105, 106, 114, 131, 183
Aquaman 42
Aristophanes 4
Aristotle 1, 5, 7, 8, 9, 11, 13, 17, 18, 19, 22, 23, 41, 45, 46, 47, 48, 50, 51, 52, 72
Arkham Asylum (graphic novel) 93, 152, 198, 200
Arkham Asylum 55, 61, 94, 99, 154

Batman and Robin 8, 41, 44, 48, 50, 51, 52, 88, 89, 92, 104, 105, 106, 107, 109, 110, 111, 112, 116, 117, 122, 190
Batman Annual 42
Batman Begins 11, 24, 25, 40, 52, 57, 58, 60, 69, 85, 91, 92, 102, 124, 126, 130, 140, 145, 149, 152, 155, 211
Batman Forever 11, 43
Batman: The New Adventures 85
Batman: Year One 24, 117, 137, 149
Bollard, Brian 185
Brody, Michael 40, 122
Brooker, Will 122, 154
Bruce Wayne 1, 8, 21, 25, 26, 27, 28, 29, 30, 31, 33, 34, 35, 36, 37, 38, 39, 42, 43, 44, 45, 46, 51, 55, 57, 58, 60, 62, 63, 64, 86, 87, 94, 96, 100, 101, 102, 105, 116, 117, 118, 119, 120, 121, 126, 131, 135, 150, 151, 152, 153, 181, 183, 212
Bukatman, Scott 154
Burton, Tim 43, 95, 148, 154

Catwoman 47
Chief O'Hara 45, 49, 89
Chopin, Kate 81
Clark Kent 36, 38, 86, 87
Clemens, Valdine 40
The Comedian 177, 179, 180, 185
Commissioner Gordon 24, 29, 86, 89, 126, 127, 129, 133, 152, 193, 196, 197
Cook, Robert 185

Cooper, Lydia 216
critical engagement approach 1, 2, 9, 13
cultural solipsism approach 9, 10, 11

Daniels, Les 154
The Dark Knight 1, 11, 17, 20, 22, 23, 24, 25, 26, 27, 28, 31, 32, 33, 34, 35, 36, 37, 38, 39, 40, 53, 54, 55, 60, 69, 70, 71, 72, 75, 76, 85, 90, 91, 92, 95, 100, 102, 103, 104, 105, 110, 111, 116, 117, 124, 125, 126, 127, 128, 129, 130, 131, 132, 133, 134, 135, 136, 137, 138, 139, 140, 144, 145, 146, 148, 151, 152, 153, 154, 155, 156, 157, 163, 164, 165, 169, 180, 182, 183, 185, 193, 195, 198, 200, 201, 206, 211, 215, 217
The Dark Knight Returns 24, 25, 26, 27, 28, 31, 33, 34, 35, 36, 37, 38, 39, 40, 55, 69, 85, 90, 95, 102, 103, 104, 105, 110, 116, 117, 137, 148, 151, 152, 153, 154, 156, 163, 164, 165, 180, 182, 185, 193, 195, 198, 200
The Dark Knight Strikes Again 157, 165
Deleuze, Gilles 78
Descartes, René 12
Detective Comics 31, 42, 104, 109, 148, 151, 154, 191
Dick Grayson 8, 31, 44, 45, 46, 51, 164
Dini, Paul 154

Ehrman, Bart 83
Ellen Yindel 32
Ellis, Warren 154
Erickson, Victoria Lee 154
eudaimonia 18
Euripides 5

Faulkner, William 8
Foucault, Michel 71, 72, 78

Gaiman, Neil 154

Hall, Stuart 165
Hallgerd 172, 173, 175
Harvey Dent 1, 17, 22, 56, 57, 58, 60, 62, 64, 65, 66, 67, 68, 70, 74, 118, 119, 126, 133, 135, 152, 181, 201, 211, 216

221

Hemingway, Ernest 81
Homer 4, 8
hooks, bell 216

Iaccino, James F. 185

Jesus 84, 150
Jimmy Olson 181
Joker 1, 11, 17, 20, 21, 22, 23, 24, 25, 31, 37, 42, 43, 47, 49, 54, 55, 56, 58, 59, 60, 61, 62, 63, 64, 65, 66, 67, 70, 72, 73, 74, 75, 76, 91, 94, 118, 126, 127, 131, 132, 133, 134, 137, 139, 146, 152, 153, 164, 182, 183, 184, 185, 187, 188, 189, 190, 191, 192, 193, 194, 195, 196, 197, 198, 199, 200, 205, 211, 212, 213, 214
Jung, Carl 93, 101, 185

Kant, Immanuel 11
The Killing Joke 59, 69, 137, 153, 154, 183, 185, 195, 196, 197, 199, 200
Kristeva, Julia 4
Kukkonen, Taneli 185

Lacan, Jacques 2, 4, 11, 93, 96, 97, 98, 99, 100, 101, 102, 103
Le Goff, Jacques 185
Lex Luthor 86, 189
Locke, John 217
Loeb, Jeph 154
Lois and Clark 86
Lucius Fox 127, 132, 133, 134

Malpas, Jeffery 154
Marx, Karl 5, 163
The Matrix 12, 144
Miller, Frank 24, 25, 26, 27, 28, 29, 30, 31, 32, 33, 34, 35, 36, 37, 40, 55, 69, 85, 90, 91, 94, 95, 102, 103, 105, 116, 117, 118, 123, 137, 146, 148, 149, 151, 152, 154, 156, 157, 158, 159, 160, 161, 162, 163, 164, 165, 180, 182, 185, 186, 193, 200
Mr. Freeze 42
Moore, Alan 59, 69, 71, 117, 129, 137, 149, 153, 154, 169, 177, 179, 183, 185, 186, 195, 196, 200
Morreall, John 186
Morrison, Grant 103, 154, 200

Nicomachean Ethics 13, 17, 45
Nietzsche, Friedrich 87, 92
Njal's Saga 169, 171, 172, 173, 174, 175, 176, 177, 181, 185, 186
No Country for Old Men 2, 201, 206, 215, 216, 217
Nolan, Christopher 10, 17, 20, 22, 23, 24, 25, 40, 42, 54, 56, 57, 69, 85, 91, 95, 102, 124, 128, 130, 131, 136, 139, 140, 144, 145, 155, 185, 201, 205, 216

Oedipus the King 9, 26, 31, 40, 130, 145

Panopticon 71, 73, 75, 78
Park, Robert 155
Penguin 42, 49, 185, 186
Plato 4, 5, 6, 7, 8, 9, 10, 12, 13, 14, 17, 49, 53, 170
Poe, Edgar Allan 98
point of departure approach 9, 11, 12
Poison Ivy 47
Propp, Vladimir 207, 217
Provine, Robert 186

Rachel Dawes 21, 22, 56, 57, 58, 59, 61, 62, 63, 64, 66, 67, 69, 126, 211, 212, 213, 214
Riddler 42, 43, 44, 47, 49, 52, 147, 154
Rivers, Shane 155

Scarecrow 20, 55
Schroeder, Fred E.H. 186
Scooby-Doo 8, 90
Shakespeare, William 186
Sigmund 97, 98, 172, 173
Skarphedin 169, 173, 174, 175, 176, 177, 180, 181, 185
Socrates 4, 8, 12
Sontag, Susan 123
Sophocles 5
Spengler, Oswald 155
Stamp, Jimmy 155
Star Trek 89, 92
Superman 3, 26, 28, 30, 35, 36, 37, 38, 42, 86, 87, 109, 111, 117, 118, 122, 149, 160, 161, 162, 163, 164, 181, 188

Talbot, Bryan 155
Tate, Chuck 186
theory exemplar approach 9, 12
Thor 42
Thrasymachus 87
Trumble, Angus 186

Uricchio, William 146, 155

V for Vendetta 117, 137
Vasey, Ruth 146
Vickie Vale 42, 44
virtue 3, 8, 17, 18, 19, 20, 21, 22, 23, 41, 47, 48, 49, 50, 51, 52, 84, 95, 110
Vollum, Scott 155

Wandtke, Terrence R. 123, 186
The Watchmen 3, 117, 137, 149, 169, 177, 180, 185, 186
Wein, Len 155
Whitehead, Alfred North 48
Wonder Woman 42, 109, 111, 160, 161, 163

X-Men 3, 93, 111

www.ingramcontent.com/pod-product-compliance
Ingram Content Group UK Ltd.
Pitfield, Milton Keynes, MK11 3LW, UK
UKHW041953140426
5217IPUK00015B/776